Especially for

....

From

....

Date

....

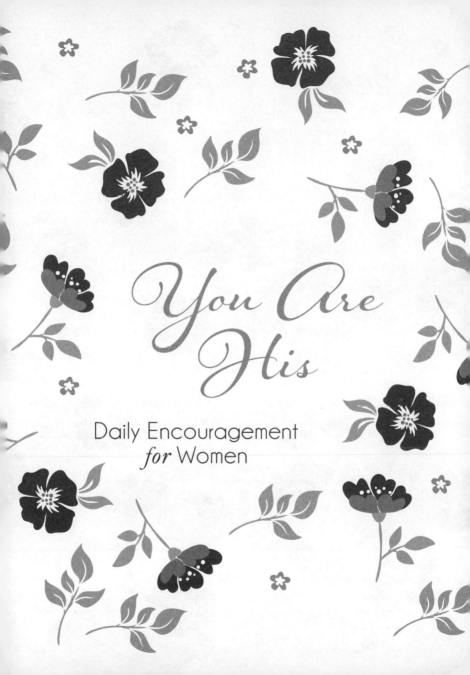

You Are His

Daily Encouragement
for Women

Darlene Sala

You Are His

Daily Encouragement
for Women

BARBOUR BOOKS
An Imprint of Barbour Publishing, Inc.

Originally published in the Philippines under the title *Refreshing Words for Busy Women,* by OMF Literature, Inc. Selections in this book previously published in the United States in the books *You Are Blessed, You Are Loved,* and *You Are Chosen* by Barbour Publishing, Inc.

Print ISBN 978-1-68322-144-9

eBook Editions:
Adobe Digital Edition (.epub) 978-1-63058-975-2
Kindle and MobiPocket Edition (.prc) 978-1-63058-976-9

Published by Barbour Books, an imprint of Barbour Publishing, Inc., P.O. Box 719, Uhrichsville, Ohio 44683, www.barbourbooks.com.

Our mission is to publish and distribute inspirational products offering exceptional value and biblical encouragement to the masses.

 Member of the
Evangelical Christian
Publishers Association

Printed in China.

*Dedicated to all busy women
who thirst for freshening,
invigorating, revitalizing,
restorative, health-giving
Living Water.*

Before You Begin

Every woman I know is a busy woman—that's the way life is in the twenty-first century. All the more important, then, to take daily breaks to "refresh your soul" (Psalm 23:3). Not meant to be a substitute for Bible study, these one-a-day short selections are written to restore and strengthen you—and sometimaes challenge you as well.

You will soon notice that every seventh selection is comprised of verses from Psalms, for you to find special refreshment in God's poetry.

Because the selections are scripture based and always encouraging, I hope they will be for you like a drink of cool water when you are thirsty and tired.

"I will refresh the weary and satisfy the faint."
JEREMIAH 31:25

Commit to the LORD whatever you do,
and he will establish your plans.

PROVERBS 16:3

A New Pencil and Notebook

When I was a kid, I always liked to get a brand-new pencil, sharpen it to a perfect point, and sit down with a fresh new notebook. Somehow that pristine pencil and paper presented so many possibilities. A new year feels like this to me, too—a fresh beginning.

I remember sitting down at the start of one new year and praying, "Lord, I want this whole year to make a difference for You." But the problem with that prayer is that it's impossible to experience the whole year in one instance. Every year comes in 365 days, each of which has 24 hours or 1,440 minutes. Unless I make those individual days and hours count for God, when December rolls around again, nothing will have changed.

Maybe one never gets to the place of total 24-hours-a-day commitment to God's will. My experience is that commitment only comes in moment-sized acts of obedience. I find no problem, personally, in committing the whole year to God—or my whole life, for that matter. It's the moments that give me trouble—the little decisions about the use of my time, money, and energy. What does God want me to do right now? Am I willing to do it?

Lord, beginning today, help me look at each moment as important to You. Your Word says, "Commit to the LORD whatever you do" (Proverbs 16:3). Help me care more about what You want than what I want. Thank You for the "new pencil and new notebook"—a fresh start.

Children, obey your parents in everything,
for this pleases the Lord.

COLOSSIANS 3:20

My Will—or God's?

One evening my daughter called my eldest grandson, who was just a toddler then, to come to the table for dinner. She was taken aback when he replied, "No, Mommy, I'm not going to come. I'm going to play now." As you can imagine, that day my grandson learned the meaning of the scripture verse that says, "Children, obey your parents in everything, for this pleases the Lord" (Colossians 3:20).

When my daughter told me about this, I felt a twinge of guilt. How many times have I said that to God when He spoke to my heart about something He wanted me to do? "No, Lord, I want to do something else right now." You see, there's another power in my life besides God—a strong one: it's my own will. While I hate to admit it, many times my will is against God's will. This battle for my own way is the essence of sin. Isaiah wrote, "We all, like sheep, have gone astray, each of us has turned to our own way" (Isaiah 53:6). My way as opposed to God's way. I have been given the ability to make the choice.

Every day I need to come to the Lord and ask, "What do You want me to do today?" Romans 12:1 tells us to present our bodies as a living sacrifice to the Lord. But as someone pointed out, the problem with living sacrifices is that they keep crawling off the altar. That's why I find I need to present myself to the Lord *every* day.

Which will it be today—God's will or yours?

*Peter got down out of the boat, walked on the water
and came toward Jesus. But when he saw the wind, he was
afraid and, beginning to sink, cried out, "Lord, save me!"*

MATTHEW 14:29–30
(THE WHOLE STORY: MATTHEW 14:22–33)

What Are You Looking At?

I'm so glad Jesus chose Peter to be one of His disciples, because he's like most of us—curious, impetuous, and sometimes weak.

Matthew 14 tells us the story of one of the best–known events in Peter's life. The disciples were in a boat, and Jesus came to them walking on the water. They thought he was a ghost, but Jesus immediately said, "Take courage! It is I. Don't be afraid" (v. 27).

"Lord, if it's you," Peter replied, "tell me to come to you on the water." Jesus said, "Come," so Peter audaciously got out of the boat and walked on the water toward Jesus (v. 28–29). When he saw the storm, however, he began to sink. Immediately Jesus reached out and caught him. As long as Peter's eyes were on Jesus, he walked on water. But when he looked at the circumstances around him, he began to sink.

When you focus your attention on how many bills you have to pay or the doctor's diagnosis of leukemia, like Peter, you'll begin to sink. Where you focus your attention makes all the difference. If you look in your own heart, you'll become depressed. If you look back to your past, you'll feel defeated by the memory of failures. If you look to others, you may be disappointed. But if you look to Christ, you will never be depressed or defeated or disappointed.

Let us fix "our eyes on Jesus, the author and perfecter of our faith," says Hebrews 12:2. When you're overwhelmed by the storm, look to Jesus. He is there. Reach for His hand.

Your hands made me and formed me.
PSALM 119:73

The Shape I'm In

Most of us are not happy with our bodies. We'd like to shed a few pounds—without effort, of course. We wish we had firmer muscles or shapelier curves. But what we have is what we've got, right?

Now, the Bible says in the beginning God formed Adam "from the dust of the ground" (Genesis 2:7). But He formed *you,* too. The psalmist echoed, "Your hands made me and formed me" (Psalm 119:73).

So if God formed you, what does that tell you about your body? Clearly, your body is exactly what God intended it to be, to accomplish His unique purpose. We can't blame God when we don't take care of ourselves. Because our bodies are tools God has given us to serve Him, we should take care of them for His purposes.

What if you are disabled? Does God still have a purpose for you? Absolutely. When she was a teen, poet Annie Johnson Flint developed crippling arthritis that worsened until her later years; a pencil had to be wedged between her fingers for her to write. Yet she authored more than seven volumes of poetry that have no trace of self-pity or railing against God's will. She wrote,

> *God hath not promised skies always blue,*
> *Flower strewn pathways all our lives through;*
> *But God hath promised strength for the day,*
> *Rest for the labor, light for the way.*[1]

Offer your body to the Lord today as a gift, "holy and pleasing to God" (Romans 12:1). You'll be amazed at what He does with it.

[1]http://www.hymnal.net/hymn.php?t=nt&n=720, accessed September 10, 2008.

My heart says of you, "Seek his face!" Your face, LORD, I will seek.
PSALM 27:8

Psalm after Christmas

One of the reasons the book of Psalms in the Bible appeals to us is that the writings touch on experiences common to us all. In the Psalms you find the entire range of human emotion: anger, love, hatred, joy, thankfulness, and more.

Once in a while I like to write a psalm-like expression of my heart to God. For instance, one January after a busy Christmas season, I wrote how I felt:

*Lord, I've spent so much money and so much time on material things
the past month that I feel out of tune. I don't think I've wasted money, really.
The things I bought were of good quality at good prices, and they were for others.
Just secular—earthly. Of course, I've eaten too much as well.
And stayed up too late. And not exercised enough.
And now deep down inside I want more than all this.*

*I know so well that lasting satisfaction comes from doing the things that count
for eternity.
So this morning I'd like my dissonant heart tuned to make harmony with Your
divine music.
The tone I made was dull and flat—though the tempo was fast enough!
Let the Holy Spirit loosen the strings that are too taut and wipe away the
smudges
where my hands have strummed the strings instead of letting You make the
music.*

Today I want my life to harmonize with You, the Master of Music.

Why don't you sit down and write what is in *your* heart now? Your words will be a prayer that God will listen to.

Brethren, I count not myself to have
apprehended: but this one thing I do.

PHILIPPIANS 3:13 KJV

This One Thing I Do

My friend Georgalyn has always been an extremely busy lady. When her husband died at a young age, she raised their two young daughters alone. Through those years, she also headed one Christian organization or another. At one time it was missionary radio, and now it is missionary printing. With her compassion for needy people, she makes a difference with her life.

While I've always admired her spunk and dedication, I observed something else in Georgalyn that spoke to my heart in a special way. Busy as she was, she made a decision to always give herself totally to her present task. For instance, whenever someone stopped her to talk, she would really listen. No matter how busy she was or how many things she had on her mind, she would give her undivided attention to that person.

The apostle Paul said, "This one thing I do" (Philippians 3:13 KJV). When you get right down to it, that's about all most of us can handle well at any one time anyway, isn't it? One thing at a time.

Jesus was the master of this. I'm sure that no matter whom He talked to, that person knew he had Jesus' undivided attention. He took time to meet each need before He went on to the next. And no one else had more people demanding His attention than Jesus did!

"This one thing I do"—may God help us to remember this thought today and put it into practice. Just maybe it will become a habit.

Selected verses from Psalm 8

Refreshing Words from Psalms

Are you discouraged? Lift up your eyes to the Lord. Yes, look up.

> *¹Lord, our Lord,*
>   *how majestic is your name in all the earth!*
> *³When I consider your heavens,*
>   *the work of your fingers,*
> *the moon and the stars,*
>   *which you have set in place,*
> *⁴what is mankind that you are mindful of them,*
>   *human beings that you care for them?*
> *⁵You have made them a little lower than the angels*
>   *and crowned them with glory and honor.*
> *⁶You made them rulers over the works of your hands;*
>   *you put everything under their feet.*
> *⁹Lord, our Lord,*
>   *how majestic is your name in all the earth!*

I feel insignificant today, Lord. Thank You for Your greatness—and Your care for me!

*"I will surely bless you and make your descendants
as numerous as the stars in the sky."*
GENESIS 22:17

How Many Stars?

In the year 125 BC, Hipparchus counted the number of stars in the heavens. He concluded that there were 1,022. Seventy-five years later, however, the astronomer Ptolemy found four more and declared that there were 1,026.

Interestingly enough, the Bible, written 2,700 years *before* Ptolemy, said that the stars were innumerable. God promised Abraham that his descendants would be "as numerous as the stars in the sky and as the sand on the seashore" (Genesis 22:17). Skeptics scoffed at such a comparison. To compare the number of stars to grains of sand on the seashore was laughable. After all, there are more grains in a handful of sand than the 1,026 stars Ptolemy claimed existed.

But only a few decades ago, on a highly acclaimed television program, the noted evolutionary scientist Carl Sagan said there are probably about as many stars in the sky as there are grains of sand on the seashores of the world. The Bible, written centuries ago, has been correct all along.

Psalm 147:4 tells us, "[God] determines the number of the stars and calls them each by name." We humans haven't yet counted them all, let alone named each star. But God has already counted and named each of them.

It's no wonder the psalmist wrote, "When I consider. . .the stars, which you have set in place, what is mankind that you are mindful of them, human beings that you care for them?" (Psalm 8:3–4).

*Jesus answered, "It is written: 'Man shall not live on bread alone,
but on every word that comes from the mouth of God.' "*

MATTHEW 4:4

The Instruction Book

When you buy a machine—whether it's a computer, a car, or a sewing machine—you receive a book of instructions. Most of us set this book aside, doubting we'll ever use it. But one day when something goes wrong with your equipment, you may wonder, *Where is that instruction book that came with this?*

You know that old saying "If all else fails, read the instructions"? Well, we'd say a person is not very wise if he knows nothing about a piece of equipment and yet refuses to refer to the directions on how to use it. Yet many people never open the instruction book that tells how to fix a human being—the Bible. It's the Book that tells where we came from, what we were made for, how we can be kept in working order—in fact, exactly what will make us most useful and effective. The great tragedy is that so many people try to live their lives without *the* instruction Book.

Jesus said, "Man shall not live on bread alone, but on every word that comes from the mouth of God" (Matthew 4:4). If you've never opened a Bible, I'd suggest beginning with the book of Mark in the New Testament. For one thing, it's short and to the point. You'll get an overview of who Jesus is and why He came to earth. Mark those verses that speak to your heart.

You will be surprised how practical God's instruction Book is. Not only will you find directions on how to live, you'll meet the One who designed you—and He can fix anything.

But Moses said to God, "Who am I that I should go
to Pharaoh and bring the Israelites out of Egypt?"

EXODUS 3:11
(THE WHOLE STORY: EXODUS 3:1–22)

Who Am I?

The bush was on fire, but it wasn't being burned up. Curious, Moses stopped to investigate. Never in a thousand years did he expect to hear what he heard—God's voice speaking aloud to him, telling him that he had been commissioned to lead the Israelites out of slavery in Egypt to the place God had promised would be their homeland.

Moses' immediate response was one of utter shock! "Who am I to do a job like that?" he asked. "Don't You remember I had to make a fast getaway out of Egypt because they wanted to kill me there? Now You want me to go back and talk Pharaoh into letting his labor force quit?"

Maybe God is speaking to your heart about something He wants you to do—something you feel is totally beyond your ability. Like Moses, you are saying, "Who am I to take on a job like that?" God reminded Moses that His name is "I AM"—that He is the God of the past, present, and future. He is the God of *your* past, *your* present, and *your* future.

When God gives you a job to do, what matters most is not who you are, but who God is. He will stand behind you with the resources you need to carry out the task He gives you—whether it's a new job, a special call to ministry, or sharing the Gospel with your coworker in the office. Don't worry about who you are; remember who God is—the great ever-present One, who will go with you as you do what He has called you to do.

When I said, My foot slippeth; thy mercy, O LORD, held me up.
In the multitude of my thoughts within me thy comforts delight my soul.
PSALM 94:18–19 KJV

The God of All Comfort

Comfort. It's a word I like to hear. It has such a—well, reassuring sound to it. It's also a Bible word. In just five verses of one chapter, 2 Corinthians 1, the word *comfort* occurs in some form seven times.

Let me give you a sample from 2 Corinthians 1:3–4: "Praise be to the God and Father of our Lord Jesus Christ, the Father of compassion and the God of all comfort, who comforts us in all our troubles." That's beautiful, isn't it?

The idea is more than just that He consoles us when we're sad or upset. Bible teacher G. Campbell Morgan writes,

> *It is the great thought of underpinned, strengthened comradeship, being by the side of, upholding. That is the great word, the upholding power that comes from God.[1]*

It's not a sign of weakness to admit you need God's help. In fact, it would be foolish to try to get through life without Him. When life piles up on us, when we face grief and difficulty, we need to turn to our Comforter. The psalmist wrote, "When I said, 'My foot is slipping,' your unfailing love, LORD, supported me. When anxiety was great within me, your consolation brought me joy" (Psalm 94:18–19).

Many years before Christ was born, the prophet Isaiah said that God would be sending Christ to earth "to bind up the brokenhearted" (Isaiah 61:1). Do you need Him to bind up your broken heart today? He is the great Comforter who will come to your side and walk with you through difficult days.

[1]G. Campbell Morgan, *The Corinthian Letters of Paul* (Grand Rapids, MI: Fleming H. Revell Company, 1946), 227.

I will instruct you and teach you in the way you should go;
I will counsel you with my loving eye on you.
PSALM 32:8

God's Gentle Pushes

My dad used to tell people of an incident that happened when our family was traveling some distance by car. It was long before the days of seat belts, and I was standing in the front seat between them. I was about four years old, and I was whistling. My mom had had ear trouble as a child, and just a sharp whistle would cause pain in her ears, so she gave me a little poke in the side with her elbow.

My dad says I immediately looked at him, and with a grin said, "Daddy, I can read Mama's pushes. That one meant stop whistling." He said they laughed about it, but as he drove, he thought, *Dear Lord, I wish I were as sensitive to Your gentle pushes so that You would not have to deal with me harshly in order for me to know what You want me to do.*

God says in Psalm 32:8, "I will instruct you and teach you in the way you should go." It is possible to have such a sensitive heart that God can communicate His will to us without having to put a major roadblock in our path to get our attention. Isaiah says, "Whether you turn to the right or to the left, your ears will hear a voice behind you, saying, 'This is the way; walk in it'" (Isaiah 30:21).

Has God been giving you one of His gentle pushes? If so, you know what He wants you to do. So why don't you act on it today?

This poor man called, and the LORD heard him;
he saved him out of all his troubles.

PSALM 34:6

R. A. Torrey's Conversion

When R. A. Torrey was a young man, he had no faith in God or the Bible. His mother, an earnest Christian, pleaded with him to turn to God.

One day he said to her, "I don't want to hear any more about my sins and your prayers. I'm leaving." His weeping mother responded, "Son, you are going the wrong way. But when you come to your darkest hour, if you earnestly call on your mother's God and seek Him with all your heart, you will get the help you need."

Torrey went deeper and deeper into sin. At last one night, weary of life, with problems pressing down on him, he decided, *I'll take that gun I have in the drawer and end my life.*

But his mother's words came rushing back to him. Convicted, he desperately cried out, "O God of my mother, if there be such a Being, I need help. I need light. If You will give it to me, I will follow You."

With tears running down his face, he put his trust in Christ as his Savior. Torrey's dark heart was filled with the light of God's love. He then hurried home to tell his mother that her prayers had been answered. Reuben A. Torrey became an outstanding evangelist and helped win thousands to Christ. He founded the Bible Institute of Los Angeles—now known as Biola University, one of the leading Christian universities in the United States.

Torrey learned the reality of the scripture that says, "This poor man cried, and the LORD heard him; he saved him out of all his troubles" (Psalm 34:6). The God who saved Torrey will save you as well!

Selected verses from Psalm 40

Refreshing Words from Psalms

Remember, no situation is too difficult for the Lord. Let us wait patiently on Him.

> *¹I waited patiently for the LORD;*
> *he turned to me and heard my cry.*
> *²He lifted me out of the slimy pit,*
> *out of the mud and mire;*
> *he set my feet on a rock*
> *and gave me a firm place to stand.*
> *³He put a new song in my mouth,*
> *a hymn of praise to our God.*
> *Many will see and fear the LORD*
> *and put their trust in him.*
> *⁵Many, LORD my God,*
> *are the wonders you have done,*
> *the things you planned for us.*
> *None can compare with you;*
> *were I to speak and tell of your deeds,*
> *they would be too many to declare.*

Lord, when I look at the situations You've helped me through in the past, my heart is filled with praise! I will trust You for today's problems.

"You are worthy, our Lord and God, to receive glory and honor and power, for you created all things, and by your will they were created and have their being."

REVELATION 4:11

In the Beginning God Created

Science writer Samuel Alibrando challenges anyone who has difficulty believing that God created the earth:

> *Let's make a huge puzzle. . . . Let's limit it to, say, one million parts. It includes chemicals, scientific properties, elements, atoms, cells, changing weather, bugs, fish, reptiles, plants, dirt, mammals, and instincts. Okay, can you put it together so that not one thing lacks what it needs. . . ?*
>
> *Well, you have it easy. You are working with things that have already been invented. Let's take it up another notch. First invent these one million things and creatures from scratch so they all work. . . . How many inventions are you going to have to create just to make the puzzle fit?*
>
> *You can't invent just ears; you have to invent sounds and sound waves. You have to invent brains to interpret the sound waves and you have to have the ability to make things and animals make sounds. . . . It has to all fit and work. . . . Now that you know how outrageously challenging it is. . .you are asked this question: What are the chances of all of this being put together by accident instead of by you? . . . Just leave those one million pieces alone and wait for all the pieces to put themselves together. Even a 5-piece puzzle won't do that.[1]*

Indeed, "You are worthy, our Lord and God, to receive glory and honor and power, for you created all things" (Revelation 4:11). Now, do you really think the same God who created the complexities of our universe will have any trouble with the puzzle pieces of your life?

[1]Samuel J. Alibrando, *Nature Never Stops Talking* (Reedley, CA: Tsaba House, 2005), 106.

Where can I go from your Spirit?
Where can I flee from your presence?

PSALM 139:7

Wherever You Go, There You Are

"Wherever you go, there you are."

What a silly saying, I thought. Of course wherever you go, there you are. Where else would you be?

But then I thought of how people try to escape from themselves and their troubles. They move to another place, thinking everything will be different there. Before long, they find the same old problems—alcohol addiction, marital troubles, busyness. That's because when they moved, they brought themselves with them. It's true—wherever you go, there you are.

There's only one way out of this dilemma: Come to God just as you are. Confess your shortcomings and failures; for He paid for your sins on the cross, and He offers forgiveness. "Therefore, since we have been justified through faith, we have peace with God through our Lord Jesus Christ" (Romans 5:1). Peace with God brings peace with yourself, too. You can stop running away.

"So don't be afraid; you are worth more than many sparrows."
MATTHEW 10:31
(THE WHOLE STORY: MATTHEW 10:26–33)

Lessons from Sparrows

When Jesus talked about God's care for the birds, He chose the humble sparrow as His illustration. That's an interesting choice, for sparrows are one of the most common birds on earth. Some people even consider them pests.

Sparrows live almost exclusively among people. According to one study, wherever the number of households increases, the sparrow population increases proportionately. Sparrows build their nests under the eaves of houses, inside shutter boxes, in holes in a wall, or in parks close to where people live.

From ancient times, sparrows have appeared in folklore, fairy tales, and proverbs. Because sparrows are so common, Jesus knew that through the centuries people would read His words and relate.

Jesus said, "Are not two sparrows sold for a penny? Yet not one of them will fall to the ground outside your Father's care. . . . So don't be afraid; you are worth more than many sparrows" (Matthew 10:29, 31). It's significant that Jesus would take note of their death since the sparrow lives only a few years.

Jesus added, "Look at the birds of the air; they do not sow or reap or store away in barns, and yet your heavenly Father feeds them. Are you not much more valuable than they? . . . So do not worry. . . . But seek first his kingdom and his righteousness, and all these things will be given to you as well" (Matthew 6:26, 31, 33). He cares for the little sparrow; imagine how much more He cares for you.

Submit yourselves, then, to God.
Resist the devil, and he will flee from you.

JAMES 4:7

When You Don't Want to Do Something

What happens when you know God wants you to do something but you don't want to do it?

Let's say that you have a friend who is sick. She *really* is your good friend, but every time you call her, she talks and talks and talks. You know God wants you to call her, but if you do, you'll be on the phone for hours. Do you:

1. Make excuses? "I can't call her today. If I do, I won't have enough time to read my Bible."
2. Rationalize? "She's probably so sick she doesn't feel like talking to me anyway."
3. Procrastinate? "I'm just too tired. I'll call her first thing tomorrow morning. I really will."

Think about an area in your life where you don't want to obey God. You know what? The devil doesn't want you to obey God either.

If you are having a hard time obeying God, James has the answer. He says, "Submit yourselves, then, to God. Resist the devil, and he will flee from you" (James 4:7). We have the mistaken idea that God and the devil are equal powers. Not so. Remember, Christ has already defeated the devil. He's sentenced and just waiting for execution. If you are a believer in Jesus Christ, God lives in you. You have the power to resist Satan, and God's promise is that Satan will flee.

When you don't want to do something you know you should do, stand firm against the devil and then submit to God. When you do, you will find the power to do that difficult thing He is asking you.

"Return home and tell how much God has done for you."

LUKE 8:39

(THE WHOLE STORY: LUKE 8:26–39)

Tell How Much God Has Done for You

After crossing the Sea of Galilee, Jesus stepped on shore and was immediately confronted by a man possessed by demons. The Bible tells us: "For a long time this man had not worn clothes or lived in a house, but had lived in the tombs" (Luke 8:27). The local people had tried to chain him and keep him under guard, but he always broke the chains and escaped.

To make a long story short, Jesus cast the demons out of the man. The townspeople found him later, dressed and calmly sitting at Jesus' feet, in his right mind and begging to go with Jesus. "No," Jesus said. "Return home and tell how much God has done for you" (Luke 8:39).

I, for one, would like to have sat at his dinner table that night and listened to him tell all the details of the story.

Think of how much God has done for you. Have you shared the details with your family recently? Tell them how God protected you when you had that close call in heavy traffic. Or perhaps how He met the urgent financial need that had been worrying you, or answered a request you'd been praying about for weeks. Or how, at last, you had a chance to share Christ with your boss at work.

Tonight, why don't *you* "return home and tell how much God has done for you"? Don't keep good news to yourself. Share it with your family. You will bless them and bring praise to God for His mighty power.

*Then you will call, and the LORD will answer;
you will cry for help, and he will say: Here am I.*

ISAIAH 58:9
(THE WHOLE STORY: ISAIAH 58:6–11)

Perspective

For a moment, pretend that you are God, and you're listening to these prayers:

"O Lord, help Danny to be the high scorer at the basketball game tonight so he can get the MVP trophy!"

What a contrast to this one: "O Lord, send us money so Danny can go to school!"

Or one family prays, "Please, God, give us sunny weather for our cruise!" while another prays, "Please, God, send rain to save our crops!"

"God, please help me lose weight so I can wear that beautiful dress to the party," a young mom prays, while another pleads, "Please, God, send us food so I can feed my family."

If you were God, it's not hard to figure out which prayers you would want to answer first, is it? Now, is it wrong to pray for good weather for your vacation or for a successful career? No, of course not. But when we get a bit demanding with God and disappointed when He doesn't give us every luxury we want, it's time to get life back in perspective.

In the Bible we're told to pray about everything, and I believe that means exactly what it says—*everything*. But don't confuse that with thinking that we *need* everything. I think God must sometimes shake His head and smile when He hears what we who have so much think our needs are.

So go ahead and pray about everything—absolutely everything. But remember that it's our needs that God has promised to supply when we are obedient to Him. The Bible says, "The LORD will guide you always; he will satisfy your needs" (Isaiah 58:11).

Selected verses from Psalm 5

Refreshing Words from Psalms

When your heart is aching, pour out your petitions to the One who can surprise you with joy.

> *¹Listen to my words, LORD,*
>   *consider my lament.*
> *²Hear my cry for help,*
>   *my King and my God,*
>   *for to you I pray.*
> *³In the morning, LORD, you hear my voice;*
>   *in the morning I lay my requests before you*
>   *and wait expectantly.*
> *¹¹But let all who take refuge in you be glad;*
>   *let them ever sing for joy.*
> *Spread your protection over them,*
>   *that those who love your name may rejoice in you.*

Turn my tears to joy, Lord, as I wait on You.

By faith the prostitute Rahab, because she welcomed the spies,
was not killed with those who were disobedient.

HEBREWS 11:31
(THE WHOLE STORY: HEBREWS 11:1–40)

Woman of Faith

The Bible has its own "Hall of Fame": Hebrews 11. It's a list of people famous for believing and trusting God. You'd expect to find Abraham and Moses there, but you may be surprised to see a woman listed who was not exactly chair of the Spiritual Life Committee of her church. In fact, she was a prostitute. Her name was Rahab.

Obviously Rahab didn't get there on the basis of purity—but then, which of us could? Here's the story: Joshua sent two spies to Jericho to assess the city before attacking. Probably in order not to arouse suspicion, the men went to Rahab's house. But word leaked out to the king, who demanded that Rahab hand over the spies. She admitted they had been there but said they already fled. Actually, she had hidden them under stalks of flax on her rooftop.

That evening, Rahab told Joshua's men, "I know that the LORD has given this land to you. . .for the LORD your God is God in heaven above and on the earth below" (Joshua 2:9, 11). Then she boldly asked that she and her family be spared when the Israelites attacked. And indeed, "By faith the prostitute Rahab, because she welcomed the spies, was not killed with those who were disobedient" (Hebrews 11:31). Rahab had a faith that gave her daring courage and earned her a place among the famous who believed God.

Rahab's fame doesn't end there. Her great-great-grandson was King David, placing her in the lineage of Jesus Himself (Matthew 1:5–6). Now that's an honor!

No, you don't have to be "perfect" to be used by God—just willing and available.

That is, that you and I may be mutually
encouraged by each other's faith.

Romans 1:12

Encouraging One Another

Sometimes I don't think we fully realize how much we encourage one another when we share about the good things God has done in our lives. I, for one, love to get a phone call or an e–mail telling me how God has met a need in a friend's life or answered a prayer. That encourages me to keep on praying until He does the same in my life. To the Christians in Rome, Paul talked about being "mutually encouraged by each other's faith" (Romans 1:12).

It's especially good to talk to our families about what the Lord has done. Moses told the people, "Be careful, and watch yourselves closely so that you do not forget the things your eyes have seen or let them fade from your heart as long as you live. Teach them to your children and to their children after them" (Deuteronomy 4:9).

I guess sometimes we're hesitant to talk about what God has done in our lives because we're afraid people will think we're trying to impress them with how spiritual we are. Don't let those fears stop you. You know that it's a great encouragement in your walk with God when someone shares with you, so don't hesitate to return the favor.

Psalm 126:3 says, "The Lord has done great things for us, and we are filled with joy." Find someone today who needs to be encouraged. Talk about the great goodness of the Lord. I think you will find, as Romans 1:12 says, that you are "mutually encouraged by each other's faith."

Taste and see that the LORD is good;
blessed is the one who takes refuge in him.
PSALM 34:8

The Challenge of Illness

My friend Louise is fighting cancer. Every three weeks she has chemotherapy that lasts the entire day and leaves her debilitated.

Yes, she gets discouraged. Numbness in her fingers and toes and the pains that accompany this treatment are certainly draining. Not one to let grass grow under her feet, she finds it hard when she doesn't have the energy to do all the things she wants to do.

But Louise is a believer in Jesus. God's Spirit in her life is evidenced by love, faith, hope, peace, friendship, courage, and a conquering spirit. She wastes little time on questions like, "Why is this happening to me?" Instead, she says,

> *I know who holds my tomorrows, and I know who holds my hand today! I praise God for the wonderful peace He gives me deep inside and for His wonderful people who walk alongside and encourage me when my body grows tired! While I am walking through the valley of the shadow of death, I know it is just a shadow, because the reality of the living Christ is with me, and His joy is my strength.*

And then she adds, "I suggest you taste and see how good the Lord really is," echoing Psalm 34:8. Meaningful advice from someone who speaks from experience.

For he is our God and we are the people
of his pasture, the flock under his care.
PSALM 95:7

Don't You Care?

The sky above the Sea of Galilee was already dark when a squall came up. Waves began to break over the boat so that it was nearly swamped. During all this, Jesus was asleep on a cushion at the back of the boat. The disciples woke Him, shouting over the howling winds, "Teacher, don't you care if we drown?" Jesus "got up. . .and said to the waves, 'Quiet! Be still!'. . .and it was completely calm" (Mark 4:38–39).

Did Jesus not care about the disciples when the storm was raging? Of course He did. It's just that He knew all along that they would safely reach the other side. But only when the disciples could see the evidence did they have peace that everything was going to be all right.

Like the disciples, we ask, "Lord, don't You care?" In other words, "Aren't You going to do something about my predicament?" We ask those words when we're in a situation where we can see no logical explanation. And the answer? Yes, God does care. Psalm 95 says, "For he is our God and we are the people of his pasture, the flock under his care" (v. 7).

Whether you're in a storm that seems like it's going to overwhelm you or you're frustrated because you're working hard and no one cares, or the rent is due and there's no way to pay it, realize God sees and cares. Jesus speaks to you those words, "Quiet! Be still!"

"Cast all your anxiety on him because he cares for you" (1 Peter 5:7). Hold on for just a little longer. Later you'll understand how great His care is for you.

"Anyone who chooses to do the will of God will find out whether my teaching comes from God or whether I speak on my own."

JOHN 7:17

How to Know

The first four books of the New Testament contain pages and pages of the teachings of Jesus. Do you want to know if all that Jesus said is true? Jesus Himself told us how to find out. He said in John, the fourth book of the New Testament, "Anyone who chooses to do the will of God will find out whether my teaching comes from God or whether I speak on my own" (John 7:17).

Sounds pretty simple, doesn't it? If you choose to do God's will, you'll know if what Jesus says is really from God. You may have heard that the Bible is a good book. You may even have read some of it. But you may wonder if what it says is true. Then ask yourself this question: Do I really want to do God's will?

If that is your attitude, then sit down with a Bible, open it to the beginning of John, and start reading. While you are reading, keep in mind that you're looking for truth, and Jesus will reveal Himself through His Word. He said that when you choose to do His will, you will know if what He said is true or not.

Brother Yun, a famous Chinese pastor often called "The Heavenly Man," said: "You can never really know the scriptures until you are willing to be changed by them." With this in mind, ask yourself: Am I willing? If so, you are about to embark on the greatest adventure of your life.

*A great and powerful wind tore the mountains apart and shattered
the rocks before the LORD, but the LORD was not in the wind.
After the wind there was an earthquake, but the LORD was not
in the earthquake. After the earthquake came a fire, but the LORD
was not in the fire. And after the fire came a gentle whisper.*

1 KINGS 19:11–12
(THE WHOLE STORY: 1 KINGS 19:1–18)

A Fast from Noise

Although not commanded directly in the Bible, you find many mentions of fasting, including Jesus' instruction about not doing it in a way that would attract people's attention.

But author Dr. Terry Teykl recommends a fast that would do many of us a lot of good. It's a fast not from food but from noise. Isn't that an interesting thought? He writes, "Decide to embark on a special kind of fast—giving up unnecessary noise and activity. Say to yourself, 'I will embrace solitude.' "[1]

Sometime today, stop long enough to really listen to what is going on around you. You may hear voices, traffic, a radio or TV, possibly the sounds of machinery running. Every day we're surrounded with unending noise.

If you set aside some time for solitude and quiet, however, you will find a fresh awareness of the presence of God. You will also find new strength, for Isaiah 30:15 says, "In quietness and trust is your strength."

There is, however, a sure way to promote God's absence, writes C. S. Lewis: "Avoid silence. . . . Concentrate on money, sex, status, health and (above all) on your grievances. Keep the radio on. Live in a crowd."[2]

There is a lot in this life that would drown out God's voice. If you're experiencing that problem, consider a fast from noise for even thirty minutes. Use earplugs if you need to. Then listen for the still, small voice of God. First Kings 19 says He sometimes speaks to us in a gentle whisper.

[1]Dr. Terry Teykl, *The Lighthouse Devotional* (Sisters, OR: Multnomah Publishers, 2000), 220.

[2]C. S. Lewis, "The Seeing Eye," in *Lewis: Christian Reflections,* ed. Walter Hooper (Grand Rapids, MI: Eerdmans, 1975), 168–69.

Selected verses from Psalm 116

Refreshing Words from Psalms

Never forget that God is compassionate and will always listen to our desperate cries for help.

> ¹*I love the* LORD, *for he heard my voice;*
>   *he heard my cry for mercy.*
> ²*Because he turned his ear to me,*
>   *I will call on him as long as I live.*
> ³*The cords of death entangled me,*
>   *the anguish of the grave came over me;*
>   *I was overcome by distress and sorrow.*
> ⁴*Then I called on the name of the* LORD:
>   *"*LORD, *save me!"*
> ⁵*The* LORD *is gracious and righteous;*
>   *our God is full of compassion.*
> ⁶*The* LORD *protects the unwary;*
>   *when I was brought low, he saved me.*
> ⁷*Return to your rest, my soul,*
>   *for the* LORD *has been good to you.*
> ⁸*For you,* LORD, *have delivered me from death,*
>   *my eyes from tears,*
>   *my feet from stumbling.*
> ¹⁷*I will sacrifice a thank offering to you*
>   *and call on the name of the* LORD.

Lord, I truly am looking to You for help. By faith, I thank You for the answer. You have never failed me.

Let us continually offer to God a sacrifice of praise.
HEBREWS 13:15

When Clouds of Depression Come

Some parts of the Bible are easy to read but hard to put into practice. Take Hebrews 13:15–16, for instance: "Let us continually offer to God a sacrifice of praise—the fruit of lips that openly profess his name. And do not forget to do good and to share with others, for with such sacrifices God is pleased."

Obeying those instructions is easy when I'm in a good mood and everything is going smoothly. Yes, praising God and doing good to others is a joy when the sun is shining. But when I'm depressed, I forget to praise the Lord, I'm not apt to think about the needs of others, and I don't really want to share.

What would happen if a depressed person actually followed those three Bible instructions?

1. Continually offer praise to the Lord
2. Do good deeds
3. Share with others

You may be thinking, *It's not possible for a clinically depressed person to do these things,* and maybe you're right. But when most of us get depressed, we *could* do something about it if we wanted to. We're depressed and don't praise God because we don't like our circumstances; we're too focused on what's happening to us.

Yet when I praise the Lord, my mood becomes lighter. When I do something kind, I'm blessed myself. Sharing gets me out of my self-centeredness.

Start with offering a sacrifice of praise to the Lord right now—whether you feel like it or not. Steps 2 and 3—good deeds and sharing—will then be a lot easier.

*"And will not God bring about justice for his chosen ones,
who cry out to him day and night? Will he keep putting them off?"*

LUKE 18:7
(THE WHOLE STORY: LUKE 18:1–8)

Possible or Impossible?

Those difficult circumstances you're dealing with right now—how do you see them? As insurmountable? Or as an opportunity for God to do the impossible?

It's amazing what a difference attitude makes. For years my husband has had a sign in his office that reads DON'T TELL ME THAT IT CAN'T BE DONE. TELL ME HOW WE'LL DO IT. Sometimes what we need to do is simply get our eyes off the difficulties and focus instead on what we can do to improve a situation.

But most times we need something more.

William Carey knew he needed something more. Throughout his forty-one years of missionary work in India, he faced many insurmountable obstacles. But he continued to press on. He said, "You have not tested the resources of God until you attempt the impossible." I like that, because it challenges my faith. If you want to bolster your own faith, read his biography and you'll find that he proved by his life that God can do the impossible. Today, Carey is known as the "Father of Modern Missions."

Right now when you pray about that overwhelming situation you're facing, don't worry that you're asking for too much. Pray big prayers because we have a big God—one who truly does the impossible.

You are judging by appearances. If anyone is confident
that they belong to Christ, they should consider again
that we belong to Christ just as much as they do.

2 Corinthians 10:7

Defeating Discouragement

Does this scenario fit you? Everything seems to have gone wrong lately. Your job is shaky, your health isn't great, your family has problems, and your finances—well, let's just say your bank account has acute anemia. You can relate to the person who prayed, "Lord, if there's any more trouble coming, send it now while I'm used to it!"[1]

What do your circumstances tell you? That there's no hope, right? But the apostle Paul said, "You are judging by appearances" (2 Corinthians 10:7).

"What do you mean, Paul? The facts are pretty plain—I'm in deep trouble!"

Yes, you are, and you're discouraged. But you may be overlooking the weapon God has given you to fight discouragement. It's "the sword of the Spirit, which is the Word of God" (Ephesians 6:17).

Sometimes we get so discouraged that we don't take hold of God's promises. When Moses told the Israelites that God was going to deliver them from Egyptian slavery, "they did not listen to him because of their discouragement" (Exodus 6:9). When depressed, we don't hear God's whispered promises of help.

But God's promises are true no matter how we feel. "The Lord himself goes before you and will be with you; he will never leave you nor forsake you. Do not be afraid; do not be discouraged" (Deuteronomy 31:8).

God's promises are the weapons He has given us to fight discouragement and renew hope. Search them out in scripture. In faith, set your mind on His promises today. God will meet you.

[1]Ray Pritchard, *The Healing Power of Forgiveness* (Eugene, OR: Harvest House Publishers, 2005), 131.

Therefore, if anyone is in Christ, the new creation has come:
The old has gone, the new is here!

2 Corinthians 5:17

A Green Bottle

A young woman in prison wrote me:

> *My life is like a bottle. I had always thought I was going to be something special. Maybe I'd be used to hold some costly medicine, or I might be a fine vase. But I ended up just a plain green bottle, sent down a conveyor belt and filled with cheap wine.*
>
> *I was packed together with a bunch of other bottles and shipped to a big city, where I sat on a dark, dusty shelf for a long time. One day, an old wino pulled me off the shelf and carried me out back into a dark alley. He finished me off, staggered to his feet and, swaying side to side, drew back and heaved me into a brick wall, smashing me to pieces.*
>
> *For years I lay there.*
>
> *Then one day someone came toward me—someone who actually kneeled down in that dirty, smelly alley and began sifting through all the broken pieces. How He did it, I don't know, but that Man found all my shattered pieces, and, one by one, He pieced me back together. It's been over two years since He found me in that alley, and He has been sealing the cracks ever since.*
>
> *The same Man who sought me out can make you whole. His name is Jesus, and He can piece anyone's life together, like He did for me. The Bible says, "Therefore, if anyone is in Christ, the new creation has come: The old has gone, the new is here!" (2 Corinthians 5:17).*
>
> *Don't stay in your broken condition. Call on Him today and let Him put your life together again.*

*I am reminded of your sincere faith, which first lived in your grandmother
Lois and in your mother Eunice and, I am persuaded, now lives in you also.*
2 TIMOTHY 1:5

Celebrate the Life

When you lose someone very close and dear to you, you naturally grieve. Something would be wrong if you didn't, for that person's input in your life has, in a very real sense, come to an end.

Yet what that person brought to your life *hasn't* really come to an end. Someone said: "A well-lived life leaves beautiful treasures shining on our shores." And like children who love to pick up shells as they amble along the scalloped edge of the ocean, we, too, can gather the beautiful qualities from a well-lived life.

The person we miss so much has truly left behind treasures that the tides of grief cannot take away. Think about just a few of these:

- The way our loved one used his or her gifts to bless others
- His or her ready smile and stories and jokes that still cheer us
- Perhaps the person's ever-constant love for the Lord—and you

Nothing can take these treasures from you if you "collect" them.

The apostle Paul reminded a young man named Timothy what he had received from others: "I am reminded of your sincere faith, which first lived in your grandmother Lois and in your mother Eunice and, I am persuaded, now lives in you also" (2 Timothy 1:5). Paul was recalling the faith that Timothy's grandmother and mother had brought to his life. Paul was convinced that that same faith was in Timothy's life, passed on from previous generations.

If you have recently lost a dear one, gather up the treasures you received from that special person. As you remember, as you mourn, celebrate his or her life.

This is what the LORD says—your Redeemer, the Holy One of Israel:
"I am the LORD your God, who teaches you what is best for you,
who directs you in the way you should go."

ISAIAH 48:17

The Weaving

Dr. Ravi Zacharias says that the most magnificent saris ever made are hand-woven in the city of Varanasi, the cultural capital of his native India. These beautiful dresses, with their gold and silver, the reds and the blues, are often chosen to bedeck brides all over the nation.

Most interesting is that these saris are usually made by just two people, a father who sits on a platform and a son who sits two steps down from him.

> *The father has all the spools of silk threads around him. As he begins to pull the threads together, he nods, and the son responds by moving the shuttle from one side to the other. Then the process begins again, with the dad nodding and the son responding. Everything is done with a simple nod from the father. It's a long, tedious process to watch. But if you come back in two or three weeks, you'll see a magnificent pattern emerging.[1]*

If only we would learn to let God direct the weaving of our lives in the same way. Only He knows the pattern He wants to create. As Dr. Zacharias says,

> *We may be moving the shuttle, but the design is in the mind of the Father. The son has no idea what pattern is emerging. He just responds to the father's nod.[2]*

You can imagine how frustrated the father would be if his son refused to follow his direction. We do best to leave the directing of our lives to the Lord.

---

[1] Dr. Ravi Zacharias *Walking From East to West,* with R.S.B. Sawyer (Grand Rapids, MI: Zondervan, 2006), 27.
[2] Ibid.

Selected verses from Psalm 119

Refreshing Words from Psalms

God's Word does so much for us—keeps us from sin, counsels us, strengthens us, lights our path, and gives us peace.

> *¹¹I have hidden your word in my heart*
> *that I might not sin against you.*
> *¹⁸Open my eyes that I may see*
> *wonderful things in your law.*
> *²⁴Your statutes are my delight;*
> *they are my counselors.*
> *²⁸My soul is weary with sorrow;*
> *strengthen me according to your word.*
> *⁸⁹Your word, LORD, is eternal;*
> *it stands firm in the heavens.*
> *¹⁰⁵Your word is a lamp for my feet,*
> *a light on my path.*
> *¹⁶⁵Great peace have those who love your law,*
> *and nothing can make them stumble.*

Lord, help me to realize that Your Word is not like any other written word. Teach me to love it and not neglect it.

For this is what the high and exalted One says—he who lives forever, whose name is holy: "I live in a high and holy place, but also with the one who is contrite and lowly in spirit, to revive the spirit of the lowly and to revive the heart of the contrite."

ISAIAH 57:15

Does God Feel at Home in Your Thoughts?

A. W. Tozer was a Bible teacher of the last century. A deep thinker whose books challenge the most experienced Bible expositors, Tozer yet expressed his thoughts in practical ways.

He was always keenly aware of the holiness of God. Isaiah 57:15 made such an impact on him: "For this is what the high and exalted One says—he who lives forever, whose name is holy: 'I live in a high and holy place, but also with the one who is contrite and lowly in spirit.'"

Tozer wrote,

> *God has been saying to me, "I dwell in your thoughts. Make your thoughts a sanctuary in which I can dwell."* [1]

If you compare your life to a cathedral, your theology is the foundation, Tozer said, but your thoughts are the high bell tower. Make sure it is a place where God can feel at home.

Having thoughts that make God feel at home is a significant concept—and a practical one. We are what we think. If our thoughts are pleasing to the Lord, so will our lives be.

So, does that mean you should *always* be thinking lofty thoughts about God? The answer is clearly "No." Isaiah tells us God lives in "a high and holy place," the high bell tower, so to speak, "but also with the one who is contrite and lowly in spirit." A humble attitude of simple dependence on our holy God keeps us in fellowship with Him through the ordinary hours of our day.

Welcome God to the bell tower of your life.

[1] A. W. Tozer, *Tozer on Worship and Entertainment,* compiled by James L. Snyder (Camp Hill, PA: Christian Publications, 1998), 10–11.

*"Indeed, the very hairs of your head are all numbered.
Don't be afraid; you are worth more than many sparrows."*

LUKE 12:7

The Beans in Our Bin

I'm always amazed when I remember that Jesus said, "Indeed, the very hairs of your head are all numbered" (Luke 12:7). My friend LuAnne learned that hairs aren't the only thing God keeps track of. Recently I received from her this urgent prayer request:

> *My husband, Bill, just came in and was very distraught. We have a grain bin that has $60,000 worth of soy beans in it. He just discovered that it has sprung a leak, and the top layer is rotten. He doesn't know how deep it has gone, but it is bad. The profit from those beans is what we will use to plant our crops next year. If we lose them, we will have to stop farming. Tomorrow he will get two men to go into the bin and scoop out the rotten beans.*

The next day I received a second e-mail from her:

> *Thanks so much for lifting our needs to the Lord. As to the loss, it is several hundred bushels, and when we sell the rest, they will be discounted. Now we wait to see what the buyer says.*

Within three days I heard from LuAnne again:

> *Today we took the first load of beans to the market. They took them at full price. We expected them to have a little mold on them, but they didn't. That was a miracle only the Lord could have done. He not only knows the hairs on our heads, but the beans in our bin.*

Yes, God keeps track of hairs and beans and bank accounts, too. You can trust Him to keep track of all that matters to you!

*So we rebuilt the wall till all of it reached half its height,
for the people worked with all their heart.*

NEHEMIAH 4:6
(THE WHOLE STORY: NEHEMIAH 2–3)

Getting the Job Done

In the fifth century BC, the walls of Jerusalem lay in disrepair. So broken down were they that the city had no protection. But under Nehemiah, the people were challenged to do something about the problem.

If the project were carried out today, a contractor and professional masons would be hired. But that wasn't an option in Nehemiah's day. The only way the wall was going to be rebuilt was for a large number of able-bodied people to pitch in. The work required people from nearby areas, too—not just the residents of Jerusalem but also citizens from surrounding cities, such as Jericho, Tekoa, Gibeon, and Mizpah.

What an interesting group of workers from all walks of life! Some were merchants, some rulers, and others were priests who ordinarily did work in the temple. Two of the most unlikely laborers were Uzziel, a goldsmith, and Hananiah, a perfume maker. And men were not the only workers. Shallum repaired a section with the help of his daughters.

In just fifty-two days, the work was completed—in spite of criticism, ridicule, interference, and even a death threat on Nehemiah. Nehemiah gave credit to God for His help and to those who participated, for as Nehemiah put it, "the people had a mind to work" (Nehemiah 4:6 NASB).

I don't know what job needs to be done where you live, but for a training manual on how to do it, read the book of Nehemiah.

Do everything without grumbling or arguing.
PHILIPPIANS 2:14

Try This for One Week

Just six little words, that's all—but they're powerful!

Here they are: "Do everything without grumbling or arguing" (Philippians 2:14).

Six words, simple to understand, but oh so hard to do! If you don't think so, I challenge you to put them into practice just for today:

1. Don't complain about anything
2. Don't argue about anything

How far do you think you'll get into your day before you flunk the challenge? Can you finish breakfast without complaining or arguing? For some of us, complaining starts early. Hearing the alarm clock ring in the morning sparks an objection that we have to get up.

Now, if only the apostle Paul hadn't included the word *everything*. Doing *everything* without protest or dispute is hard. Some situations just call for complaining or arguing—I want to reserve the right under certain conditions.

Just think, though, what could happen in our relationships if we took this verse seriously. How peaceful our families would be if we didn't argue! Sit down with your family and show them this verse. See if you can get everyone to agree to practice it for one week. You may even make a rule that if anyone complains or argues, he or she has to put money in a fund to buy ice cream for the family at the end of the week. You may be surprised at the difference this verse will make!

The righteous will flourish like a palm tree, they will grow like a cedar of Lebanon; planted in the house of the LORD, they will flourish in the courts of our God. They will still bear fruit in old age, they will stay fresh and green.

PSALM 92:12–14

What Is Ahead

Have you noticed how fast birthdays seem to keep coming year after year after year? That means, if we live long enough, each of us is going to grow old. I, for one, want to make the best of those golden years. I hope what Psalm 92:14 says about old age will be true in my life: "They will still bear fruit in old age, they will stay fresh and green." Now that's the way to live! Not worrying about wrinkles or aches and pains, but radiant with a desire to live life to its fullest.

We may be nearing old age, but that shouldn't stop us from setting goals for the future. *The Message* paraphrase of Paul's words to the Philippians says, "Friends, don't get me wrong: By no means do I count myself an expert. . .but I've got my eye on the goal, where God is beckoning us onward—to Jesus. I'm off and running, and I'm not turning back" (Philippians 3:13–14 MSG).

High in the Swiss Alps, a monument has been erected in honor of a mountain guide who died during his attempt to rescue a stranded tourist. The message inscribed on the stone reads, "He Died Climbing." That's the motto I would like to leave behind when my time on earth ends. So, I'm off and running. I hope to still bear fruit in old age—and stay fresh and green.

Simon Peter answered him, "Lord, to whom shall we go?
You have the words of eternal life."

JOHN 6:68

Bad Things Happen

God could have prevented it—why didn't He? He can change any circumstance I face.

Do thoughts like these ever go through your mind? If you're honest, you'll have to admit they do. You don't like what God is allowing in your life. So what are your options?

You have two choices: either to turn away from God and become bitter, or to turn to God and rely on Him even though you don't understand why you're suffering.

It's pretty obvious that option 1—turning away from God and becoming bitter—is not a good choice. That leaves option 2—turning to God. When you choose to rely on God, you give up relying on any logical reason for what is happening. You simply say, "God, I am going to rely on You and no one else. I ask You to solve this problem. But if You don't, I will trust You anyway."

Like the three Israelites in the book of Daniel who were thrown into the fiery furnace, you say, "If we are thrown into the blazing furnace, the God we serve is able to deliver us from it. . .but even if he does not. . .we will not serve [other] gods" (Daniel 3:17–18). If you think they burned, read their story.

Let's say you decide you can't trust God. Whom will you trust? When some of the crowds turned back and no longer followed Jesus because they didn't like His teachings, He asked the disciples if they wanted to leave, too. Peter answered, "Lord, to whom shall we go? You have the words of eternal life" (John 6:68).

When disaster happens, to whom will *you* go?

Selected verses from Psalm 3

Refreshing Words from Psalms

When things are grim, He is the lifter of our heads. He answers, delivers, and sustains us.

> ¹LORD, how many are my foes!
>   How many rise up against me!
> ²Many are saying of me,
>   "God will not deliver him."
> ³But you, LORD, are a shield around me,
>   my glory, the One who lifts my head high.
> ⁴I call out to the LORD,
>   and he answers me from his holy mountain.
> ⁵I lie down and sleep;
>   I wake again, because the LORD sustains me.

Lord, You are intimately aware of things "rising up against me." I know You will sustain me as I give those troubles to You.

We remember before our God and Father your work produced by faith,
your labor prompted by love, and your endurance inspired
by hope in our Lord Jesus Christ.

1 THESSALONIANS 1:3

When You Need Reasons to Keep Going

At 5:30 a.m. our daughter Nancy called us for help. The family dog had quit breathing. Since her husband had to leave immediately for the airport, could my husband take the dog out of the house before their four children awoke? Fortunately, by the time he was dressed, the dog had revived. But the next morning brought another crisis: a woman drove directly into Nancy's brand-new car. The following day, her daughter called from school with severe stomach pains. Could she please come pick her up? It was one of those weeks when Nancy felt like giving up.

The early Christians had reasons for giving up. They faced suffering, persecution, and constant threats, yet they kept on. How?

In 1 Thessalonians 1:3, Paul speaks of three practical qualities Christians should have: faith, love, and hope. First, he says their work was produced by faith. That means they did what they did, believing that someday it would all make a difference. Caring for toddlers, going to work every day, making sacrifices for other people—they all have to be done by faith.

Next, Paul talks about "labor prompted by love." I think of labor as any work that is superhard. What kept the early believers going was that Jesus had done so much for them; no sacrifice was too great if they would do it for Him.

The last quality is hope—the hope of heaven. Author Tim LaHaye says, "For the believer, this life is as bad as it gets!" But we can endure because we have a future with the Lord.

*"The eternal God is your refuge,
and underneath are the everlasting arms."*

DEUTERONOMY 33:27

Underneath Are the Everlasting Arms

When the airplane I'm in hits turbulence during a flight, I'm a candidate for the "Chicken of the Air" award. I just don't like being tossed around. But I've found a verse in the Bible that helps a lot: "The eternal God is your refuge, and underneath are the everlasting arms" (Deuteronomy 33:27). Picturing God's big arms underneath that bouncing plane calms my emotions. God's everlasting arms hold the plane as a loving father holds his newborn child.

Although air travel was several thousand years in the future when he wrote these words, David tells us that there is no place we can go that we will not find God already there. He writes, "If I go up to the heavens, you are there; if I make my bed in the depths, you are there. If I rise on the wings of the dawn, if I settle on the far side of the sea, even there your hand will guide me, your right hand will hold me fast" (Psalm 139:8–10).

Maybe it's not plane travel that makes you feel insecure. Maybe your job is shaky. Or you dread going to the doctor. Or your marriage is rocky.

Read these verses. David said, "Though an army besiege me, my heart will not fear; though war break out against me, even then will I be confident. . . . For in the day of trouble he will keep me safe in his dwelling; he will hide me in the shelter of his sacred tent and set me high upon a rock" (Psalm 27:3, 5).

Remember, God is our refuge, and we're in His everlasting arms!

For I am convinced that neither death nor life, neither angels nor demons, neither the present nor the future, nor any powers, neither height nor depth, nor anything else in all creation, will be able to separate us from the love of God that is in Christ Jesus our Lord.

ROMANS 8:38–39

He Loves Me

When writer Elizabeth Prentiss was a teenager in the 1800s, she became so disgusted with her temper and lack of self-control that she was sure God could never love her. She told a minister friend, "I can't be good two minutes at a time. I do everything I do not want to do and do nothing I try and pray to do."

The minister replied, half to himself, "Poor child. . . All you say may be true. I dare say it is. But God loves you. He loves you."

Then he told her, "Go home and say over and over to yourself, 'I am a wayward, foolish child. But He loves me! I have disobeyed and grieved Him ten thousand times. But He loves me! I have lost faith. . .I do not love Him; I am even angry with Him! But He loves me!'"

At home Elizabeth knelt down to pray. As she tells it, "All my wasted, childish, wicked life came and stared me in the face. I looked at it and said with tears of joy, 'But He loves me!'"

Absolutely nothing you can do will keep God from loving you. The apostle Paul wrote, "I am convinced that neither death nor life, neither angels nor demons, neither the present nor the future, nor any powers, neither height nor depth, nor anything else in all creation, will be able to separate us from the love of God that is in Christ Jesus our Lord" (Romans 8:38–39).

When you are tempted to despair at the long list of your shortcomings, no matter what you have done wrong, friend, don't forget to add, "But He loves me—unconditionally!"

One thing God has spoken, two things I have heard:
"Power belongs to you, God, and with you, Lord, is unfailing love";
and, "You reward everyone according to what they have done."

PSALM 62:11–12

Strong and Loving

When we think of masculine and feminine characteristics, we often think of strength as masculine and love as feminine. Of course, that's an oversimplification. But I find it interesting that the Bible says God has both of these traits. Psalm 62:11–12 says, "Power belongs to you, God, and with you, Lord, is unfailing love."

If God were only strong, I might be afraid of Him. I'm well aware He could zap me into eternity in a split second. If He were only loving but not strong, He might not be able to help me. His love would reach out to me in compassion. He would feel sorry for me, but that's as far as it would go. Instead, He is the ideal Father—both strong and loving. He is loving enough to care and strong enough to help.

I'm encouraged when I read verses about God's strength, like: "What god is there in heaven or on earth who can do the deeds and mighty works you do?" (Deuteronomy 3:24), and "Your arm is endowed with power; your hand is strong" (Psalm 89:13).

And I am comforted when I find verses that tell me that my strong God is also loving: "You are my strength, I watch for you; you, God, are my fortress, my God on whom I can rely" (Psalm 59:9–10).

A loving God who is strong! That's exactly what we need. Take a moment right now to acknowledge that He is strong enough to help you in the situation you face today. Then thank Him that He loves you and cares for you. As the psalmist said, "He is my loving God. . .and my deliverer" (Psalm 144:2).

*"I know your deeds, that you are neither cold nor hot.
I wish you were either one or the other!"*

REVELATION 3:15
(THE WHOLE STORY: REVELATION 3:14–22)

A Famous Church

Of the many well-known churches in the world, one became famous for all the wrong reasons. The apostle John tells us about it in Revelation 3. It's the church of Laodicea, located in what is now Turkey.

God says about the people in this church: "I know your deeds, that you are neither cold nor hot. I wish you were either one or the other! So, because you are lukewarm—neither hot nor cold—I am about to spit you out of my mouth" (v. 15–16). Strong words!

The worst thing was that these people didn't realize how bad they were. Because they had money, they didn't think they needed anything else. The Bible says, "You do not realize that you are wretched, pitiful, poor, blind and naked" (v. 17).

Many Christians today are like the people of that church. Their relationship with God has grown distant. No longer do they enjoy a sense of God's presence or do the things that please God. Yet God doesn't give up on them. He stands at their hearts' door, knocking—"If anyone hears my voice and opens the door, I will come in and eat with that person, and they with me" (v. 20). Instead of rejecting them, He wants to nurture them by His presence. He offers them His companionship, knowing that the fire in their hearts will be rekindled by the warmth of His love.

If you have grown lukewarm in your relationship with God, open the door of your heart and invite Him in. Listen to His words in the Bible, and share your deepest thoughts with Him in prayer. He's knocking on your heart's door right now.

*And my God will meet all your needs according
to the riches of his glory in Christ Jesus.*

PHILIPPIANS 4:19

Potatoes

The Great Depression hung over America in the 1930s when my dad accepted the pastorate of a small church with a weekly salary of only $10—barely enough to buy groceries and pay the rent.

One day, Mr. Smith, a farmer in the church, backed his little white pickup truck into my parents' yard and unloaded a hundred-pound sack of potatoes, saying, "When these are gone, let me know, and I'll bring you another sack." My parents thanked him gratefully.

One hundred pounds of potatoes! They felt like millionaires. You can do so many different things with potatoes: boil them, bake them, fry them, stuff them, and more. They really enjoyed those potatoes.

But as the weeks went by, the number of potatoes in the sack dwindled. My dad remembered Mr. Smith's offer to bring another sack. He said he didn't know whether it was pride or stubbornness, but he simply could not bring himself to ask Mr. Smith for more potatoes. But he did get down on his knees and ask God to tell Mr. Smith that they needed more potatoes.

Do you know in less than two weeks Mr. Smith unloaded another one hundred-pound sack of potatoes? There were exactly two potatoes left in the original sack.

How amazing to think that they had a God who loved them so much that He would even keep track of the number of potatoes in their sack! God knew exactly how and when to meet my parents' needs. Take heart, He will meet your needs as well. As the apostle Paul said, "My God will meet all your needs according to the riches of his glory in Christ Jesus" (Philippians 4:19).

Selected verses from Psalm 34

Refreshing Words from Psalms

Nothing. That's what I'll lack if I turn to God for deliverance, refuge, and blessing.

> ¹*I will extol the LORD at all times;*
>   *his praise will always be on my lips.*
> ⁴*I sought the LORD, and he answered me;*
>   *he delivered me from all my fears.*
> ⁸*Taste and see that the LORD is good;*
>   *blessed is the one who takes refuge in him.*
> ⁹*Fear the LORD, you his holy people,*
>   *for those who fear him lack nothing.*
> ¹⁰*The lions may grow weak and hungry,*
>   *but those who seek the LORD lack no good thing.*
> ¹⁵*The eyes of the LORD are on the righteous,*
>   *and his ears are attentive to their cry.*
> ¹⁸*The LORD is close to the brokenhearted*
>   *and saves those who are crushed in spirit.*
> ¹⁹*The righteous person may have many troubles,*
>   *but the LORD delivers him from them all.*

Thank You, Jesus, that You knew I'd have trouble. Thank You that You knew I'd cry out to You. And thank You that You promised to be close to me.

When Jesus spoke again to the people, he said,
"I am the light of the world. Whoever follows me will
never walk in darkness, but will have the light of life."

JOHN 8:12

God Intervenes

At the age of ten, my dad dedicated his life to serving the Lord and longed to go to Bible college. His parents, however, thought he should go to a secular college.

One day, toward the end of his senior year of high school, he was standing waist deep in a swimming pool during physical education class. My dad felt a strange sensation and began to lose consciousness. He remembered praying, "Lord, save me!" as he slipped under the water. An alert lifeguard saw him lying at the bottom of the pool and rescued him.

In June of the following year, he fell unconscious again. There was no logical explanation for either incident, but a day or so later, his mother greeted him as he arrived home, tears streaming down her face. Throwing her arms around him, she said the Lord showed her that these incidents had occurred because she wanted him to go to secular college. She said, "You can go to Bible school tomorrow if you want to."

When the fall semester began, you can be sure that my dad was in the front row of the student assembly at Bible school. For the remaining seventy-four years of his life, he faithfully served the Lord as an evangelist, pastor, author, and seminary professor.

Incidentally, my dad was never unconscious again in his entire life of eighty-nine years. His favorite Bible verse when it came to guidance for life was John 8:12, where Jesus said: "I am the light of the world. Whoever follows me will never walk in darkness, but will have the light of life." How wonderful to have a God who personally directs our lives!

The fruit of the righteous is a tree of life,
and the one who is wise saves lives.

PROVERBS 11:30

The Job Is Too Small

Several years ago, the board of the Standard Oil Company was looking for a manager for their new office in China. He or she had to be able to speak Chinese fluently, be a qualified businessman, a born leader, and be under age thirty. After much deliberation, there was still no one who met the requirements.

Finally one of the board members spoke: "I do know a man who fits the qualifications. He is twenty-eight years old, he was valedictorian of his class, he is a born leader, and he speaks Chinese fluently and lives in China."

The board was at once interested and commissioned the member to go to China and offer the man the job. He was instructed to get him at any price.

After traveling halfway around the world, the man presented the opportunity to his friend, offering him a comfortable salary. But his friend, a missionary, shook his head, "No." The man raised the amount several times, but each time the answer was "No!"

"What *will* you take?" the man asked.

The missionary replied, "Oh, there is nothing wrong with the salary. It is magnificent, but the job is too small. I have a small salary but a big job. You offer me a big salary but a little job. I would be foolish to stop winning people to the Lord and start selling oil."

Whether you are a missionary or a layperson, it is just as true today. In Proverbs 11 King Solomon, who was both wise and rich, wrote, "The one who is wise saves lives" (Proverbs 11:30). Winning souls to the Lord is the biggest job in the world.

And this is love: that we walk in obedience to his commands. As you have heard from the beginning, his command is that you walk in love.

2 JOHN 1:6

Excusitis

Missionary Chris Pilet was browsing through a bargain book table one day when he spotted a book entitled *The Magic of Thinking Big* by David J. Schwartz. He figured it was probably a sort of humanistic self-help book, but since the price was only a dollar, he decided to buy it. Surprisingly, he found it challenging on many levels. One concept that impressed him was "excusitis," something the author calls "the failure disease":

> *Study the lives of successful people and you'll discover this: all the excuses made by the mediocre fellow could be but aren't made by the successful person.*
>
> *I have never met nor heard of a highly successful. . .leader in any field who could not have found one or more major excuses to hide behind. Franklin D. Roosevelt could have hidden behind his lifeless legs; [Harry] Truman could have used "no college education;" John F. Kennedy could have said, "I'm too young to be president."*
>
> *Like any disease, excusitis gets worse if it isn't treated properly. A victim. . .goes through this mental process: "I'm not doing as well as I should. What can I use as an alibi that will help me save face? Let's see: Poor health? Lack of education? Too old? Too young? Bad luck? Personal misfortune? Wife? The way my family brought me up?"*
>
> *Once the victim of this failure disease has selected a "good" excuse. . .he relies on the excuse to explain to himself and others why he is not going forward.[1]*

Have you ever suffered from excusitis? The cure is very straightforward: simple obedience to what God wants you to do. John wrote, "And this is love: that we walk in obedience to his commands" (2 John 1:6).

[1]David J. Schwartz, *The Magic of Thinking Big* (New York: Simon & Schuster Adult Publishing Group, 1987), 29–30.

He saved us, not because of righteous things
we had done, but because of his mercy.

TITUS 3:5

Saved by Good Deeds or God's Mercy?

My grandfather was the son of an Episcopalian minister. Though he was brought up in a strict environment, he had never truly had a relationship with Jesus Christ. In fact, Grandpa made up his mind that when he left home, he was going to live it up. But when he did, he found no real satisfaction, so he returned to church. Being a traveling salesman, he joined the Gideons, that fine organization of Christian businessmen who place Bibles in hotel rooms around the world.

Grandpa made a trip to collect the annual donation of a Mr. Noble to the Gideons. After presenting his check to Grandpa, this elderly gentleman asked him, "Are you saved?" to which Grandpa replied, "I'm doing the best I can, and I hope to get to heaven."

The white-haired gentleman said, "That's a sure ticket to hell for you. Tell me, what are you doing to get to heaven?" Grandpa said he was striving to live a good life, to be a good husband and father, and to be a respectable citizen.

The old gentleman snapped his fingers and said, "That won't count that much toward getting you to heaven." Then Mr. Noble told him that salvation did not depend on what *he* did, but what Jesus had done *for* him on the cross. Soon they were both on their knees, praying, and my grandfather finally surrendered his life to Christ.

The Bible says God saves us "not because of righteous things we [have] done, but because of his mercy" (Titus 3:5). We *all* qualify for that!

We love because he first loved us.
1 JOHN 4:19

Loving Obedience

I attended a conference where one of the speakers asked an interesting question: "Which are you more afraid of—breaking God's commandments or breaking His heart?" That hit home with me. Most of us know that God wants us to do right and reject wrong.

But even beyond obedience, God wants an intimate relationship with us. There is such a need for us to obey God because we love Him, because we don't want to do anything that would bring heartache to our loving heavenly Father.

We need loving obedience in five areas of our lives: our mind, our will, our emotions, our body, and our time. Now, if you're alive and breathing, you struggle in one or more areas. I struggle with lovingly obeying God when it comes to taking care of my body. Exercise? I don't want to do it. I also struggle with wanting to play when I should work. And most of all, I struggle when I need to confront someone about an issue and I don't want to.

A friend struggles with her mind and emotions. She has a fear of serious illness. She can convince herself that she has the symptoms of nearly every illness she hears about. My friend has to lovingly obey God by focusing on God's promises to care for her.

I challenge you to listen, to be sensitive, to God's voice and then lovingly obey Him—not because He's going to punish you if you don't, but because you love Him so much that you don't want to break His heart. John said, "We love him, because he first loved us" (1 John 4:19 KJV). What motivation for us!

Jesus said to [Zacchaeus],
"Today salvation has come to this house."
LUKE 19:9
(THE WHOLE STORY: LUKE 19:1–10)

God Seeks the Lost

One day, while swimming along the bottom of the ocean, a professional diver noticed an oyster with a piece of paper in its mouth. He opened the oyster and held the paper close to his goggles. To his surprise, he found it was a Gospel tract explaining how to become a Christian.

Amazed, the diver realized, *I cannot hold out against God any longer since He has gone to so much trouble to track me down.* At the bottom of the ocean he repented of his sins and placed his faith in Jesus Christ.

Zacchaeus was a tax collector who was short on morals and in stature. He was in Jericho when Jesus arrived but couldn't see him over the crowd, so he ran ahead and climbed a tree. When Jesus reached the tree, He looked up, saying, "Zacchaeus, come down immediately. I must stay at your house today."

The people began to mutter, "He has gone to be the guest of a sinner."

Zacchaeus said, "Look, Lord! Here and now I give half of my possessions to the poor, and if I have cheated anybody out of anything, I will pay back four times the amount."

Jesus said, "Today salvation has come to this house. . . . For the Son of Man came to seek and to save the lost" (Luke 19:1–10, excerpted).

If God is speaking loud and clear to you today, don't you think it's time for you to respond? Whether you are at the bottom of the ocean or in a tree or driving your car to work, He's calling you.

Selected verses from Psalm 10

Refreshing Words from Psalms

Have you ever felt helpless, victimized, or fatherless? Psalm 10 tells us God sees, He hears, He helps.

> *12 Arise, LORD! Lift up your hand, O God.*
>   *Do not forget the helpless.*
> *14 But you, God, see the trouble of the afflicted;*
>   *you consider their grief and take it in hand.*
> *The victims commit themselves to you;*
>   *you are the helper of the fatherless.*
> *17 You, LORD, hear the desire of the afflicted;*
>   *you encourage them, and you listen to their cry.*

Lord, I do commit myself to You. Thank You for Your promises of encouragement.

I plead with Euodia and I plead with
Syntyche to be of the same mind in the Lord.
PHILIPPIANS 4:2

Women Who Can't Get Along

When they came to me, the two women were at a heated impasse. They were both Sunday school leaders in a large church. The dilemma was that one strongly believed hexagonal crayons were best for young children to use, while the other insisted that round crayons were the only way to go. As ridiculous as it sounds, neither woman would give in.

A similar thing happened to two women in the Bible. Paul wrote, "I plead with Euodia and I plead with Syntyche to be of the same mind in the Lord" (Philippians 4:2). Like the two Sunday school leaders, these women were both energetic workers for the Lord. Many had come to faith in Christ through their efforts. But some difference of opinion had grown into an impasse.

I hate to admit it, but I've observed that this problem happens more often among women than men. In a board meeting, for instance, two men can argue vehemently about an issue. But when the meeting is over, they can go out and play basketball together without holding on to hard feelings. When two women disagree, they don't even want to talk to each other, let alone have lunch.

Yes, it's possible to believe in Christ, work hard for His kingdom, and yet have strong disagreements with others who are committed to the same cause. But there is no excuse for remaining unreconciled.

Psalm 133:1 says, "How good and pleasant it is when God's people live together in unity!" Do you need to iron out your differences with someone today?

The LORD is good, a refuge in times of trouble.
He cares for those who trust in him.
NAHUM 1:7

A Refuge in Times of Trouble

You're leaving on a trip abroad when you learn there is a travel warning posted for your destination. Upon arriving at the airport, a bomb scare empties the terminal. Metal detectors, dogs sniffing your luggage—like it or not, the world is an uncertain place.

As never before, we need to hold on to the assurance that God cares for those who trust in Him. It's not enough to know that this promise is in the Bible. You need to know it's in your heart—internalized and made your own.

The short Old Testament book of Nahum was written about the Middle Eastern city of Nineveh whose people were cruel and wicked. Through the prophet Nahum, God graphically warned the Ninevites that they would be destroyed.

Yet smack-dab in the middle of all the bad news is one of the most beautiful promises in the Bible. It's in Nahum 1:7, "The LORD is good, a refuge in times of trouble. He cares for those who trust in him."

God is a good God. When you have a personal relationship with Him, you have a refuge in trouble—a haven, a sanctuary, a place of safety, a shelter. I love the image in Psalm 91:4 of God as a mother hen protecting her chicks: "He will cover you with his feathers, and under his wings you will find refuge."

We live in a scary world, but remember that you have a God who "cares for those who trust in him."

"Know this, you and all the people of Israel: It is by the name of Jesus Christ of Nazareth, whom you crucified but whom God raised from the dead, that this man stands before you healed."

ACTS 4:10

In the Name of Jesus

Veteran missionary Greg Fisher relates that when he was growing up in the US, his dad was a street evangelist.

Greg tells about going with his dad to a spot in Hollywood in front of Grauman's Chinese Theatre when he was only seven years old. As his dad preached to the crowds lined up for the Sunday matinee, one bystander yelled at his dad—not a rare experience for street preachers. But what amazed Greg, even at that young age, was that what set the man off was the mere mention of the name of Jesus.

So, too, in New Testament days when Peter and John healed a lame man, the religious leaders were up in arms. They questioned: "By what power or what name did you do this?" Peter answered unequivocally, "It is by the name of Jesus Christ of Nazareth" (Acts 4:10).

Today some would say that we should not use the name of Jesus in the public arena for fear of offending those of other religions. Yet as Greg points out,

> *It is the name of Jesus that carries real power to transform darkness—power to heal broken bodies and restore crushed and mutilated souls. Ultimately, what we are announcing is that the name of Jesus has power to save.[1]*

He sums it up with this powerful statement:

> *As a Christian. . .I can have no other program, no other cure, no other agenda than to announce—from every point possible—that there is salvation in the Mighty Name of Jesus Christ of Nazareth.[2]*

[1]Greg Fisher, http://africathoughts.blogspot.com, December 1, 2005, accessed October 21, 2008.

[2]Ibid.

And so we will be with the Lord forever.

1 Thessalonians 4:17
(the whole story: 1 Thessalonians 4:13–18)

With the Lord

Everybody wants to go to heaven when they die. Or at least, they certainly don't want to go to hell! But have you ever thought that one day you might suddenly find yourself in heaven, not knowing your way around? Common belief is that the apostle Peter will welcome us, but actually the Bible doesn't confirm this.

You don't have to worry about feeling lost when you die. The Bible says that because Jesus is our Savior, we will be with Him. Paul says that to be away from the body is to be at home with the Lord (2 Corinthians 5:8). There is no intermediary place, no time lapse in between.

Notice Paul doesn't say, "To be absent from the body is to be in heaven." He says something far more fantastic: when we die, we'll instantly be in Jesus' presence—with Him.

Paul also tells us what will happen if we are still alive when Jesus returns. He says that "God will bring with Jesus those who have fallen asleep in him" (1 Thessalonians 4:14). He continues, "After that, we who are still alive and are left will be caught up together with them in the clouds to meet the Lord in the air. And so we will be with the Lord forever" (1 Thessalonians 4:17).

Just think of it! The One who walked with you through your problems and to whom you have spoken countless times in prayer, the One who died for you, the One who loves you more than anyone else—you're really going to be with Him, at home with Jesus forever. Magnificent promise!

By the word of the LORD the heavens were made,
their starry host by the breath of his mouth.

PSALM 33:6

Bigger Than the Sombrero Galaxy

One of the most beautiful galaxies viewable from earth is the Sombrero Galaxy. This brilliant heavenly mass got its interesting name from its resemblance to a broad-rimmed Mexican hat. Even though this galaxy is just beyond what the naked eye can see, data from the Hubble Telescope has determined that it's actually a massive object equivalent to eight hundred billion suns. If you were to travel from one side to the other of the Sombrero Galaxy, it would take you fifty thousand light years![1]

Our minds have trouble wrapping themselves around anything of such large dimensions. But even if we can't truly grasp how massive eight hundred billion suns are, just *trying* to understand is good for us because the effort enlarges our concept of how big God is. If God made the heavens, He must be bigger than, greater than, and superior to anything He has made, right? Does it not follow, then, that He must be bigger than our problems?

"By the word of the LORD the heavens were made, their starry host by the breath of his mouth" (Psalm 33:6). *Poof!* Just like that, God created our tremendous heavens and earth! Even a glimpse of how big our God is makes trusting Him easier.

Check out a book on astronomy. If you have access to the Internet, search the size of the universe. Investigate the heavens, and I can pretty well guarantee that your faith in God will grow.

[1]http://hubblesite.org/newscenter/archive/releases/2003/28/image/a/, accessed September 17, 2008.

"Father, I have sinned against heaven and against you."
LUKE 15:21
(THE WHOLE STORY: LUKE 15:11–24)

Mature Prayer

Jesus told a story about a son who said to his father, "Give me my share of the estate," and the father did so. The son then set off and squandered all his wealth. Reduced to taking a job feeding pigs, he was so hungry that even the pigs' slop looked good to him.

Eventually he came to his senses and said, "How many of my father's hired men have food to spare, and here I am starving! I will go back to my father and say to him: 'Father, I have sinned against heaven and against you. I am no longer worthy to be called your son; make me like one of your hired men.'" So off he went.

But while he was still a long way off, his father ran to him and threw his arms around him. The father told the servants, "Bring the best robe and put it on him. Put a ring on his finger and sandals on his feet. Let's have a feast and celebrate. For this son of mine was dead and is alive again; he was lost and is found" (Luke 15:12–24, excerpted).

Beyond this story of forgiveness and restoration is a lesson on prayer. The young son started out saying, "Father, give me my share of the estate." But his request changed to: "Father, make me like one of your hired men." Immature prayer stops with "Father, give me"—the long list of everything we want from God. Mature prayer goes on to say, "Father, make me—exactly what You want me to be."

After you've brought all your "give-me" requests to God, don't forget the "make-me" part.

Selected verses from Psalm 28

Refreshing Words from Psalms

Our incomparably awesome Creator God is never too busy running the universe to hear our cries for help!

> *¹To you, Lord, I call;*
>   *you are my Rock,*
>   *do not turn a deaf ear to me.*
> *For if you remain silent,*
>   *I will be like those who go down to the pit.*
> *²Hear my cry for mercy*
>   *as I call to you for help,*
> *as I lift up my hands*
>   *toward your Most Holy Place.*
> *⁶Praise be to the Lord,*
>   *for he has heard my cry for mercy.*
> *⁷The Lord is my strength and my shield;*
>   *my heart trusts in him, and he helps me.*
> *My heart leaps for joy,*
>   *and with my song I praise him.*

Lord, I am awed at Your care and concern for me. Thank You for hearing and helping me. May my heart "leap for joy" when I see Your hand in my life today.

*Do not be anxious about anything, but in every situation, by prayer
and petition, with thanksgiving, present your requests to God.*

PHILIPPIANS 4:6

Anything and Everything

I'll give you a verse in the Bible that covers anything and everything that will happen to you today. You'll find it in Philippians 4:6 (TLB). The first part says, "Don't worry about anything." Now, that sounds simple to do—but only until something major strikes at the center of what you care most about. It could be the business you just started or a family relationship. Then you find yourself thinking about the problem nonstop.

How can God tell you not to worry about anything when what you really care about most is falling apart? Well, the verse doesn't stop there. God goes on to say, "Instead, pray about everything." Prayer is the antidote God gives for worry. The big question is, have you tried it? Today, every time that worry pops in your mind, immediately turn it into a prayer for God's help. Our human tendency is to think that our worry is either too small to bother God about or too big for us to expect Him to fix. But nothing is too large or too small for God. That's why He tells us to pray about *everything*—yes, every worry that comes to mind.

The biggest problem most of us have with prayer is giving up too soon. We think that once we have prayed about a problem, that should take care of it. But it doesn't work that way. Remember, we need to pray every time we worry—and that can be pretty often on any day. God urges us to turn every worried thought into a prayer.

After that, we who are still alive and are left will be caught
up together with them in the clouds to meet the Lord in the air.
And so we will be with the Lord forever.

1 Thessalonians 4:17

Ready at a Moment's Notice

William, our oldest grandson, has worn glasses since he was a baby. Though he wears contact lenses now, as a toddler he loved his glasses because they helped him see better. Every night he wanted those glasses near his bed so he could put them on first thing in the morning.

When William was very young, he had a photo taken with James Irwin, a committed Christian and one of only twelve Americans who have walked on the moon.

The following conversation between six-year-old William and his dad took place while they were looking out the car window at the moon.

"Daddy, what's the moon made of?"

"Rocks and dust. Astronaut James Irwin went to the moon and walked around on it, and that's how we know. Do you remember that he held you in his arms?"

"No, Daddy, I don't remember."

"He's gone to heaven, and he's with Jesus now."

"Daddy, I don't think I'll recognize him in heaven."

"Oh yes, William, we'll all be able to recognize each other in heaven. Astronaut Irwin will say, 'Oh, I know you—you were the little boy I held in my arms.'"

"Then I'm going to sleep with my glasses in my hand from now on," responded William, "so I'll be able to recognize him!"

The Bible says one day we who have put our faith in Jesus Christ "will be caught up. . .in the clouds to meet the Lord in the air. And so we will be with the Lord forever" (1 Thessalonians 4:17). Keep in mind that *today* just might be the day we see Christ. Like William, let's be ready at a moment's notice.

And Noah and his sons and his wife and his sons' wives
entered the ark to escape the waters of the flood.

GENESIS 7:7
(THE WHOLE STORY: GENESIS 6:1–8:18)

Mrs. Noah

All the people of the world trace their lineage to this woman. She lived during a period when morals sank to an all-time low and the earth was filled with violence.

She is a descendant of Eve and lived at least ten generations after her. Her husband is mentioned over fifty times in the Bible. "Noah was a righteous man, blameless among the people of his time, and he walked faithfully with God" (Genesis 6:9). But she is only identified as "the wife of Noah."

When God told Noah He was going to destroy the world by a flood, the peoples of the earth had never even seen rain. For 120 years Noah warned of God's coming judgment, but no one listened. Can you imagine how hard it must have been for Mrs. Noah when people made fun of her husband, how she had to encourage him when he got tired of preaching with no results? Realize, too, her boys had no "good" kids to play with. Yet she must have raised her kids to be godly, because when the world was destroyed, God saved her three sons.

Life on the ark? Imagine living in a floating zoo with the windows closed for forty days and nights of rain. And they had to wait inside the ark for 150 more days before they could step out on dry land and begin a new life.

Mrs. Noah surely exemplified 1 Corinthians 15:58: "Let nothing move you. Always give yourselves fully to the work of the Lord, because you know that your labor in the Lord is not in vain." You, Mrs. Noah, belong in the Faith Hall of Fame.

"When the people willingly offer themselves—praise the LORD!"
JUDGES 5:2
(THE WHOLE STORY: JUDGES 5:1–9)

Volunteers

Every organization that touches people's lives depends on a select group to help make it happen: the volunteers. Organizations also have paid staff, but they would never be able to accomplish what they do if it were not for hard-working, selfless volunteers who stuff envelopes, make repairs, count donations, and do anything that needs to be done. I know, because I've seen them at work in our own organization, Guidelines International Ministries.

In the Bible I found two verses about volunteers, and both times, the author was prompted to say, "Praise the Lord!" for them. Barak and Deborah were leading an important battle against Sisera, a Canaanite king who had cruelly oppressed Israel for twenty years. The leaders couldn't win the battle alone—volunteers made the difference that led them to victory.

After the battle, the leaders sang a song declaring, "When the princes in Israel take the lead, when the people willingly offer themselves—praise the LORD!" (Judges 5:2). I think the leader of any organization would heartily agree with that sentiment. When people offer to help, the battle can be won! In another part of the song, the leaders exclaimed, "My heart is with Israel's princes, with the willing volunteers among the people. Praise the LORD!" (Judges 5:9).

If you volunteer your time to make a difference in the lives of people, I want to say, "Thank you," to you today. Everything you do may be behind the scenes. But one day God will acknowledge what you have done, and then we will all say, "Praise the Lord!"

When your words came, I ate them; they were my joy and my heart's delight,
for I bear your name, LORD God Almighty.

JEREMIAH 15:16

Spiritual Survival

The flight attendant recited the instructions as the plane was taking off. "If loss of cabin pressure occurs, oxygen masks will drop. If you are traveling with a child, secure your own mask before putting the mask on your child." If you black out, you would not be able to help your child. It makes sense.

Yet when it comes to parenting, we mothers usually feel we must always tend to our children's needs before our own. Sometimes we're pretty close to blacking out from exhaustion.

Moms often come up short in availing themselves of spiritual resources. When I was mothering three young children, I wondered if it were possible to have a deep spiritual life. There simply was no time for extensive Bible study or long periods of prayer. The best I could do was grab a few verses on the run and send up prayers of desperation, saying, "Lord, help me!"

So my advice to moms is don't panic when a few days go by when you can't complete a Bible study and your prayers are very short. Consider a psalm as you brew the coffee, a prayer of praise as you look into your baby's face during a diaper change, or uplifting words from scripture tapes or CDs as you drive.

The same principle is true if you're responsible for the employees of a large corporation. You can't go very long without spiritual nourishment. The prophet Jeremiah said, "When your words came, I ate them; they were my joy and my heart's delight" (Jeremiah 15:16).

Make sure you keep spiritually "nibbling" daily when a "sit-down dinner" isn't possible!

And over all these virtues put on love,
which binds them all together in perfect unity.
COLOSSIANS 3:14

God's Wardrobe

In Colossians 3 we're told to clothe ourselves with seven characteristics. If we do, we'll have an entire outfit—and all of the highest quality!

The first on the list is *compassion*. That's the shirt because it's worn close to the heart. When our hearts are filled with compassion, we'll reach out to others.

The second is *kindness*. Since it's our legs that carry us to do helpful things for others, kindness must be the skirt or pants.

The belt that secures kindness in place is *patience*! With patience, we have the grace to continue to treat others kindly even when they're unresponsive.

Humility certainly must be the shoes, the items closest to the ground. Shoes of humility will take us to help those who are less fortunate than us.

For accessories, try *gentleness*. It's not very flashy, but oh so attractive. Peter says, "Your beauty should not come from outward adornment. . . . Rather, it should be that of. . .a gentle and quiet spirit, which is of great worth in God's sight" (1 Peter 3:3–4).

Item number six is *forgiveness*. This is the hat because forgiveness is first a decision you make in your head, then an emotion of the heart.

How about a coat to keep out the cold? Scripture says, "Over all these virtues put on love, which binds them all together in perfect unity" (Colossians 3:14). *Love* absolutely radiates warmth.

Don't you agree that the person wearing compassion, kindness, humility, gentleness, patience, forgiveness, and love is well dressed for any occasion? Let's wear God's wardrobe!

Selected verses from Psalm 37

Refreshing Words from Psalms

Stop. Stop and take refuge in Him today. His Word tells us that He delivers and saves those who do.

> *³Trust in the L*ord *and do good;*
>   *dwell in the land and enjoy safe pasture.*
> *⁴Take delight in the L*ord*,*
>   *and he will give you the desires of your heart.*
> *⁵Commit your way to the L*ord*;*
>   *trust in him and he will do this.*
> *⁷Be still before the L*ord
>   *and wait patiently for him;*
> *do not fret when people succeed in their ways,*
>   *when they carry out their wicked schemes.*
> *³⁹The salvation of the righteous comes from the L*ord*;*
>   *he is their stronghold in time of trouble.*
> *⁴⁰The L*ord *helps them and delivers them;*
>   *he delivers them from the wicked and saves them,*
>   *because they take refuge in him.*

Lord, thank You for the "safe pasture" that awaits me every time I stop long enough to be with You. Teach me that I can't live without the refuge of You.

In everything [Amaziah] followed the example of his father Joash.

2 KINGS 14:3

(THE WHOLE STORY: 2 KINGS 14:1–4)

The Power of Example

Steve Maxwell, a leader in the homeschool movement, tells of a lesson he learned from his son.

While moving his family to a new home, they stopped at a restaurant to eat. When the waiter took their order, Nathan, their eldest son, spoke up. He told the waiter that they would be asking the Lord to bless their food and asked if there was anything they might pray about for him. The waiter was taken aback. Recovering, he said that his girlfriend's father was in the hospital with a serious heart problem, and they would appreciate prayer for him. After the prayer, the waiter was clearly moved and grateful.

Steve told his son Nathan how thankful he was for his example, and that he was looking forward to asking others this same question in the future. Nathan explained that he had been with someone else who had done this, and he decided he would do it himself. Someone had set an example for Nathan, and Nathan learned from the example he saw.

The power of example! It is passed from person to person. Whether you realize it or not, you are mentoring people by your life. Some of the finest teaching is done not with words but by example.

You may never have heard of kings by the name of Amaziah or Joash, but we can learn something from them. Scripture says Amaziah "did what was right in the eyes of the LORD. . . . In everything he followed the example of his father Joash" (2 Kings 14:3). So Joash set the example, and his son Amaziah followed in his footsteps.

Be encouraged—people do notice what you do. Your example has the power to shape their lives.

"Your Father knows what you need before you ask him."
MATTHEW 6:8

God Is a Great Accountant

My dad, who was in ministry for seventy-four years, began preaching during the difficult days of the 1930s, when money was hard to come by.

Dad told about one day when he had to mail an important letter. It had to be posted that day, but he did not have three cents to buy the necessary stamp. When the mailman came that very morning, Dad received a letter from a friend, and there, between the pages of the letter, was a three-cent stamp. No mention of the stamp was made in the letter, but the Lord had known, several days before, that he was going to need a postage stamp. The Lord had graciously put it into the heart of this friend to drop a stamp into the envelope.

Dad also remembered a time when he needed ten cents for something important—just ten cents, but he did not have it. Again a letter came with a dime thrown in. He used to exclaim, "How wonderful the Lord is to His children!"

I'm glad he told us these experiences, because it taught me that God is a great accountant. He knows exactly how much you have and how much you need at any given moment. The Bible says, "Your Father knows what you need before you ask him" (Matthew 6:8). And if God has supplied His children's needs in the past, you can be sure that He will also meet their present needs.

You may think, *God answers prayer for other people, but I don't know if He will for me.* Just try Him. For He knows what you need even before you ask Him.

Indeed, we felt we had received the sentence of death. But this happened that we might not rely on ourselves but on God, who raises the dead.

2 CORINTHIANS 1:9

Three Reasons Why This Happened

When you're deeply hurting, the question that immediately comes to mind is: *Why? Why did this happen to me?* Three examples in the Bible give us three answers to this troubling question.

The first is that pain comes because of sin. Jeremiah 13:22 says, "And if you ask yourself, 'Why has this happened to me?'—it is because of your many sins." We may see this connection in others, but sometimes we're not so quick to see this truth in ourselves.

Another reason God allows pain is so that He will be praised. Does that seem strange to you? Just before Jesus healed a blind man, the religious leaders asked whose sin had caused the blindness. Jesus answered, "Neither this man nor his parents sinned. . .but this happened so that the work of God might be displayed in his life" (John 9:3). God may want you to be a showcase of His supernatural power so that people will acknowledge Him.

Third, Paul said that painful experiences happen to us "that we might not rely on ourselves but on God" (2 Corinthians 1:9). We quickly realize, *I can't fix this! I really need God's help!* There's nothing like an impossible situation to make us realize how helpless we are.

If right now you are dealing with a painful problem, God may be saying, "There's sin here that we need to talk about." Or maybe He's going to send such a miraculous solution that all you can say is, "Praise Him!" Or maybe He's helping you realize how totally dependent you are on Him and how totally dependable He is. Just listen!

*A young girl from Israel. . .served Naaman's wife. She said to
her mistress, "If only my master would see the prophet who
is in Samaria! He would cure him of his leprosy."*

2 Kings 5:2–3
(THE WHOLE STORY: 2 Kings 5:1–15)

Where's the Piccolo?

The famous conductor Sir Michael Costa was leading an orchestra rehearsal with hundreds of instruments and voices. The choir sang at full voice, accompanied by the thundering of the organ, the rolling of drums, and the blaring of horns.

In the midst of the music, the piccolo player, far up in a corner, said to himself, "It doesn't matter what I do," and he stopped playing. Suddenly, the great conductor flung up his hands and brought the rehearsal to a complete standstill. "Where is the piccolo?!" he cried. His sharp ear had noticed its absence. And so, for him, the whole piece had been spoiled.[1]

What about you? In life's orchestra, have you ever felt like the piccolo player—insignificant and hidden?

The Bible tells the story of how a simple servant played an important role in the life of a highly regarded man. Naaman was commander of the army of the king of Aram. Then he contracted leprosy.

His armies had taken a young Israeli girl captive, and she became a servant to Naaman's wife. She was definitely "just" a piccolo player—a prisoner, a slave. But she spoke up and said to her mistress, "If only my master would see the prophet [Elisha] who is in Samaria! He would cure him of his leprosy" (2 Kings 5:3). Naaman did just that. Through Elisha, God healed Naaman of the disease. From that point on, Naaman said he would worship only the true God. God used a simple captive maid to draw an important man to Himself.

You make a difference in this life. Keep playing your piccolo. The Divine Conductor of life's orchestra is listening for your part.

[1]Corrie ten Boom, *Not I but Christ* (Nashville, TN: Thomas Nelson Publishers, 1984), 135.

Then they cried to the LORD in their trouble, and he saved them from their distress. He brought them out of darkness, the utter darkness, and broke away their chains.

PSALM 107:13–14

No Pit Too Deep

By her own admission, she was a prostitute, a lesbian, an alcoholic, and a stripper. Only twenty-four years old and in prison for a year now on a murder charge, she was also a single mom with two kids.

She wrote me from prison to tell me that, four months previously, Jesus had given her a new life. When she thought she was "finished," God rescued her, and now, she writes, "I am so happy to be alive in Jesus Christ."

While she was in prison, someone sent her my book *Created for a Purpose*. She read it and then wrote to say that she now knows God has a unique purpose for her life. My eyes filled with tears of joy when I read her letter. What a miracle God has done in her life!

This young woman is a glowing example of Psalm 107:13–14: "Then they cried to the LORD in their trouble, and he saved them from their distress. He brought them out of darkness, the utter darkness, and broke away their chains."

Maybe you, too, are chained in a pit. You're feeling that you've wasted your days—that you've gone too far for even God to restore your life. Dear friend, that simply is *not* true. Corrie ten Boom, a Dutch Christian who survived the horrors of the Ravensbrück concentration camp in World War II, said, "There is no pit so deep that God's love is not deeper still." God can change your life; turn to Him with all your heart.

It was good for me to be afflicted so that I might learn your decrees.

PSALM 119:71
(THE WHOLE STORY: PSALM 119:67–71)

Getting My Attention

Her name was Carol, and she was in her eighties. The thing that impressed me most about her was the sweet attention she devoted to the Lord. Every morning during her quiet time with God, after she read some scripture, she would write a letter to Him. In these letters she would thank God for His goodness to her and ask Him for her needs. She would also tell Him about the circumstances that she didn't like. Each letter was Carol's prayer to the Lord, and this practice prepared her to face each day.

Carol was a volunteer at our Guidelines Ministries office for almost twenty years. So many times when she was going through difficult circumstances, I've heard her say something like: "The Lord is so good. If necessary, He wakes me up at two o'clock in the morning to talk to me. He loves me too much to let go my own way. So if I know what's good for me, I'll listen to Him and learn what He wants to teach me so He doesn't have to keep trying to get my attention."

Yes, God has interesting ways of getting our attention. Sometimes He speaks softly in our hearts. Other times He stops us in our tracks with a roadblock so big, we have no choice but to turn to Him. Either way, His motivation is love.

The writer of Psalm 119 said, "It was good for me to be afflicted so that I might learn your decrees" (v. 71). Thanks, Carol, for being a living example of that truth.

Selected verses from Psalm 25

Refreshing Words from Psalms

Need help navigating your life today? The Lord is ready and willing to show you His paths and guide you step by step.

> ¹*In you, Lord my God,*
>   *I put my trust.*
> ²*I trust in you;*
>   *do not let me be put to shame,*
>   *nor let my enemies triumph over me.*
> ³*No one who hopes in you*
>   *will ever be put to shame,*
> *but shame will come on those*
>   *who are treacherous without cause.*
> ⁴*Show me your ways, Lord,*
>   *teach me your paths.*
> ⁵*Guide me in your truth and teach me,*
>   *for you are God my Savior,*
>   *and my hope is in you all day long.*
> ⁶*Remember, Lord, your great mercy and love,*
>   *for they are from of old.*
> ⁷*Do not remember the sins of my youth*
>   *and my rebellious ways;*
> *according to your love remember me,*
>   *for you, Lord, are good.*

Lord, I lift my day, I lift my very soul up to You. Please show me Your paths. Guide and teach me, for my hope is in You and Your goodness.

Therefore encourage one another and build
each other up, just as in fact you are doing.
1 THESSALONIANS 5:11

Ten Things I Love about You

When birthdays or Christmas roll around, do you ever wonder what to give that special person in your life who seems to have everything? My friend Angie suggests an album or scrapbook or card entitled "Ten Things I Love about You." Although this gift will not cost you much money, it will require time for reflection as you go through the memories of your relationship and choose ten things that are special about that person.

This beautiful gift of "Ten Things I Love about You" can be given to your eight-year-old son or your ninety-year-old grandma—it fits all sizes and ages perfectly.

It's strange, but we presume that those we care about already know their strengths and lovable qualities. But that's not necessarily true. Sometimes those closest to us have struggled in certain areas and don't realize how successful they have become in conquering their difficulties. Instead of obstacles, those areas of their lives are now blessings—and they need you to tell them.

The Bible says, "Encourage one another and build each other up" (1 Thessalonians 5:11). Each of us would benefit from this kind of encouragement, and that's why this gift is so special.

Another plus is that whenever the recipient of your gift hurts you or needs your forgiveness—as eventually happens in every relationship—thinking of the ten things you love about that person will help your anger fade.

Take time to encourage that special person with a priceless gift that no one else can give. Both of you will be blessed.

"There is no one like the God of Jeshurun, who rides across the heavens to help you and on the clouds in his majesty."

DEUTERONOMY 33:26

Superman

Superman began as a comic book character in June 1938. He grew in popularity, appearing in comic books, radio programs, newspaper comic strips, graphic novels, TV programs, movies, and even a Broadway musical. Wearing his familiar costume of red, blue, and yellow with the stylized *S*, he has been a hero figure to millions.

In some versions of the story, his arrival on earth hints at parallels to the birth of Jesus. In the original movie version, Superman's father, played by Marlon Brando, tells his son to lead ordinary men to righteousness, saying, "For this reason above all—their capacity for good—I have sent them to you, my only son."

There is certainly a hunger in the human heart for somebody bigger than we are. We want someone to look up to, someone who can accomplish incredible feats that we cannot, someone to fight the evil forces we see furiously at work in the world.

Fortunately, we have Someone who can do exactly those things. The Lord God Almighty is His name. "There is no one like the God of Jeshurun, who rides on the heavens to help you and on the clouds in his majesty" (Deuteronomy 33:26). And who was Jeshurun? Scholars tell us it was a poetic name for the people of Israel, used to express affection. It means "the dear upright people" (Deuteronomy 32:15, 33:5, 26; Isaiah 44:2).

Superman can't be everywhere at once, and there are feats that Superman can't do, but "nothing will be impossible with God" (Luke 1:37 ESV). He is the real Superhero. Aren't you glad you know Him?

Jesus answered. . . "What is that to you?
You must follow me."

JOHN 21:22
(THE WHOLE STORY: JOHN 21:1–25)

What Is That to You? Follow Me!

I love the story of the conversation between Simon Peter and Jesus on the shores of the Sea of Galilee after Jesus rose from the dead.

Peter and Jesus had some unfinished business. Remember what happened? Peter had denied Jesus three times before Jesus was crucified. But now Jesus turns to Peter and asks, "Simon, do you love Me?" Peter answers, "Yes, Lord, You know that I love You." Jesus asks the question three times. Three denials and three professions of love. Then Jesus tells Peter ahead of time that when he is old he will glorify God by being executed—tradition says by crucifixion. Jesus then adds a command, "Follow Me!" (John 21:19).

You can always count on Peter to ask the questions you would have liked to ask if you had the nerve. Peter sees his fellow disciple John and asks, "What about him, Lord?" (John 21:21). Don't you love his audacity? It's as if he is saying, "Lord, is he going to have to suffer as much as I?" In our day, we compare ourselves with other Christians and ask, "Why do I have more problems than she has?"

Jesus answers, "If I want him to remain alive until I return, what is that to you? You must follow me" (John 21:22).

Jesus would say the same thing to us today: "Don't compare My work in your life with the way I work in the lives of others." Your experience with God is made specifically for you. Our job is simply to follow the Lord wherever He leads us. Thank God for His custom-designed plan for you! Just obey Him one day, or even one hour, at a time. Who knows how He will use your life to bless others!

"His master replied, 'Well done, good and faithful servant! You have been faithful with a few things; I will put you in charge of many things. Come and share your master's happiness!' "

MATTHEW 25:21

Florence Nightingale

Florence Nightingale, the founder of modern nursing, was born in 1820 to a wealthy English family.

When Florence was seventeen, she heard God call her for a special purpose in life. That calling was to help the sick and poor by becoming a nurse—in those days a lowly position that was considered to be "working–class."

When England entered the Crimean War, Florence and a team of thirty-eight nurses went to Turkey, and later Crimea, to help the wounded soldiers. The military hospitals were filthy, infested with rats and fleas that brought typhus and cholera. Florence herself contracted Crimean Fever. She made improvements, however, that helped bring the death rate down from 40 percent to 2 percent. Her work there was the inspiration for the founding of the International Red Cross.

Returning to England after the war, Florence campaigned for improving hospitals so that they would become places where lives were saved, not lost. Three years before she died, she received the Order of Merit, making her the first woman ever to receive it.

Florence wrote,

> My life. . .show[ed] how a woman of very ordinary ability has been led by God in strange and unaccustomed paths to do in his service what he has done in her. And if I could tell you all, you would see how God has done all, and I nothing. I have worked hard, very hard, that is all; and I have never refused God anything.[1]

The Lord must have surely told her, "Well done, good and faithful servant!" (Matthew 25:21). Think about the circumstances God has placed you in. What can you do in His service to show all that He has done in you?

[1]Killy John and Alie Stibbe, *Bursting at the Seams* (Oxford, UK: Monarch Books, 2004), 12.

Therefore, I urge you, brothers and sisters, in view of God's mercy, to offer your bodies as a living sacrifice, holy and pleasing to God—this is your true and proper worship. Do not conform to the pattern of this world, but be transformed by the renewing of your mind. Then you will be able to test and approve what God's will is—his good, pleasing and perfect will.

ROMANS 12:1–2

Living Sacrifices

It was one of those days when I felt pressured by too much to do, and I was working hard to complete each task. Just then, my husband asked me if I had time to run an errand for him. Something flared up inside me, and in my mind I immediately answered him with a very firm "no." My answer wasn't audible, but I'm sure by the look on my face, he detected that I didn't want to do what he asked.

As I quickly thought it over, I realized that I was the logical person to run the errand. After all, I had more time than he did. So I said "yes," and started for the car.

But inside I was still resentful of being interrupted. I climbed in the driver's seat, and as I started the car, I turned on the radio. Immediately I heard the words, "Have you ever presented your body to the Lord as a living sacrifice?" *Okay, Lord,* I thought. *I hear You.*

In Romans 12:1 Paul says, "Therefore, I urge you, brothers and sisters, in view of God's mercy, to offer your bodies as a living sacrifice, holy and pleasing to God." Yes, I had made that commitment. But doing it in a beautiful, candlelit service is one thing; living out that commitment in everyday life is another. I confessed my lack of willingness and asked His forgiveness.

You, too, at one time or another may have offered your life to the Lord as a living sacrifice. But maybe you, like me, need to go back to the altar from time to time and do it again.

To this you were called, because Christ suffered for you,
leaving you an example, that you should follow in his steps.

1 PETER 2:21

The Power of Touch

Missionary doctor Paul Brand is famous for his contributions to stopping leprosy in poor areas of the world. Dr. Brand worked with lepers who had been ostracized by their communities, for the disease had long been incorrectly thought to be contagious.

Dr. Brand tells about one day in India when he was examining the hands of a man, trying to explain to him that he could halt the progress of the leprosy and perhaps restore some movement. But he could do little about the man's facial deformities. Dr. Brand joked with him a bit, laying his hand on the man's shoulder. "Your face is not so bad," he said with a wink, "and it shouldn't get any worse if you take the medication. After all, we men don't have to worry so much about our faces. It's the women who fret over every bump and wrinkle." He expected the man to smile, but instead he began to shake with muffled sobs.

"Have I done something wrong?" Dr. Brand asked his assistant in English. "No, doctor," said the nurse. "He says he is crying because you put your hand around his shoulder. Until he came here, no one had touched him for many years."[1]

Jesus touched people—the blind, the disabled, and yes, even people with leprosy—giving us an example that we "should follow in his steps" (1 Peter 2:21).

Sometimes we just don't realize how much someone needs our touch. Of course, it should be appropriate—the right person at the right time in the right way. See if there is someone in your life who needs this loving encouragement today.

[1]Dr. Paul Brand and Philip Yancey, The Gift of Pain (Manila, Philippines: OMF Literature Inc., 2000), 106

Selected verses from Psalm 31

Refreshing Words from Psalms

Have things ever looked so dark for you that you surely thought you were cut off from God? Impossible, assures Psalm 31.

> *¹In you, LORD, I have taken refuge;*
>   *let me never be put to shame;*
>   *deliver me in your righteousness.*
> *²Turn your ear to me,*
>   *come quickly to my rescue;*
> *be my rock of refuge,*
>   *a strong fortress to save me.*
> *¹⁵My times are in your hands;*
>   *deliver me from the hands of my enemies,*
>   *from those who pursue me.*
> *¹⁶Let your face shine on your servant;*
>   *save me in your unfailing love.*
> *¹⁹How abundant are the good things*
>   *that you have stored up for those who fear you,*
> *that you bestow in the sight of all,*
>   *on those who take refuge in you.*
> *²²In my alarm I said,*
>   *"I am cut off from your sight!"*
> *Yet you heard my cry for mercy*
>   *when I called to you for help.*
> *²⁴Be strong and take heart,*
>   *all you who hope in the LORD.*

I feel insignificant today, Lord. Thank You for Your greatness—and Your care for me!

Then Peter came to himself and said, "Now I know without a doubt that the Lord has sent his angel and rescued me from Herod's clutches and from everything the Jewish people were hoping would happen."

ACTS 12:11
(THE WHOLE STORY: ACTS 12:1–11)

What a Difference a Year Makes!

It was Passover, and the apostle Peter was in prison sleeping between two soldiers, bound with chains, with sentries standing guard. No Passover meal for Peter.

Where had Peter celebrated the previous Passover just a year ago? At that unforgettable meal with Jesus, the Last Supper. In prison, Peter had all the time in the world to remember.

He must have remembered that Jesus washed his feet that night. Remembered that he told Jesus he would rather die than deny Him. With what shame he must have remembered that three times he denied even knowing Him—then wept bitterly.

The crucifixion followed, and afterward Jesus' body was put in a tomb. But then came Resurrection Day! Peter saw for himself that the tomb was empty. There was that thrilling moment when Jesus appeared in front of him and the other disciples. Later, the risen Savior ate breakfast with them on the shores of Galilee, and Jesus told Peter, "Follow me" (John 21:22).

Peter's trial was to be very soon (Acts 12:4). He might shortly suffer the same fate as his Lord. Now in prison, waiting for the outcome, Peter had the peace of knowing he had been obedient and that his life was in God's hands. And so he slept soundly—even in prison.

Later, after his miraculous release, he wrote: "In all this you greatly rejoice, though now for a little while you may have had to suffer grief in all kinds of trials" (1 Peter 1:6). "Cast all your anxiety on him because he cares for you" (1 Peter 5:7).

Like Peter, may we, too, obey Jesus' command: "Follow Me."
Let the peace of Christ rule in your hearts, since as members of
one body you were called to peace. And be thankful.

COLOSSIANS 3:15

Let the Peace of God Rule—and Be Thankful

Two of my grandchildren, ages six and nine at the time, were fighting. Heated words flew back and forth. Finally, I interrupted them. "Carson, tell me one thing you like about Ryan—just one." It took awhile before he could think of anything, but finally he admitted, "Well, he helps me rollerblade."

I can't remember now if Ryan, in turn, came up with anything or not, but they did quit arguing. It's almost impossible to stay angry with someone when you're thinking about one thing you like about that person.

The apostle Paul must have known that when he wrote to the Colossians, "Let the peace of Christ rule in your hearts, since as members of one body you were called to peace. And be thankful" (Colossians 3:15).

Anger and thankfulness are almost mutually exclusive. You can't be angry with someone and thankful for that person at the same time. Paul was saying, "Let the peace of Christ be the umpire in your disputes."

When we think of peace, we often think of an image, like a perfectly calm lake. But preacher G. Campbell Morgan said that the word for peace used in the Bible is "not a stillness in which there is no movement at all. . . . It is the ending of strife and conflict."[1] It's that blessed relief that comes when the conflict is over.

That person you're angry with right now—isn't there one thing that you're thankful for about him? You may have to think very hard to come up with something. But if you do, your anger will begin to subside. Try it!

[1] G. Campbell Morgan, *The Corinthian Letters of Paul* (Westwood, NJ: Fleming H. Revell Company, 1946), 15.

He appointed twelve that they might be with him
and that he might send them out to preach.

MARK 3:14

Oh, How I'll Love You!

Richard Abanes wrote a beautiful love song meant to be sung at weddings. The refrain goes,

> *And I'll honor you, I'll comfort you, abide with you forever.*
> *I'll be true to you, stay near to you, forsake you never.*
> *I will laugh with you, I will cry with you,*
> *We will walk through life together;*
> *And I'll love you, oh, how I'll love you.[1]*

What bride wouldn't want to hear her groom pledge his love so beautifully? I couldn't help thinking that this is also the kind of relationship God wants with each of us. God has demonstrated that He desires a bond with us. Why else does God call Himself our Father? Why else is the Body of Christ, made up of all believers, pictured as the bride of Christ?

When Jesus called the disciples, "He appointed twelve that they might be with him" (Mark 3:14). Oh yes, after that He sent them out to preach. But first, He called them to be with Him. That's how we get to know the Lord—by being with Him.

Two men in the Bible, we're told, walked with God—Enoch and Noah (Genesis 5:22, 24; 6:9). No wonder they knew Him so well. If we just spend time walking and talking with God, we, too, will grow to be more like Him.

Here's another thought. My husband knows beyond the shadow of a doubt that I love him. But he still wants to hear me tell him so every day—and so does God. Sit quietly for a moment and tell Him today.

[1]"Oh, How I'll Love You," music and lyrics by Richard Abanes © 1998. Used by permission.

My guilt has overwhelmed me like a burden too heavy to bear.

PSALM 38:4

God's Hook

When she entered college, Pamela's relationship with her mom started to become strained, and from that point on, things only grew worse. She remembers, "We just kept trying to be close, only to hurt each other again and again."[1] Both mother and daughter genuinely wanted to restore the broken relationship. So they decided to take a car trip together to patch things up.

The tension was pretty bad at first, but while they were in a restaurant, Pamela finally poured out her heart about the things for which she needed forgiveness. To her surprise, her mother responded, "Sweetheart, I forgave you for all of those things years ago. You just didn't take them off of your hook and put them on God's."[2]

I love that word picture—taking your sins off your hook and putting them on God's! Sometimes we ask God to forgive our failures, but then we continue to carry guilt for them. Like David, we could say, "My guilt has overwhelmed me like a burden too heavy to bear" (Psalm 38:4). But God never intended it that way. Jesus said, "Come to me, all you who are weary and burdened, and I will give you rest" (Matthew 11:28). God is ready to carry your burdens for you, even the burden of guilt.

When I was a kid, I remember a wall plaque that said LET GO AND LET GOD. Could this be the day that you would do just that? Right now let go of your failure and let God take care of it. Accept His forgiveness. Take your load off your hook and put it on God's!

---

[1] Pamela Sonnenmoser, "Road Trip to Forgiveness," in *The Gift of Letting Go: Powerful Stories of Forgiveness* (Colorado: Honor Books, 2005), 204.

[2] Ibid., 205.

*What, then, shall we say in response to these things? If God is for us,
who can be against us? He who did not spare his own Son, but gave him up
for us all—how will he not also, along with him, graciously give us all things?*

ROMANS 8:31–32

Ten Ways to Reduce Stress

A friend recently sent me a list of "Thirty-Six Ways Christians Can Reduce
Stress." No, I won't list all thirty-six, but let me share just ten ideas with you.

1. *Get up on time so you can start the day unrushed.* Let me add that it
   would be great if, before you tackle your responsibilities, you
   include time for Bible reading and prayer.
2. *Simplify and unclutter the rest of your day.* Allow more time than you
   think you need to do things and to get to places.
3. *Take one day at a time, separating worries from concerns.* If the situation
   is a concern, ask God what to do about it. If it's a worry, turn it
   over to Him and forget it.
4. *Delegate tasks to others who are more capable.* It's an ego trip to think
   you're the only one who can do the job.
5. *Carry a Bible with you to read while waiting in line.* That's a great
   way to use time. Another good use of time is to listen to an
   inspirational CD or MP3 while driving.
6. Having problems? *Talk to God on the spot.*
7. *Keep on hand a folder of favorite scripture verses or encouraging quotations.*
   You can also write them on cards you can carry with you.
8. *Be kind to unkind people*—they probably need kindness the most.
9. *Remind yourself that you are not the general manager of the universe.* God
   is quite capable of taking care of what you can't.
10. *Every night before going to sleep, think of one thing you're grateful for that
    you've never thanked God for before.* You'll sleep well.

Praise be to the God and Father of our Lord Jesus Christ,
the Father of compassion and the God of all comfort,
who comforts us in all our troubles, so that we can comfort those
in any trouble with the comfort we ourselves receive from God.

2 CORINTHIANS 1:3–4

GALS

Fifty ladies attended the luncheon that day. They all had something in common. Each of them has experienced how it is to wake up one morning and realize she is starting a new chapter in her life—as a widow.

Most married women will know how it is to live without husbands. Currently, three-fourths of the people who are living at age seventy-five are women.

These women inspire me. They call themselves GALS ("Get a Life, Sister"). I see them using their gifts, time, and resources to bless others. Some have a ministry of prayer. Some minister to the elderly. Many are using their influence to impact their grandchildren. Each lives with precious memories, not "getting over" grief but getting on with living a life of meaning.

My friend Dee Green is such a person. For many years she worked alongside her husband, Paul, in ministry. Then with little warning, Paul went to be with the Lord. At first Dee didn't even want to live. But then God spoke to her heart and reassured her that He had a plan and unique work for her to do.

Many times I've called on Dee for help when a friend of mine has lost her husband. Dee knows how to rejoice with those who rejoice and weep with those who weep. She herself knows well the One the apostle Paul calls "the God of all comfort, who comforts us in all our troubles, so that we can comfort those in any trouble with the comfort we ourselves receive from God" (2 Corinthians 1:3–4). Thanks, Dee, for modeling how to reach out to others who are in need.

Selected verses from Psalm 27

Refreshing Words from Psalms

Does today hold something scary for you? Family stress, medical tests, or a "besieging army"? You can be confident the Lord will see you through the day.

> *¹The LORD is my light and my salvation—*
>   *whom shall I fear?*
> *The LORD is the stronghold of my life—*
>   *of whom shall I be afraid?*
> *³Though an army besiege me,*
>   *my heart will not fear;*
> *though war break out against me,*
>   *even then I will be confident.*
> *⁵For in the day of trouble*
>   *he will keep me safe in his dwelling;*
> *he will hide me in the shelter of his sacred tent*
>   *and set me high upon a rock.*
> *¹⁰Though my father and mother forsake me,*
>   *the LORD will receive me.*
> *¹³I remain confident of this:*
>   *I will see the goodness of the LORD*
>   *in the land of the living.*
> *¹⁴Wait for the LORD;*
>   *be strong and take heart*
>   *and wait for the LORD.*

Lord, I place my confidence in You today! I wait on You for strength.

The LORD said, "I have indeed seen the misery of my people."

EXODUS 3:7
(THE WHOLE STORY: EXODUS 3:7–8)

God Is Concerned about You

Are you going through a time when you're feeling down—below sea level—struggling just to stay alive in the middle of your problems? I wish I could change your circumstances, but I can't. But I do have some words from the Bible to encourage you.

First, here's what I want you to do. Think back to the time when God's people, the Israelites, were slaves in Egypt. Just think of how life was for them as they suffered under the tyranny of the pharaohs. Maybe there are some parallels between their troubles and what you are going through.

For instance, you're stuck in this impossible situation where you don't see any way out, right? That's how the Israelites felt. When they cried out to God, nothing seemed to happen.

But then something *did* happen. God intervened. And everything changed fast. "The LORD said, '*I have indeed seen* the misery of my people. . . . *I have heard* them crying out. . .and *I am concerned* about their suffering. So *I have come down to rescue* them'" (Exodus 3:7–8, italics added).

Dear friend, God has not forgotten you. As He told His people so long ago, He does see you, He hears you, He is concerned, and He will rescue you. Cast your load of cares on the Lord and see if He doesn't bring you into a place of blessing in your life.

God says, "Remember. . .I have made you, you are my servant. . .I will not forget you" (Isaiah 44:21).

And whatever you do, whether in word or deed, do it all in the name of the Lord Jesus, giving thanks to God the Father through him.
COLOSSIANS 3:17

Small Obediences

As a woman, every day you do so many *little* things, don't you? You see to it that dirty clothes are laundered, groceries are bought, meals are prepared, dental appointments are made, homework is done. The list goes on and on. A woman's life is made up of seemingly endless little things to do.

But little things are important. Evangelist F. B. Meyer said,

> *Do not try to do a great thing; you may waste all your time waiting for the opportunity which may never come. But since little things are always claiming your attention, do them. . .for the glory of God.*

Meyer echoes what the apostle Paul wrote in Colossians 3:17: "And whatever you do, whether in word or deed, do it all in the name of the Lord Jesus, giving thanks to God the Father through him."

I like to think of little things as "small obediences." Cardinal John Henry Newman said that taking up the cross of Christ consists of the continual practice of small duties that may be distasteful to us.

When I was caring for my young children, one of them was always needing Mom—not for anything "important"—just to settle an argument or mop up a spill, while the phone was ringing and the pasta was boiling over on the stove. I had little time to do anything "spiritual," such as long periods of prayer or lengthy Bible study.

I finally realized that in that particular season of my life, the best thing I could do was to meet each demand with the right attitude—doing each task for the Lord with my heart in tune to Him. Small obediences! Today, why don't you offer those little things to the Lord?

But let all who take refuge in you be glad; let them ever sing for joy. Spread your protection over them, that those who love your name may rejoice in you.
PSALM 5:11

What to Do in Adversity

How do you cope in times of difficulty? My friend recounts this experience in the hospital after his dad's stroke:

> *Yesterday was Christmas day—a truly wonderful day. We had brought Dad's favorite Christmas music to the hospital room and cranked up the volume on the little boom box as loud as we dared. We played a version of "Joy to the World" done with a massive choir and orchestra. The finale is the word* joy *repeated five times, each one building louder until the final* joy *is sung with the orchestra playing furiously, bells chiming, cymbals crashing, timpani pounding, and trumpets blasting! It's amazing how worship can transform any place into the throne room of God.*
>
> *After we had asked permission from the staff, we walked up and down the long halls, singing carols to the open doors we found. It was a deeply moving experience as people in the beds would join our singing. In one room, all we could see was the end of a bed, but the owner's feet were moving in time with the music. In another room a croaky voice joined us behind a curtain. We decided we couldn't stop until we had sung for every room. I learned again that for Christians, when we face adversity or trials, our response should be: Sing louder! Worship with more intensity! Love with more abandon! That Christmas couldn't have been a better day.*

That's great advice for times of adversity! Sing louder, worship with more intensity, and love with more abandon! As the psalmist wrote, "Let all who take refuge in you be glad; let them ever sing for joy" (Psalm 5:11)!

*Since we have now been justified by his blood,
how much more shall we be saved from God's wrath through him!*

ROMANS 5:9

You Can Know

Do you truly know that God has forgiven you for *all* the wrong you've ever done? You can know—beyond the shadow of a doubt!

Most of us are aware that God is perfect. He has never done anything wrong. And most of us are equally aware that we have done wrong—*we are sinners*. So God has a "problem" in that He wants us to live with Him forever, but holiness and sin cannot live together. There's that issue of you and I being sinners.

That is exactly the reason why Jesus came to earth—to live with us and die and pay the price for our sins. We should have been the ones crucified on the cross because we've sinned. We should have been the ones to pay the penalty of death. But Jesus died in our place.

The apostle Paul wrote, "Since we have now been justified by his blood, how much more shall we be saved from God's wrath through him!" (Romans 5:9). Did you notice the phrase "justified by his blood"? That means that with His blood, Jesus paid for our sins so that we don't have to. By simply believing in what He did for us, we find eternal life and full forgiveness. We don't have to pretend we never did anything wrong. We don't have to cover up our sins. And we don't have to catch God in a good mood for Him to forgive us. Forgiveness is based on a fact of history—Jesus' death on the cross for us—not on any frame of mind.

Don't spend another day wondering if you have forgiveness. Place your faith in what Jesus did on the cross. You can know that you are forgiven.

Give thanks in all circumstances;
for this is God's will for you in Christ Jesus.

1 THESSALONIANS 5:18

The Hat

"When I became pastor of my first church in Canada," related my dad, "I noticed that virtually every man wore a hat. So I decided that if I wanted to be a respectable member of Canadian society, I should purchase a hat—and I did: a beautiful light tan fedora.

"After about two years, I noticed that my hat had become terribly dirty, and I began to pray for the money to get it cleaned. Somehow I managed to get seventy-five cents together and had my hat cleaned.

"The next Monday night I wore my hat to church for what we called a fellowship service—a specially-blessed time. I was praising the Lord as I walked home—when all of a sudden, the most cantankerous wind came and lifted my beautiful, clean hat off my head and deposited it in a mud puddle.

"Resentment welled up and the blessedness I felt quickly leaked out. As I picked up my hat, I fully expected to see the underside completely muddy. But as I turned it over, to my amazement there was just one little piece of dirt. I flicked it off with my finger and it was gone.

"I said, 'Why, you dirty old devil. You almost robbed me of a great blessing over absolutely nothing.' I put my hat on my head and walked home with joy."

Then Dad concluded, "Whatever you do, do not allow some petty annoyance to rob you of the sweetness of God's blessing in your life."

As the apostle Paul said, "Give thanks in all circumstances; for this is God's will for you in Christ Jesus" (1 Thessalonians 5:18).

Teach us to number our days,
that we may gain a heart of wisdom.

PSALM 90:12

The Death Clock

Among the strangest of websites is Deathclock.com. When you visit that site, you will be greeted with the message, "Welcome to the Death Clock, the Internet's friendly reminder that life is slipping away. . .second by second. The Death Clock will remind you just how short life is."

You can type in your birth date, gender, weight, height, and interestingly, whether you are a smoker or nonsmoker, and also your general outlook in life. The Death Clock will then give you a "guesstimate" of your day of death, down to exactly how many seconds you have left to live. (The date is purely a guess based on life expectancy tables.) Then the number runs down before your eyes.

Why contemplate the shortness of life? One Bible verse answers that question. Moses prayed, "Teach us to number our days, that we may gain a heart of wisdom" (Psalm 90:12). I wrote down the estimated date of my death, not because I believe it's accurate, but to remind myself that each day is God's gift to be used wisely.

I want to encourage you to live today fully, appreciating each moment. Anna Lindsay said, "That we are alive today is proof positive that God has something for us to do today."[1] Don't waste precious seconds in bitterness or feeling sorry for yourself. Don't let anger or revenge rob you of even one day. Life is much too priceless for that.

Today God has given you 86,400 seconds. Embrace the day, and with a wise heart, use those seconds to make a difference.

[1]Quoted in *Joy and Strength,* ed. Mary Wilder Tileston (Boston: Little, Brown, and Company, 1901), 47.

Selected verses from Psalm 90

Refreshing Words from Psalms

God is familiar with every single day of your life. He offers you wisdom for today.

> *¹Lord, you have been our dwelling place*
>   *throughout all generations.*
> *²Before the mountains were born*
>   *or you brought forth the whole world,*
>   *from everlasting to everlasting you are God.*
> *¹²Teach us to number our days,*
>   *that we may gain a heart of wisdom.*
> *¹³Have compassion on your servants.*
> *¹⁴Satisfy us in the morning with your unfailing love,*
>   *that we may sing for joy and be glad all our days.*

Lord, please lead me today with Your wisdom that created the world! Only You will truly satisfy me.

But the fruit of the Spirit is. . .self-control.
GALATIANS 5:22–23
(THE WHOLE STORY: GALATIANS 5:16–26)

Self-Discipline

I was taking care of our daughter's four children by myself. Because the oldest was six and the twins were one-year-olds, I needed eyes in the back of my head to keep up with them! While I was upstairs helping three of them get dressed, one of the twins decided he would help me by pouring his own orange juice for breakfast. He managed to open the refrigerator and drag the half-gallon carton of juice from the shelf. You've already guessed what happened. As he poured the juice into his cup, the weight shifted in the carton, and soon *all* the juice was on the floor. I can't remember how many times I washed the sticky floor that day, trying to get it clean.

I have found from my experience as a mother of three and grandmother of eight that I need self-discipline—lots of it—when everything is hectic. Self-discipline makes the difference between exasperation and restraint, between lashing out in impatience and controlling my anger.

But frankly, the thought of self-discipline turns me off. I immediately think of a straitjacket—of spending my days only thinking, *What is the next thing I must do?* How am I supposed to live that way?

The truth of the matter is that self-discipline, or self-control, is part of the fruit of the Spirit listed in Galatians 5. The fruit of the Spirit are qualities that God's Holy Spirit produces in our lives. I can no more produce self-discipline in my life by my own efforts than I can tie an apple on a tree and expect it to grow. God has to do it.

Ask God to fill you with His Spirit and strengthen you to obey Him. Then you will find self-discipline becoming more and more a natural part of your life.

Thomas said to him, "Lord, we don't know where you are going, so how can we know the way?"

JOHN 14:5
(THE WHOLE STORY: JOHN 14:5–14)

The Jesus Road

An old Indian chief had been told the story of Jesus and how He sacrificed His life on the cross to pay for our sins. A missionary tried to persuade the chief to accept Christ as his only hope of eternal life, but the elderly man shook his head, saying, "The Jesus road is good, but I have followed the Indian road all of my life, and I will follow it to the end."

One year later, the old chief was on the brink of death. "Can I turn to the Jesus road now?" he asked the missionary. "My road stops here. It has no path through the valley."

What a tragedy if we put our faith in a belief system that offers nothing beyond the end of life's road! The good news is that the Jesus road has a path through the valley.

Psalm 23:4 tells us, "Even though I walk through the darkest valley, I will fear no evil, for you are with me." The Jesus road is open to you. Jesus travels with you through the valley, into the bright sunshine of heaven at the other end.

How do you find the Jesus road? Jesus said, "I am the way and the truth and the life. No one comes to the Father except through me" (John 14:6). Don't wait until you're near the end of your life to settle the matter. Take your first steps today on the Jesus road. Ask Him to come into your life and be your Savior and Guide. He will be with you—in life and in death.

"The King will reply, 'Truly I tell you, whatever you did for one of the least of these brothers and sisters of mine, you did for me.'"
MATTHEW 25:40
(THE WHOLE STORY: MATTHEW 25:31–40)

Do It for Me

In the first months when Anita Septimus began caring for babies with AIDS, she wanted to quit. Three of the babies had already died. *Why go on with such painful work? What difference did my love and intervention make if the babies died anyway?* she asked herself. "You have not chosen a pretty profession," friends reminded her.

But Anita didn't give up. She continued to minister not only to the children but to their families. She taught them how to prevent AIDS so that other family members wouldn't contract it. She grieved with them as only parents can grieve when they lose a child.

Anita continued her labor of love to more than three hundred families of children with AIDS. When one of the babies who would have died without her intervention celebrated her tenth birthday, Anita knew her work was worthwhile. Since 1985, Anita has devoted herself to this life-giving ministry.

She lived out her life following what Jesus taught. "Truly I tell you," said Jesus, "whatever you did for one of the least of these brothers and sisters of mine, you did for me" (Matthew 25:40).

Jesus said that one day we will stand before His presence to receive rewards for what we have done. If you are going through the monotony of helping someone who doesn't show appreciation, and you feel like you're wasting your time, remember that God is watching. He's keeping a record of your kindness. Keep on going, and one day you will hear Jesus tell you those words Himself.

You were running a good race. Who cut in
on you to keep you from obeying the truth?
GALATIANS 5:7

Who Cut In on You?

The 3,000-meter women's race in the 1984 Los Angeles Olympics turned out to be one of the most dramatic moments in sports history. Favored to win the gold medal was American Mary Decker. A strong competitor was Zola Budd, the young barefoot-running, record-breaking athlete originally from South Africa, now running for Great Britain.

Shortly after the halfway point of the race, Budd and Decker collided. Decker crashed down onto the inner field, clutching her right thigh in pain. Budd recovered her balance and continued with the race amid the booing of the crowd who thought she had intentionally tripped Decker. Budd, who was leading when the race began, finished seventh. Decker was carried off the track in tears, unable to finish the race.

Every time I hear that story, it reminds me of a verse in the book of Galatians. Young Galatian Christians were being sidetracked from their spiritual progress by an issue in the church. The apostle Paul asked them, "You were running a good race. Who cut in on you to keep you from obeying the truth?" (Galatians 5:7).

We're very much like those Galatians. We allow conflicts and disappointments with people to throw us off course. Sometimes, all it takes is for someone to bump into us with criticism, and we're ready to quit. I think Paul would have also said to us, "You were running a good race. Who cut in on you?" No matter who hurts or disappoints you, it's not enough reason to quit. Take heart. Get up, refocus, and keep running.

"For I know the plans I have for you," declares the LORD, *"plans to prosper you and not to harm you, plans to give you hope and a future."*
JEREMIAH 29:11

Celebrate Your Femininity

Have you ever seriously thought that your being a woman and not a man is God's distinct plan for you? If God needed another man in the world, you would have been one, for there are about 104 boy babies born for every 100 girl babies. " 'For I know the plans I have for you,' declares the LORD, 'plans to prosper you and not to harm you, plans to give you hope and a future' " (Jeremiah 29:11).

Since your gender is God's direct, individual plan for you, I encourage you to celebrate your femininity and not let anything steal your pride or enjoyment of His gift of womanhood. God gave you a beautiful body in spite of how media and today's culture have endeavored to make you feel deficient and in need of "fixing" with Botox injections and surgery. We came from the drawing board of heaven to be lovely creations of God's handiwork. Appreciate your body. Take good care of it with proper nutrition and enough exercise. Enjoy pretty clothes and feminine things.

Shortly after we were married, Harold and I visited France. I had heard about the prostitutes in Paris, but I was not prepared to see how beautiful they were—well groomed, slender, stylish, and walking with pride. *If they can look like that while making their living in that disgraceful, exploitative way,* I thought, *I can keep myself attractive for my wonderful husband who is faithful to me and loves me with all his heart.*

Enjoy your femininity not extravagantly or with self-centeredness, but with freedom to be the woman God has created you to be.

Jesus said, "Truly I tell you, this poor widow has put more into the treasury than all the others. They all gave out of their wealth; but she, out of her poverty, put in everything—all she had to live on."

MARK 12:43–44

(THE WHOLE STORY: MARK 12:41–44)

The Most Valuable Donation Ever Given

One day, Jesus was sitting near the temple in Jerusalem, watching the people as they put their money into an offering box placed close to the entrance. He noticed that many rich people put in large amounts. But then a poor widow came and put in two very small copper coins worth only a fraction of a penny.

Calling His disciples to Him, Jesus said, "Truly I tell you, this poor widow has put more into the treasury than all the others. They all gave out of their wealth; but she, out of her poverty, put in everything—all she had to live on" (Mark 12:43–44).

The other day I got to thinking about how much money has been given to the Lord's work as a result of this widow's example. We don't even know her name, but no doubt millions of dollars have been given because of her willingness to give all she had. Her tiny gift has been multiplied countless times. Wouldn't she be surprised if she knew?

Jesus still sees what we give. He knows how much we give and how much we have left after we give. He also knows our motive for giving. He looks at our hearts and knows whether we do it for Him or only to impress other people— or perhaps to assuage feelings of guilt about how blessed we really are.

Yes, God sees when you sacrifice in order to give to Him. And one day He will reward you. Give—you never know how your example will influence others.

Selected verses from Psalm 61

Refreshing Words from Psalms

He knows that life is full of days that cause our hearts to grow faint. He offers us a rock, a refuge, a strong tower to run to.

> *¹Hear my cry, O God;*
>   *listen to my prayer.*
> *²From the ends of the earth I call to you,*
>   *I call as my heart grows faint;*
>   *lead me to the rock that is higher than I.*
> *³For you have been my refuge,*
>   *a strong tower against the foe.*
> *⁴I long to dwell in your tent forever*
>   *and take refuge in the shelter of your wings.*

Lord, help me turn to You for refuge today and not try to handle things on my own.

For since the creation of the world God's invisible qualities—
his eternal power and divine nature—have been clearly seen, being
understood from what has been made, so that people are without excuse.

ROMANS 1:20

Dr. Nadia

Nadia Panchenko was a shining inspiration to me. A doctor of biology, Nadia was the director of the Medico-Ecological Center in Ukraine, which researched health problems that developed from the nuclear disaster at Chernobyl. One of the first to help victims after the meltdown, Dr. Nadia refused to stop her mission in order to protect herself. As a result, she incurred high doses of radiation and her own life was shortened by cancer.

But in the intervening years, Dr. Nadia operated a clinic in Kiev to treat the people who had been relocated there from the radiation area. She cared for them for free since they had no money to pay. Children especially touched her heart because she knew they would suffer ever-increasing health problems during their lifetime.

Dr. Nadia authored more than ninety scientific publications and held patents for ten discoveries relating to the blood. If she had sought popularity and status, she could have become world famous—but instead, she stayed with those who needed her most. Growing up in the former USSR, Dr. Nadia had learned only atheistic evolution. But when she began to study blood cells, she became amazed at the precision, order, and interdependence of processes in the cells. "The blood cell 'witnessed' to me about the Creator," she said. This ultimately led her to faith in Christ.

Dr. Nadia discovered the Creator in His creation. "For since the creation of the world God's invisible qualities—his eternal power and divine nature—have been clearly seen, being understood from what has been made" (Romans 1:20). Her faith, in turn, made her reach out to those who so desperately needed help. Yes, Dr. Nadia, your life truly is still an inspiration!

"Blessed is the one whose sin the
Lord will never count against them."
ROMANS 4:8

Forgiving Yourself

The woman wept as she said, "What I have done is so awful! I can accept that God has forgiven me, but I can never forgive myself." Sadly, she was setting herself up for a lifetime of misery.

Many people don't understand the concept of forgiveness. When God forgives, He does not merely say, "What you did is not so bad—and besides, I love you; I won't hold this sin against you this time." No, that's not what forgiveness is. Sin is bad and forgiveness was costly. It took the death of Jesus on the cross to pay the penalty for our sin. When God forgives us, He does so not because He "feels" like forgiving us. He forgives us based solidly on the fact that Jesus paid the sentence for sin so that we don't have to pay.

Why, then, do people not forgive themselves? My friend Dr. Richard Smith, who counsels people with forgiveness issues, says that in his experience, the people who have problems forgiving themselves don't really understand that God has fully forgiven them. God no longer looks on us as sinners but as *saints*, the biblical term for believers forgiven by Jesus Christ. And if that is the way God see us, what right do we have to see ourselves in any other way? In God's eyes our sins no longer exist. Romans 4:8 says, "Blessed is the one whose sin the Lord will never count against them."

Forgiven sin is gone forever! You are wasting your time punishing yourself for it. More than that, you are dishonoring God who paid the price for your forgiveness. It's time to let your guilt feelings go! Time to forget what is behind, as Paul said, and press toward what is ahead (Philippians 3:13). Go to God in prayer and ask Him to help you finally, fully forgive yourself, now.

"But be sure to fear the LORD and serve him faithfully with all your heart; consider what great things he has done for you."

1 SAMUEL 12:24
(THE WHOLE STORY: 1 SAMUEL 12:19–24)

When You've Wronged God

The people of Israel wanted a king so they could be like the pagan nations around them. At the time they were a theocracy—a government with God as the head and human judges to advise the people.

But now they wanted a monarchy because everybody else had one. In effect they said, "God, You're not good enough for us." They made a serious mistake.

Samuel, their judge at the time, helped them restore their relationship with God. What he said to them in 1 Samuel 12 gives us a pattern to follow when we have wronged the Lord:

1. First, admit your wrongdoing. The people said to Samuel, "We have added to all our other sins the evil of asking for a king" (v. 19).
2. Second, turn with all your heart to the Lord.
3. Third, understand that when you repent, God will restore you. Samuel said, "For the sake of his great name the LORD will not reject his people, because the LORD was pleased to make you his own" (v. 22).
4. Fourth, let mature Christians pray for you, and humbly accept their instruction. Samuel said, "As for me, far be it from me that I should sin against the LORD by failing to pray for you. And I will teach you the way that is good and right" (v. 23).
5. Finally, thank God for His forgiveness and determine to serve Him. "Be sure to fear the LORD and serve him faithfully with all your heart," said Samuel (v. 24).

When we have wronged God, it's not the end. In fact, it can be a new beginning if we turn back to the Lord.

"I called but you did not answer, I spoke but you did not listen."
Isaiah 65:12

Answering and Listening

In these days of voice mail and caller ID, people often do not answer their phones until they know who is calling.

Surprisingly, there's a verse in the Bible about God calling us and not getting an answer. Isaiah 65:12 says, "I called but you did not answer, I spoke but you did not listen." How sad! Almighty God, the Creator of heaven and earth, called the people He loves, but they neither answered Him nor listened to what He had to say. In other words, they hung up on God.

Let's be honest. Has there been a time when you heard God's voice speak to you in your heart, but you didn't want to listen? So you let the call go on the answering machine, so to speak, and ignored God's voice. I admit I have done that.

How different is the way God deals with our calls. In the same chapter of Isaiah, God says, "Before they call I will answer; while they are still speaking I will hear" (v. 24). When we call God, He answers even before we call, not ignoring us like we sometimes ignore Him.

When you call God, you can be sure you'll get through to Him. David said, "In my distress I called to the LORD; I cried to my God for help. From his temple he heard my voice; my cry came before him, into his ears" (Psalm 18:6). God has no answering machine, no receptionist taking the call. Your cry comes directly to His ears.

The next time you sense God speaking to you, do Him the courtesy of answering.

The LORD said to me, "You have seen correctly,
for I am watching to see that my word is fulfilled."
JEREMIAH 1:12

Forty-Seven Kings

We usually think of the Bible as a book that teaches us principles for living—the divine Handbook for life. But sometimes we forget that the Bible is also an accurate record of history.

For instance, the historical books of the Old Testament (from Joshua to 2 Chronicles) record the names of forty-seven kings besides those who reigned in Israel and Judah. Strangely, for some 2,300 years, secular scholars did not recognize them as men who actually lived and ruled. In spite of these rulers' greatness, the scholars relegated them to the sphere of mythology because they simply had not found evidence outside the Bible that they had actually existed.

But archaeologists began to make new discoveries. One by one these kings made their appearance in universally accepted historical records. Now all forty-seven of them have been authenticated by archaeological evidence. Each king has been recognized as a person who lived and ruled, just as the Bible says he did.

Aren't you glad that the words God inspired the writers of the Bible to record are true and reliable? That's a wonderful comfort when you're going through difficult times. The God who made sure that history was recorded accurately in the Bible is the same God who promises, in that same Bible, that "the LORD himself goes before you and will be with you; he will never leave you nor forsake you. Do not be afraid; do not be discouraged (Deuteronomy 31:8).

You can rest on His promises for He said, "I am watching to see that my word is fulfilled" (Jeremiah 1:12).

We will not hide them from their descendants;
we will tell the next generation the praiseworthy deeds
of the LORD, *his power, and the wonders he has done.*

PSALM 78:4

The Ethical Will

A new type of will is becoming popular: the Ethical Will. In this will the author bequeaths to his heirs his values rather than his valuables. It's a documentation of a person's beliefs, desires, and love for his family and friends, in either written or video format.

Spurred by 9/11 and the tsunami disaster in Asia, people have come to look their mortality in the face. Realizing with new clarity that life is short, people desire to express who they are and what they stand for to those they care about.

"We have lawyers to make sure our property will be taken care of, but what will happen to our values after we've gone? People are starting to make an accounting of their lives, share with their children who they are, what they stand for and what they've learned in life," says Rabbi Jack Riemer of Boca Raton, Florida.[1]

Though not a legal document, an Ethical Will can be the most significant thing you leave behind. Your family may be scattered, and you may seldom have the chance to be together and talk to them in one place. An Ethical Will may communicate all that is important to you, especially your faith in Jesus Christ and your desire that each one of them have a personal relationship with Him. We must live each day sharing our faith with our loved ones, but an Ethical Will is a concrete legacy that we can give to future family members as well. The psalmist declared, "We will tell the next generation the praiseworthy deeds of the LORD, his power, and the wonders he has done" (Psalm 78:4).

If there is something of eternal value you'd like to say to your family and heirs, put it in writing today.

[1] Jeffrey Steele, "The Ethical Will: Bequeathing Values Rather Than Valuables," *Los Angeles Times,* June 21, 2005, Y4.

Selected verses from Psalm 71

Refreshing Words from Psalms

We have a God who has done great things! And He is near to us.

> ¹*In you, LORD, I have taken refuge;*
>   *let me never be put to shame.*
> ³*Be my rock of refuge,*
>   *to which I can always go;*
> *give the command to save me,*
>   *for you are my rock and my fortress.*
> ¹²*Do not be far from me, my God;*
>   *come quickly, God, to help me.*
> ¹⁸*Even when I am old and gray,*
>   *do not forsake me, my God,*
> *till I declare your power to the next generation,*
>   *your mighty acts to all who are to come.*
> ¹⁹*Your righteousness, God, reaches to the heavens,*
>   *you who have done great things.*
>   *Who is like you, God?*

Lord, help me to remember as I go through my day that You are near—You will come quickly to help me if I call.

*[David] died at a good old age, having enjoyed long life,
wealth and honor. His son Solomon succeeded him as king.*

1 Chronicles 29:28

How Old Are You?

The only time in our lives when we like to get older is when we're kids. The often-irreverent comedian George Carlin observed that when you're a kid, you're so excited about aging that you think in fractions. He said:

"How old are you?" "I'm four-and-a-half!" You're never thirty-six-and-a-half.

Once you get into your teens, they can't hold you back. "How old are you?" "I'm gonna be sixteen!" And then the greatest day of your life—you become twenty-one. Yes!

But then you turn thirty. What happened there? It makes you sound like bad milk! He turned [sour]; we had to throw him out.

You become twenty-one, you turn thirty, then you're pushing forty. Whoa! Put on the brakes. Before you know it, you reach fifty. But wait! You make it to sixty.

So you become twenty-one, turn thirty, push forty, reach fifty, and make it to sixty. You've built up so much speed that you hit seventy! You get into your eighties. Into the nineties, you start going backwards: "I was just ninety-two."

Then a strange thing happens. If you make it over one hundred, you become a little kid again. "I'm one hundred-and-a-half!"[1]

Whether you're thirty or fifty, what counts is not how many years you live, but how you live those years. King David of Israel "died at a good old age, having enjoyed long life, wealth and honor" (1 Chronicles 29:28). Though he was far from perfect, God called him "a man after his own heart" (1 Samuel 13:14).

May God grant you a full and long life that glorifies Him every day you live!

[1]Excerpted from "George Carlin's Views on Aging," http://www.guidepostmag.com/spirit/passalongs-archive/?i=2705, accessed September 9, 2008.

*This inheritance is kept in heaven for you, who through
faith are shielded by God's power until the coming of
the salvation that is ready to be revealed in the last time.*

1 PETER 1:4–5

(THE WHOLE STORY: 1 PETER 1:3–9)

Good Things in Heaven

Armin Gesswein was a godly man known for prayer—and coffee. He not only led the prayer support for some of Billy Graham's early crusades, but he also spent almost his entire life teaching and preaching about prayer.

Much of his life, Armin ministered in Norway. There, he married a beautiful Norwegian girl, Reidun. Armin and Reidun both deeply enjoyed cups of hot, strong coffee.

They're with the Lord now, but I often exchange e–mails with their daughters, Carol and Sonja. In one exchange with Carol, I mentioned that it would be great if we could get together for a cup of coffee. Since she lives many miles from where I live, I casually added, "Maybe in heaven? Or do they drink coffee in heaven?"

Carol wrote back, "Well, my dad sure loved his coffee, and since there's no unhappiness in heaven, there must be coffee in heaven!"

I wish we could peek into heaven and see what it's like. I'm looking forward to that cup of coffee with the Gessweins.

"Our citizenship is in heaven. And we eagerly await a Savior from there, the Lord Jesus Christ" (Philippians 3:20). The apostle Peter says there's "an inheritance that can never perish, spoil or fade. . .kept in heaven for you" (1 Peter 1:4). John added, "No longer will there be any curse. The throne of God and of the Lamb will be in the city, and his servants will serve him. They will see his face. . . . And they will reign for ever and ever" (Revelation 22:3–5).

I can hardly wait!

Godly men buried Stephen and mourned deeply for him.
But Saul began to destroy the church.

ACTS 8:2–3
(THE WHOLE STORY: ACTS 7:1–8:3)

Life-Changing Power

The evangelist Dwight L. Moody once accepted the challenge to debate with an atheist. He agreed, however, on one condition—that the atheist produce ten or more people whose lives had been changed by atheism. Moody said, "I will have at least one hundred people on the platform who will testify to the fact that belief in Christ has changed their lives." Not able to produce even ten examples, the atheist withdrew his offer.

The apostle Paul himself was a prime example of Christ's life-changing power. When we first find him in the Bible, he is a young man named Saul watching Stephen being stoned to death. The witnesses laid their outer clothes at Saul's feet. But Saul was not merely a spectator. Scripture says he was giving approval to Stephen's death (Acts 8:1). After this, Saul himself began to go from house to house, "breathing out murderous threats" (Acts 9:1) and putting Christians in prison (Acts 9:3).

Little did he know that before he could reach Damascus, he would be forever changed by an encounter with the Lord. His vocation would be changed from persecutor to preacher, his name changed from Saul to Paul, and his heart changed from burning with the desire to see Christians dead to the willingness to give his life that others might hear the Gospel.

Paul declared, "I am not ashamed of the gospel, because it is the power of God that brings salvation to everyone who believes" (Romans 1:16). The Gospel is still powerful enough to change lives for all eternity.

"I myself said, 'How gladly would I treat you like my children and give you a pleasant land, the most beautiful inheritance of any nation.' I thought you would call me 'Father' and not turn away from following me."

JEREMIAH 3:19

Call Me Father

To me, one of the most heartrending verses in the Bible is Jeremiah 3:19.

Here you have God, the Supreme Being of the universe, the Creator of all that is, yearning for a father-child relationship with us. And so He grieves. He owns everything but the affection of His children.

Many women tell me they have trouble thinking of God as their heavenly Father because they have had such despicable earthly fathers. Rather than loving, cherishing, and encouraging them, their dads molested and abused them or simply disappeared from their lives. They have no concept of what it is like to have a father who protects and can be depended on.

Author Hannah Whitall Smith helps us conceptualize God the Father's love:

> *Put together all the tenderest love you know of, the deepest you have ever felt and the strongest that has ever been poured out on you; heap on it all the love of all the loving human hearts in the world; then multiply it by infinity, and you will have a faint glimpse of the love and grace of God![1]*

Clearly, God wants a relationship with us, and His Father-heart yearns for us to want to be close to Him. He says it in His Word. What can we do but believe Him?

Take a moment today to thank God for being your heavenly Father. He's waiting to hear you call His name.

[1]Melvin E. Dieter and Hallie A. Dieter, *God Is Enough—Selections from Published and Unpublished Devotional Writings by Hannah Whitall Smith* (Longwood, FL: Xulon Press, 2003), 97.

"Now this is eternal life: that they know you, the only true God, and Jesus Christ, whom you have sent."

JOHN 17:3
(THE WHOLE STORY: JOHN 17:1–5)

The Need to Know

Lynn, a mother, writes,

> *I can nearly remember the exact moment. . .when I began to lose credibility with my children. When they turned into teenagers, I started having difficulty functioning. . . . Once, in a hotel room, I refused to try to set the digital clock. Of course, my teenagers. . . seemed to be able to work every button.*[1]

It's so true. A teenager knows how to find his way around technology. Lynn notes that her son "can hook up all kinds of wires to stereos. . .guitars and amplifiers without instructions."[2] Yet she observes he can't aim and hit the wastebasket, turn off a light switch, drink from a glass instead of the milk container, or write legibly.

We learn—and do—what is important to us. A teenager needs to know about wires and computers to communicate with his friends. "He will learn to turn off the lights when *he* is paying the light bill," Lynn notes. "He will learn to have plenty of gas in the car when *he* is traveling with his own teenagers."[3]

It's true that we learn what is necessary in our lives, and there are also things and people we can live without knowing. But there is a *Person* we cannot afford *not* to know, and that is God. You don't have to be college educated or computer savvy to know Him. He is inviting you to have a relationship with Him.

Knowing Him will make a difference in your life for all eternity.

[1] Lynn Assimacopoulos, "When I Lost the Need to Know," in *Humor for a Mom's Heart* (West Monroe, LA: Howard Publishing Company, 2002), 161.

[2] Ibid., 162.

[3] Ibid.

I have been crucified with Christ and I no longer live, but Christ lives in me.
The life I now live in the body, I live by faith in the Son of God,
who loved me and gave himself for me.

GALATIANS 2:20

When God Intervenes

The three young men—Matt, Steve, and Cole—were best friends. On a trip to Las Vegas, however, they were involved in a serious car accident. Matt and Cole survived, but Steve did not.

The experience of losing their best buddy, Steve, caused Matt and Cole to bond as only those who have gone through tragedy together do. The two enjoyed riding dirt bikes, and finally they planned the big trip—an entire weekend riding in the area of an old gold mining town in the desert. Scott, a third friend, went too.

They were down to the final ride. Matt rode his bike up the hill first—and disappeared from view. As Cole crested the hill, he saw nothing but a massive hole in the ground. Frantically he and Scott began to look for Matt, but then the horror of reality set in. Matt had fallen 780 feet straight down into an abandoned, unmarked mine shaft and did not survive.

"I could feel sorry for myself, blame God, and maybe start drinking," Cole said. "Or I could do something with my life." At twenty-one, Cole made the decision to honor Steve and Matt by living a God-centered life. He began to share his testimony at churches and schools.

Cole said, "I vowed. . .that no matter how uncomfortable it may be, if I feel the Lord calling me to do something, never again will I let an opportunity pass me by."[1] Cole can now say with Paul, "I have been crucified with Christ and I no longer live, but Christ lives in me" (Galatians 2:20).

When God clearly intervenes in a person's life, it's for a purpose. Has He been speaking to you through the circumstances in your life? Listen to what He is telling you.

[1]Taken from Cole Hatter's prayer letter, 2005.

Selected verses from Psalm 100

Refreshing Words from Psalms

You are His lamb. . .and His love for you never ends. Say thank You, and do it out loud!

> ¹*Shout for joy to the* LORD, *all the earth.*
> ²*Worship the* LORD *with gladness;*
> *come before him with joyful songs.*
> ³*Know that the* LORD *is God.*
> *It is he who made us, and we are his;*
> *we are his people, the sheep of his pasture.*
> ⁴*Enter his gates with thanksgiving*
> *and his courts with praise;*
> *give thanks to him and praise his name.*
> ⁵*For the* LORD *is good and his love endures forever;*
> *his faithfulness continues through all generations.*

Lord, I am glad to be Yours. I thank You and praise Your name today.

They said, "The land we explored devours those living in it.
All the people we saw there are of great size. . . . We seemed like
grasshoppers in our own eyes, and we looked the same to them."

NUMBERS 13:32–33
(THE WHOLE STORY: NUMBERS 13:16–33)

Grasshopper Faith

The people of Israel stood on the border of the land God had promised them. But before they went in, they sent an investigating committee of twelve men to assess the land.

All twelve saw that it was good; all twelve knew that God had promised to give it to them. But only two said, "We should go up and take possession of the land, for we can certainly do it" (Numbers 13:30). The other ten said, "We saw the Nephilim [giants] there. . . We seemed like grasshoppers in our own eyes" (Numbers 13:33).

My dad used to say, "I don't think any child of God ought to think of himself as a grasshopper. You and I have been redeemed with the precious blood of the Lord Jesus Christ. I believe in humility, but being humble does not mean showing disrespect for what God has done for you."

The ten spies reported, "The cities are large, with walls up to the sky" (Deuteronomy 1:28). Do you know why they thought that? "Because they were grasshoppers," my dad would say. "Just imagine a grasshopper down at the base of a walled city. He turns his eyes enough to look up at that wall, and it goes up, up, up, and never stops until it touches the sky. That's a grasshopper's view of a wall."

Are you facing giants and walled cities? How are you looking at them— from a grasshopper's viewpoint? God looks down from heaven and sees the same giants and the same walls, but from His vantage point, they don't look very big. Be encouraged: our God is bigger than anything we will ever face.

Remember your leaders, who spoke the word of God to you.
Consider the outcome of their way of life and imitate their faith.

Evaluating Christian Leaders

Every so often you hear about a Christian leader who has failed morally. You may ask, "How can I know that any Christian leader has integrity? How can I count on what he says to be true?"

A verse in Hebrews gives guidance on this point. Hebrews 13:7 says, "Remember your leaders, who spoke the word of God to you. Consider the outcome of their way of life and imitate their faith."

A closer look can help us evaluate our Christian leaders. First, we're to keep in mind the leaders who spoke the Word of God to us. Have you ever thanked God for the teachers who have contributed to your knowledge of the Bible and your spiritual progress? We owe much to them. Paul says, "How beautiful are the feet of those who bring good news!" (Romans 10:15).

Then we're told to consider the outcome of their lives. Are they a good model to follow? Are they consistent in what they say and how they live?

Finally, we're told to imitate their faith. Notice that we're not told to copy their conduct but their faith. No one is perfect, and if you really get to know any Christian leaders, you will find they all have flaws. If they have truly relied on God through the ups and downs of life and found Him to be faithful to His promises, then you have a model to follow. John writes, "Dear friend, do not imitate what is evil but what is good" (3 John 1:11). Good advice!

The fruit of that righteousness will be peace;
its effect will be quietness and confidence forever.

ISAIAH 32:17

No More Guilty Feelings

A young woman we'll call Beth was listening to Guidelines' *Commentary* on the radio when God reminded her of the shoplifting she had done thirteen years before. She knew God wanted her to make restitution.

The shoplifting had occurred when Beth switched the box of the item she was buying with that of a cheaper item. Over the years, however, whenever she recalled what she had done, she felt guilty.

When she went back to the store, however, to pay for what she had stolen, the store staff would not accept her money because it would throw off their accounting system. So Beth sent a letter with a check for the amount she owed to the general manager of the company, explaining how this had happened when she had fallen away from her Christian faith. Having asked for forgiveness from the Lord, she wrote that she felt a deep conviction that she should make restitution.

Beth received a letter from the company praising her for her honesty and saying that her check would be donated to a charity. Then they added that because her letter was such a wonderful contrast to the letters they usually received, they would frame it and hang it on their office wall. Beth says that she finds it embarrassing to picture her confession hanging on a wall, but if it brings glory to the Lord, it's okay with her. She says, "I am finally at peace."

The Bible tells us, "The fruit of righteousness will be peace; its effect will be quietness and confidence forever" (Isaiah 32:17). Is God speaking to you about anything in your past you need to settle so you will be free from guilty feelings?

I press on toward the goal to win the prize for which
God has called me heavenward in Christ Jesus.

PHILIPPIANS 3:14

Success or Significance?

It's exciting that many people in the world are thinking about their life purpose since reading Rick Warren's bestselling 2002 book *The Purpose-Driven Life.*

Are you one of those who have discovered their life purpose? Are you pursuing success or significance?

Many of us think that in order to be significant, we have to accomplish something great that makes us famous. In reality, many famous people have never accomplished significance, and conversely, some significant people are unknown outside the walls of their home or organization.

If you're feeling unsuccessful or insignificant, be encouraged to know that your goal in life should not be to pursue what the world says is important, but to be what God says is valuable. Endeavor to take hold not of someone else's reason for being, but of God's purpose for *you*. Your job is to "press on toward the goal" (Philippians 3:14) of God's purpose for you and to leave the rest to Him.

In *Dear God, It's Me Again!* Gail Ramsey reminds us of the *Peanuts* cartoon where Charlie Brown holds out his hands to Lucy and says, "Look at these hands! These hands may someday build big bridges! These hands might hit home runs! These hands could one day write important books, or heal sick people. . .or drive a rocket ship to Mars!" Looking at Charlie Brown's hands, Lucy retorts, "They've got jelly on 'em."[1]

Lucy didn't see what Charlie Brown saw. She saw only the jelly. When others look at you, many will see just the jelly. But don't let that destroy the dream that God has put in your heart. Live out His purpose for you.

[1]Gail Ramsey, *Dear God, It's Me Again!* (New Kensington, PA: Whitaker House, 2004), 79.

Be strong and take heart, all you who hope in the LORD.
PSALM 31:24

Attitude Makes All the Difference

A delightful ninety-two-year-old lady who was legally blind was moving to a nursing home. Her husband of seventy years had recently passed away. As she maneuvered her walker to the elevator, the staff member accompanying her described her tiny room.

"I love it!" she stated with the enthusiasm of an eight-year-old who had been given a new puppy.

"Mrs. Jones, you haven't seen the room," the staff member said.

"That doesn't have anything to do with it," she replied. "Happiness is something you decide on ahead of time. Whether I like my room or not doesn't depend on how the furniture is arranged—it's how I arrange my mind. I've already decided to love it. It's a decision I make every morning when I wake up. I have a choice: I can spend the day in bed recounting the difficulty I have with the parts of my body that no longer work, or get out of bed and be thankful for the parts that do. Each day is a gift, and as long as I live, I'll focus on the new day."

What a beautiful attitude to have! I'm sure we all hope that in the final years of our lives we'll reflect the positive mind-set of this dear lady.

One of the best things we can do to prepare for our golden years is to look to God as our source of hope. The God who has been faithful to us will not abandon us in the years to come. The psalmist wrote, "Be strong and take heart, all you who hope in the LORD" (Psalm 31:24), for each day is a gift from Him to be enjoyed.

The Lord is full of compassion and mercy.
JAMES 5:11

Mercy

A woman had her picture taken by a photographer. When she went back to see the proofs and make her selection for the final portrait, she was very disappointed with the pictures.

"Sir, these pictures do not do me justice!" she exclaimed.

"Madam, it's not justice you need but mercy."

We laugh at that, but honestly, we're all in the same position. Because we have sinned and none of us is perfect, we need mercy, not justice. And when we come to God for mercy, we have come to the right source. The Bible says, "The Lord is full of compassion and mercy" (James 5:11).

God's mercy refers to His tender caring, His forgiveness and amazing kindness toward undeserving men and women.

Even if you think your sin is too great for God to forgive, think again! The psalmist wrote, "Let the wicked forsake their ways and the unrighteous their thoughts. Let them turn to the LORD, and he will have mercy on them, and to our God, for he will freely pardon" (Isaiah 55:7). For "the LORD is compassionate and gracious, slow to anger, abounding in love. He will not always accuse, nor will he harbor his anger forever; he does not treat us as our sins deserve or repay us according to our iniquities" (Psalm 103:8–10).

You and I can find God's mercy whenever we need it. "Let us then approach God's throne of grace with confidence, so that we may receive mercy and find grace to help us in our time of need" (Hebrews 4:16). Thank God today for His bountiful mercy!

Selected verses from Psalm 130

Refreshing Words from Psalms

Are you in darkness, longing desperately for this blackest night to give way to shining dawn? Put your hope in God's unfailing love.

> *¹Out of the depths I cry to you, LORD;*
> *²Lord, hear my voice.*
> *Let your ears be attentive*
> *to my cry for mercy.*
> *³If you, LORD, kept a record of sins,*
> *Lord, who could stand?*
> *⁴But with you there is forgiveness,*
> *so that we can, with reverence, serve you.*
> *⁵I wait for the LORD, my whole being waits,*
> *and in his word I put my hope.*
> *⁶I wait for the Lord*
> *more than watchmen wait for the morning,*
> *more than watchmen wait for the morning.*
> *⁷Israel, put your hope in the LORD,*
> *for with the LORD is unfailing love*
> *and with him is full redemption.*

Lord, I wait and I watch. I watch for the dawn of Your unfailing love in dark areas of my life, knowing it will come. Thank You for the assurance of Your Word.

I will be joyful in God my Savior.

HABAKKUK 3:18

Yet, I Will Rejoice

The prophet Habakkuk lived in a day of uncertainty. Babylon was growing as a world power, and the people of Judah were afraid for their lives. Yet for all his questions about the future, the prophet ends his writings with a song of encouragement, which confidently declares that God will protect and sustain His people. He writes,

> *Though the fig tree does not bud*
> *and there are no grapes on the vines,*
> *though the olive crop fails*
> *and the fields produce no food,*
> *though there are no sheep in the pen*
> *and no cattle in the stalls,*
> *yet I will rejoice in the LORD,*
> *I will be joyful in God my Savior.*
> HABAKKUK 3:17–18

I have homework for you today. Before you go to sleep tonight, please open your Bible, read Habakkuk, and write your own paraphrase of the last verses of this book. Substitute your problems for Habakkuk's. When you get to the part where Habakkuk says he will still be joyful and rejoice in the Lord in spite of all the problems, tell God. I believe you will be encouraged.

Let us then approach God's throne of grace with confidence, so that we may receive mercy and find grace to help us in our time of need.

HEBREWS 4:16

Reasons for Praying

Why do we pray? Probably for at least one of five reasons. Let me explain. First, we pray because *we can pray*. God desires to have a relationship with us and so created us with the ability to communicate with Him. He gave us brains that form ideas and shape words.

Also, we pray because *we may pray*. Our holy God gives us access to the very throne room of heaven—an amazing opportunity for imperfect human beings like us. "Let us then approach God's throne of grace with confidence," the Bible says (Hebrews 4:16).

Third, we pray because *we should pray*. Prayer is a command. Jesus told his disciples that "they should always pray and not give up" (Luke 18:1).

Then, we pray because *we want to pray*. We have needs that we want God to meet and expressions of thankfulness, too. We can bring those needs and praises to our living God, who listens to those who call on Him.

Last, we pray because *we must pray*. Pastor Jim Cymbala says, "If I say, 'I *ought* to pray,' I will soon run out of motivation and quit. . . . I have to be *driven* to pray."[1]

That's one reason God allows trouble in our lives—to drive us to seek Him. When you need God's help, you don't stop to think of reasons why you believe in prayer—you just frantically call to Him.

We pray because we can, we may, we should, we want to, and we must. It's a great privilege. As Moses told Israel, "What other nation is so great as to have their gods near them the way the LORD our God is near us whenever we pray to him?" (Deuteronomy 4:7).

[1] Jim Cymbala *Fresh Wind, Fresh Fire,* with Dean Merrill (Grand Rapids, MI: Zondervan Publishing House, 1997), 49.

Likewise, the tongue is a small part of the body, but it makes great boasts.
Consider what a great forest is set on fire by a small spark.

JAMES 3:5

If You Can't Say Something Nice

An elderly grandfather who was wealthy but quite deaf decided to buy a hearing aid. Several weeks after his purchase, he stopped by the store where he had bought the device and told the manager that he could now pick up conversations easily, even from the next room.

"Your relatives must be very happy to know that you can hear so much better," beamed the manager.

"Oh, I haven't told them yet," the man chuckled. "I've just been sitting around listening—and you know what? I've changed my will twice!"

Yes, we should be careful about what we say. Did your mother ever tell you, "If you can't say something nice, don't say anything at all"? Well, it *is* scriptural! Perhaps your mom knew that the Bible says: "Sin is not ended by multiplying words, but the prudent hold their tongues" (Proverbs 10:19).

The book of James says, "The tongue is a small part of the body, but it makes great boasts. Consider what a great forest is set on fire by a small spark" (James 3:5). Words are powerful. The psalmist notes that men "sharpen their tongues like swords and aim cruel words like deadly arrows" (Psalm 64:3).

On the other hand, the tongue can bring great comfort and hope. "The tongue of the wise brings healing," says Proverbs 12:18. We would do well to start our day with David's prayer: "May these words of my mouth and this meditation of my heart be pleasing in your sight, LORD, my Rock and my Redeemer" (Psalm 19:14).

This is what God the LORD says—the Creator of the heavens,
who stretches them out, who spreads out the earth with all that springs
from it, who gives breath to its people, and life to those who walk on it.

ISAIAH 42:5

When Your Prayers Hit the Ceiling

Have you ever felt that you just didn't want to talk to God? And when you did, it seemed to you that your prayers went no farther than the ceiling? Probably it's because you've lost your perspective of Him.

When I was growing up, someone who didn't attend church would give the excuse, "I worship God in nature." Yet, as I've gotten more years behind me, I've learned that in addition to worshipping in church, we can worship God as we delight in the world He has created. When I feel that God is remote—somewhere deep in space—if I go outside and look at nature and what He has made, my outlook changes.

In Romans 1:20, the apostle Paul says, "Since the creation of the world God's invisible qualities—his eternal power and divine nature—have been clearly seen, being understood from what has been made." All God has made points us back to the One who made it all.

If your perspective of God is skewed, take a closer look at what God has created. Go outside and really *look* at a flower—its details, its shading, its texture.

Or just look at the stars tonight. Author Philip Yancey says that a small coin "held out at arm's length would block fifteen million stars from view, if our eyes could see with that power."[1] It's hard to digest that fact without regaining your perspective on the One who created those stars.

And what about those prayers that seemed so trite and mechanical? By the time you reflect on God's wonders, I think your heart will be filled with worship.

[1]Philip Yancey, *Finding God in Unexpected Places* (Manila, Philippines: OMF Literature Inc., 2000), 21.

Oh, the depth of the riches of the wisdom and knowledge of God!
How unsearchable his judgments, and his paths beyond tracing out!

ROMANS 11:33

The Owner of the Bible

The following is a true story told by Bill Bright, founder of Campus Crusade for Christ.

In the 1930s, Stalin ordered a purge of all Bibles in the former Soviet Union. He had millions of Bibles confiscated. In Stavropol, Russia, this order was carried out with a vengeance.

A few years ago, a missions team was sent to Stavropol. When the team couldn't get Bibles from Moscow, someone mentioned that the Bibles confiscated in Stalin's day had been stored in a warehouse outside of town.

One member finally got up the courage to ask government officials if the Bibles were still there and could be distributed to the people. The answer was "Yes"!

The missions team arrived at the warehouse with a truck and a young Russian who was hired to help load the Bibles. A hostile, skeptical, agnostic collegian, he had come only for the day's wages.

As the team was loading the Bibles, the young man disappeared. Eventually they saw him in a corner of the warehouse, weeping. He had slipped away hoping to quietly take a Bible. What he found shook him. Inside the Bible he had picked up was the handwritten signature of his grandmother! Out of the many thousands of Bibles in the warehouse, he had stolen the one belonging to her. She had no doubt prayed for him, and now this young man's life was being transformed by the very Bible that his grandmother found so dear.

"Oh, the depth of the riches of the wisdom and knowledge of God!" the Bible says. "How unsearchable his judgments, and his paths beyond tracing out!" (Romans 11:33). In His wisdom He answers our prayers with perfect timing.

For the LORD *loves the just and will not forsake his faithful ones.*

PSALM 37:28

❀

Facing Loneliness with Courage

In his book *Facing Loneliness,* J. Oswald Sanders tells of visiting Hannah Higgens, a woman who for sixty-nine of her eighty-two years was in constant pain from a progressive bone disease. Because of the disease, she lost both arms and legs.

For forty-three years Hannah lived in one room, but she didn't let her isolation or the fact that she had no arms limit her reach. She had a special attachment fixed to the stump of her right arm so that she could write with a pen. Using her whole body to form words, she wrote thousands of letters to people all over the world. The walls of her room were covered with the photographs of people she had encouraged and, in many cases, led to a relationship with God.

"I have so much to be thankful for, so many mercies," Hannah said. "Although I am deprived of health and strength and my limbs, Jesus is far more precious than ever. . . . I can truthfully say that I never feel lonely."[1]

How could Hannah be so isolated and yet not be lonely? She had discovered a secret—the truth that God was with her every moment. Most of us know about God's presence in theory, but Hannah knew it as reality. She knew that God meant it when He said, "For the LORD loves the just and will not forsake his faithful ones" (Psalm 37:28).

Loneliness and sorrow will no doubt come to all of us. You can run away from the troubling emotions of life or look the facts in the face with the courage God gives you.

[1]J. Oswald Sanders, *Facing Loneliness* (East Sussex, England: Highland Books, 1988), 54–55.

Selected verses from Psalm 118

Refreshing Words from Psalms

He made today—your day. Whom better to trust with all of its details?

> *¹Give thanks to the LORD, for he is good;*
> *his love endures forever.*
> *⁵When hard pressed, I cried to the LORD;*
> *he brought me into a spacious place.*
> *⁶The LORD is with me; I will not be afraid.*
> *What can mere mortals do to me?*
> *⁸It is better to take refuge in the LORD*
> *than to trust in humans.*
> *¹³I was pushed back and about to fall,*
> *but the LORD helped me.*
> *²⁴The LORD has done it this very day;*
> *let us rejoice today and be glad.*

Lord, thank You for the freedom I can experience when I remember You made this day and nothing can happen to me today outside of Your love.

*So God created mankind in his own image, in the image of
God he created them; male and female he created them.*

GENESIS 1:27

Women—God's Special Creation

Elayne Boosler says, "When women are depressed, they either eat or go shopping. Men invade another country." We laugh at that, but it's true—men and women are different. The Bible says, "God created mankind in his own image . . .male and female he created them" (Genesis 1:27).

But are women better than men? A historian in England found a book called *Womans Worth* that dates back to the early 1600s. Its subtitle states that it is "A treatise proveinge by sundrie reasons that woemen do excel men" [A treatise proving by sundry reasons that women do excel men].[1]

Whether or not women excel men, science has recently proven what men have believed for a long time—that women are far more complex than men. Here's how. A man has an X and a Y chromosome. The Y chromosome determines maleness but little else, scientists say. Men are largely products of one chromosome, the X. But women have two X chromosomes, and the genes in them are highly influential. That means each woman is the product of about twice as many genetic instructions as any man. Researcher Huntington Willard of Duke University said, "Every one of the females we looked at had a different genetic story."[2]

So the Bible is right. Women are different—and more complicated! Yet when men and women understand how different we really are and respect our differences, we will know that each has what the other needs and will value the unique qualities that each brings to a relationship.

Never forget it, dear lady, you are truly God's special creation!

[1]"Women Better Than Men," *Philippine Star,* April 22, 2002, 32.

[2]"Why Women Are So Complicated," *The Week*, April 8, 2005, 23.

*For the L*ORD *God is a sun and shield; the L*ORD *bestows favor and honor;*
no good thing does he withhold from those whose walk is blameless.

PSALM 84:11

Making Beautiful Music

When a composer visited the cathedral at Friedberg, Germany, he heard the magnificent sounds of the great organ there. Climbing up to the loft, he asked permission to play it. The old organist refused but was finally persuaded. After listening with delight and amazement to the glorious music, the old man laid his hand on the shoulder of the inspired musician and exclaimed, "Who are you? What is your name?"

"Felix Mendelssohn," replied the player.

Like the organist, control can be such an issue for us. How many of us let God, the Master Musician of the universe, have full access to the keyboard of our lives? Often we hesitate to get off the organ bench and let Him compose our life's music.

When will we learn that God wants only the best for us? The Bible is full of verses that tell us this:

- *No good thing will he withhold from them that walk uprightly*
  (Psalm 84:11 KJV).
- *Every good and perfect gift is from above, coming down from the*
  Father of the heavenly lights, who does not change like shifting
  shadows (James 1:17).
- *Those who seek the L*ORD *lack no good thing* (Psalm 34:10).
- *"If you, then, though you are evil, know how to give good gifts*
  to your children, how much more will your Father in heaven give
  good gifts to those who ask him!" (Matthew 7:11).

With promises like these, how can we afford to run our own lives? We'd be fools to try. Get off the organ bench and listen to the beautiful music God will make out of your life.

And the peace of God, which transcends all understanding,
will guard your hearts and your minds in Christ Jesus. Finally,
brothers and sisters, whatever is true, whatever is noble, whatever
is right, whatever is pure, whatever is lovely, whatever is admirable—
if anything is excellent or praiseworthy—think about such things.

PHILIPPIANS 4:7–8

Stressed Out

I have come to accept that life now moves at such a fast pace that stress can't be totally avoided.

One reason we should learn to handle stress well is that stress makes us old. Scientists learned that constant stress causes the tiny caps of chromosomes that govern cell regeneration to get smaller. When the tiny caps get too small, the cells stop dividing and eventually die.

Dr. Thomas Peris, director of the research project, says that the greater people perceived their stress to be, the "older" their cells were. And those who didn't perceive their lives as stressful? Stress didn't age them nearly as much.[1]

The study cited examples of people living well into their eighties and nineties who had successfully coped with stress in a number of ways: sports, games, humor, optimism, a sense of purpose, close friendships, music, finding meaning in life, and prayer.

When I read this, I thought about what Paul said to the Philippians: "Brothers and sisters, whatever is true, whatever is noble, whatever is right, whatever is pure, whatever is lovely, whatever is admirable—if anything is excellent or praiseworthy—think about such things. . . . And the God of peace will be with you" (Philippians 4:8–9). The God of peace is the One who can relieve us of stress. A relationship with Him is our best stress buster!

[1]Sarah Mahoney, "10 Secrets of a Good, Long Life," *AARP* Magazine, July–August 2005, 66.

The LORD is my shepherd. . . . He refreshes my soul.

PSALM 23:1, 3

(THE WHOLE STORY: PSALM 23)

Room Enough for God

Mary Southerland tells about visiting Amish country in Pennsylvania one summer. The Amish are a conservative Christian group who dress simply; work without electricity, cars, and other modern equipment; and whose homes are known for simple furnishings.

Wanting to buy a souvenir to remind them of their trip, Mary and her husband began to travel down hidden back roads. Finally she spotted a small white sign that said AMISH CRAFTS on the fence of a quaint house with a porch filled with lovely handmade items. Walking up the stone walk, they were greeted by a woman with a beautiful smile.

The house was sparsely furnished, but the homeowner described her life with words like "calm, uncomplicated, and serene." When asked why she had chosen such a lifestyle, she responded: "I have discovered that when my life and my heart get too crowded, there is not enough room for God."

What a thought to ponder! Mary reminds us, "It is so easy to relegate our spirituality to religious activity when all [God] wants is to spend time with us."[1]

If our lives are too crowded for God, they're too crowded—period. If you want to change that, start spending time with the Lord; you may be amazed at the peace that comes to your heart.

[1]Mary Southerland, *"For Women in Ministry: A Balanced Life—the Impossible Dream,"* from www.pastors.com, March 20, 2004.

*As you do not know the path of the wind, or how the body
is formed in a mother's womb, so you cannot understand
the work of God, the Maker of all things.*

ECCLESIASTES 11:5

God Makes No Mistakes

Kim's brother, Steve, was born with cerebral palsy and confined to a wheelchair. When she was younger, Kim remembers going out to play and then coming back to check on Steve—feeling guilty.

During her freshman year of college, the women's chaplain, wanting to get to know Kim better, asked about her family. Kim described how guilty she felt when she thought of Steve. Because his life was so restricted, Kim felt undeserving when anything good happened to her.

To her amazement, the chaplain exclaimed, "Kim, now I understand why you're such a special person. It must be because of Steve." The chaplain went on: "You are sensitive to others. You take the time to connect with people. You were forced to think and care for others because of your brother's unusual needs. It seems to me that Steve is one of the greatest gifts you've been given."[1]

That day Kim began to look at her life differently. She had not fully recognized the gift her brother had been in her life. She was able to forgive herself and let go of the guilt. Kim said, "God has so tenderly crafted me to be exactly what He wants and needs me to be."[2]

Romans 8:28 says, "We know that in all things God works for the good of those who love him, who have been called according to his purpose." Those words were true for Kim, and they're true for you, too.

[1]Kim Ford, "A Journey of the Heart," in *The Gift of Letting Go* (Colorado Springs, CO: Honor Books, 2005), 154.

[2]Ibid.

*"Now, Lord. . .enable your servants to
speak your word with great boldness."*
ACTS 4:29

Speaking with Boldness

Frances Havergal, an English hymn writer and musician in the 1800s, gave singing lessons to a group of young girls. After the lessons, Frances would walk with them to chat so they could be together a bit longer.

A few years later, Frances was at the bedside of one of these girls who was seriously ill. The girl had become a Christian. She shared with Frances that during the singing lessons, she had been looking for a relationship with Christ but had been too shy to tell Frances. She had kept hoping that Frances would talk to her about it. Of course, Frances had not known of the girl's hunger for Christ and felt terribly sorry that she had not shared about Christ during their hours together. For years afterward, when tempted to ignore an opportunity to talk about the Lord with another person, the girl's words would ring in Frances's ears: "Ah, Miss Frances, I ought to have been yours!"[1]

What if no one else had talked to the girl about the Lord—what would have been her eternal destiny? What an encouragement to us to speak boldly about our Savior!

"Now, Lord. . .enable your servants to speak your word with great boldness" (Acts 4:29), prayed Peter and John, leaders of the early Christian Church. Peter and John actually prayed that prayer from prison. If they could show such courage for the Gospel in jail, surely we, too, can pray, "Lord, help us to speak Your word with great boldness." It can make an eternal difference for someone.

[1]Frances Ridley Havergal, *Opened Treasures,* compiled by William J. Pell (Neptune, NJ: Loizeaux Brothers, 1962), February 7.

Selected verses from Psalm 105

Refreshing Words from Psalms

Remember. Remember today what God has done for you—His strength, His wonders, His miracles, and His promises. He is the Lord, *your* God!

> ^{1}*Give praise to the LORD, proclaim his name;*
> *make known among the nations what he has done.*
> ^{2}*Sing to him, sing praise to him;*
> *tell of all his wonderful acts.*
> ^{4}*Look to the LORD and his strength;*
> *seek his face always.*
> ^{5}*Remember the wonders he has done,*
> *his miracles, and the judgments he pronounced.*
> ^{7}*He is the LORD our God;*
> *his judgments are in all the earth.*
> ^{8}*He remembers his covenant forever,*
> *the promise he made, for a thousand generations.*
> ^{45}*Praise the LORD.*

I do praise You! You are the Lord whose judgments are in all the earth and whose promises are to a thousand generations. You have also done wonderful things in my life. Amazing!

Whatever you do, work at it with all your heart,
as working for the Lord, not for human masters.

COLOSSIANS 3:23

What Are You Going to Be When You Grow Up?

"What are you going to be when you grow up?" we often ask kids. Depending on their ages, their answers progress from "I'm going to be a fireman" to "I have no idea—I don't even know what classes to register for."

We start out with big dreams and plans for the future. But sometimes the further we go in life, the more we realize our dreams are not realistic. That's the time when we need to reevaluate our gifts and opportunities. Jane Chesnutt says, "To dream is a wonderful thing, but to make the very best out of a reality is ultimately more special, I think."[1]

I once gave a talk on being all God created us to be. I asked, "What do you want to do more than anything else?" Afterward a girl came to me and shared her dream: to be President of the United States. The sad part was that as we talked, I realized she had mental limitations. She was dreaming but not dealing with reality. I asked her about what she could do with her life right now. Maybe God created her to help with children or with church hospitality. I urged her to go to work for God now.

If you don't have an ideal marriage or ideal career or ideal kids, don't let that stop you from making the best of your life. The Bible is very practical. Colossians 3:23 says, "Whatever you do, work at it with all your heart, as working for the Lord, not for human masters." Remember, making the best out of reality is more special than dreaming impossible dreams.

[1]Jane Chesnutt, *Woman's Day Magazine,* 1994, opening editorial.

I will extol the LORD *at all times; his praise will always be on my lips.*

PSALM 34:1

At All Times and in All Places, Give Thanks

Author Elizabeth Sherrill was frustrated. Having flown in to speak at a seminar for Christian writers, she was annoyed that part of her luggage had not arrived, including her dress shoes.

"Of *all times* for this to happen," she said to herself. Then a phrase came to her mind: "We should at all times, and in all places, give thanks unto Thee."

So Elizabeth went ahead with her session. At the end of the seminar, several writers came up to the platform. Suddenly there was the sound of gunfire and breaking glass. A woman shouted, "Lie down everyone!"

Outside, two drunk men were taking potshots at telephone poles. One of the shots had come through a window, and the "bullet," which was the tip of an electric screwdriver shot from a homemade gun, lodged in the wall behind the speaker's stand.

As police reports were being filled out, Elizabeth traced the trajectory of the bullet from the window to its resting place, just one inch above her head. Her mind went immediately to a pair of shoes with two-and-a-half-inch heels in a missing suitcase and a prayer, "We should at all times, and in all places, give thanks unto Thee, O Lord."[1]

How many times have we come close to death and not even realized it? A car accident that didn't happen. An armed robbery that God prevented. On an occasion when King David had just experienced one of his many close calls with death, he said, "I will extol the LORD at all times; his praise will always be on my lips" (Psalm 34:1). Let's remember to give thanks to the Lord at all times and in all places.

[1]Elizabeth Sherrill, "The Missing Shoe," in *His Mysterious Ways,* vol. 2 (Carmel, NY: Guideposts Associates, Inc., 1991), 46–47.

"Do not store up for yourselves treasures on earth, where moths and vermin destroy, and where thieves break in and steal. But store up for yourselves treasures in heaven, where moths and vermin do not destroy, and where thieves do not break in and steal."

MATTHEW 6:19–20

Send It on Ahead

Alexander the Great left specific orders that when he died, his hands were not to be wrapped in the specially treated cloths that embalmers used in his day. He wanted his hands to be exposed so that all could see that they were empty.[1]

The writer of Psalms said, "Do not be overawed when others grow rich. . . they will take nothing with them when they die" (Psalm 49:16–17). It's true—you can't take anything with you when you die. Jesus said, "Do not store up for yourselves treasures on earth, where moths and vermin destroy, and where thieves break in and steal. But store up for yourselves treasures in heaven" (Matthew 6:19–20).

How do we do this? The apostle Paul instructed, "Command those who are rich in this present world not to be arrogant nor to put their hope in wealth, which is so uncertain, but to put their hope in God, who richly provides us with everything for our enjoyment. Command them to do good, to be rich in good deeds, and to be generous and willing to share. In this way they will lay up treasure for themselves as a firm foundation for the coming age, so that they may take hold of the life that is truly life" (1 Timothy 6:17–19). You may not take earthly treasure to heaven, but you can always have God's treasure. You can send it on ahead!

Jim Elliot sacrificed his life while taking the Gospel to the Auca Indians of Ecuador. Before he died, he wrote these words, "He is no fool who gives what he cannot keep to gain what he cannot lose." Nothing given to God is ever lost.

[1]H.G.B., "Death, the Leveler," in *Our Daily Bread Magazine* (Grand Rapids, MI, date unknown).

Who is a God like you, who pardons sin and forgives the transgression of the remnant of his inheritance? You do not stay angry forever but delight to show mercy. You will again have compassion on us; you will tread our sins underfoot and hurl all our iniquities into the depths of the sea.

MICAH 7:18–19

What God Does with Our Sins

Have you just done something you know you shouldn't have done? Are you afraid God will never forgive you for it? Then read these encouraging verses written by the Old Testament prophet Micah: "Who is a God like you, who pardons sin and forgives the transgression. . . ? You do not stay angry forever but delight to show mercy. You will again have compassion on us; you will tread our sins underfoot and hurl all our iniquities into the depths of the sea" (Micah 7:18–19).

I love the word pictures Micah used. He said that God, in His compassion, grinds our sins into the ground under His great foot. As you would step on a poisonous spider so that you would never have to deal with it again, God tramples our sins underfoot.

In the next word picture, Micah said God hurls all our sins into the depths of the sea. Notice that God doesn't deposit them near the shoreline, where they might be washed ashore with the tide. Nor does He merely drop them into the sea. No, He *hurls* them. And then, as Corrie ten Boom said, He puts up a sign that reads No FISHING.

Other verses in the Bible tell us that God sweeps away our sins like the morning mist that evaporates so quickly (Isaiah 44:22)—that He blots out our sins and remembers them no more (Isaiah 43:25).

That thing you know you shouldn't have done? Admit right now that you did wrong and ask God to forgive you. Then watch as He hurls your sin into the deepest sea.

"Here I am! I stand at the door and knock. If anyone hears my voice and opens the door, I will come in and eat with that person, and they with me."

REVELATION 3:20

The Prison Walls of Loneliness

Can you imagine being in solitary confinement for years? That was the experience of Madame Jeanne Guyon, a French mystic in the seventeenth century. Madame Guyon was imprisoned in the infamous Paris Bastille for her belief that anyone can directly enjoy God's presence through constant, reflective, and intimate prayer. Madame Guyon was in prison, but her attitude made all the difference. She believed that she was there in the will of God. The reality that God was with her helped her survive the terrible living conditions.

She learned that moment-by-moment communication with God banishes loneliness. Madame Guyon chose to accept everything that happened to her as from the hand of God. She learned not to fight difficulties but to live with them, believing that since God allowed them, He would supply the strength she needed. She had such great delight in God that her spirit soared far above the prison walls. In fact, she said the stones in her prison shone like rubies. She wrote:

> *A little bird am I.*
> *Shut out from fields of air,*
> *Yet in my cage I sit and sing*
> *To him who placed me there!*
> *Well pleased a prisoner to be,*
> *Because, my God, it pleaseth Thee.*[1]

Are you feeling isolated and alone? Jesus said, "Here I am! I stand at the door and knock. If anyone hears my voice and opens the door, I will come in and eat with that person, and they with me" (Revelation 3:20). When you make Him your dearest friend, you, too, can soar above the prison walls of loneliness.

[1]http://www.cowart.info/John's%20Books/Guyon/Guyon.htm, accessed September 9, 2008.

My dear brothers and sisters, take note of this: Everyone should be quick to listen, slow to speak and slow to become angry.
JAMES 1:19

Quick to Listen

A high school student asked her mother if she could drop her Spanish class. Her mom immediately reacted, "No, why should you drop a class?" End of discussion. The girl knew it was a waste of time to talk about it further. She finished the class, but never again did she take a Spanish class, even though she was fluent enough to have taken part in an exchange student program.

How miserable her mom felt when she learned later that two-thirds of the students had dropped the class because of the teacher's bad attitude. If only she had listened to her daughter before jumping to conclusions!

Do you know what our problem is? Like the mother, we'd rather talk than listen. I remember a cartoon of two people talking, but the dialogue was pretty one-sided. The caption read, "I'd let you talk more—but you're not as interesting as I am!"

The apostle James wrote, "Everyone should be quick to listen, slow to speak and slow to become angry" (James 1:19). We nod our heads when we hear that verse, but we forget to close our mouths. How hard it is to put this verse into practice!

The next time someone wants to tell you something, look directly at him—even if what he is saying is boring. Look at his eyes. Concentrate on what he is saying. When he finishes, pause before replying. As James suggests, be quick to listen and slow to speak.

Wouldn't there be fewer misunderstandings in our relationships if we would only learn to really listen?

Selected verses from Psalm 142

Refreshing Words from Psalms

Need to register a few complaints? Lift up your voice to the Lord, for He knows them already. He longs to be *your* refuge.

> ¹*I cry aloud to the LORD;*
>   *I lift up my voice to the LORD for mercy.*
> ²*I pour out before him my complaint;*
>   *before him I tell my trouble.*
> ³*When my spirit grows faint within me,*
>   *it is you who watch over my way.*
> *In the path where I walk*
>   *people have hidden a snare for me.*
> ⁵*I cry to you, LORD;*
>   *I say, "You are my refuge,*
>   *my portion in the land of the living."*
> ⁶*Listen to my cry,*
>   *for I am in desperate need;*
> *rescue me from those who pursue me,*
>   *for they are too strong for me.*
> ⁷*Set me free from my prison,*
>   *that I may praise your name.*
> *Then the righteous will gather about me*
>   *because of your goodness to me.*

Lord, thank You for listening. Thank You for setting me free from the prison of my cares. You are my sustenance, and I praise Your name.

But thanks be to God, who always leads us as captives
in Christ's triumphal procession and uses us to spread
the aroma of the knowledge of him everywhere.

2 CORINTHIANS 2:14

Lives That Tell the Truth about God

"A saint is someone who makes it easy to believe in Jesus," said an anonymous writer. Did you know that the Bible says that all those who have put their faith in Christ are "saints"? But not all of us attract others to the Lord. That makes me ask myself, when people look at me, knowing that I am a child of God, do they see any family resemblance? It's a penetrating thought, isn't it?

Like it or not, people are watching us. Are our lives telling the truth about God?

Ruth Graham, wife of evangelist Billy Graham, recalled a morning when her children were young. Billy was out of town, and she had been up with one of the kids about five times in the night. Tired and sleepy, she picked up the baby from his bed and didn't bother to change him—just plunked him down in the high chair.

She grabbed the closest bathrobe, her hair and face both a mess. At the breakfast table, every time Gigi, her eldest, started to say something, Bunny, the youngest daughter, would interrupt. Finally Gigi banged down her fork, pushed back her chair, and said, "Mother, between looking at you, listening to Bunny, and smelling the baby, I'm just not hungry!"

Ruth challenges us with a question: "Are you taking away someone's appetite for Christ?"[1]

Let's live our lives in a way that tells the truth about God and "spread the aroma of the knowledge of [Christ] everywhere" (2 Corinthians 2:14).

[1]Ruth Bell Graham, "Husbands, Children and God," *Decision Magazine*, June 1967, 8.

We are therefore Christ's ambassadors, as though God were making his appeal through us. We implore you on Christ's behalf: Be reconciled to God.

2 CORINTHIANS 5:20

Christ's Ambassadors

We were in Vladivostok, Russia, where we had just spent some very special time listening to pastors share their hearts about their needs as they try to live on about $200 a month.

Late that evening, we went to the airport to catch the night flight to Siberia. You've never seen such pushing and shoving! The plane was old, and safety rules were not followed. The biggest problem, though, once we got on board, were the huge Siberian mosquitoes. My husband is good at swatting them but not before I had some pretty big welts on my arms and neck. I was feeling culture shock and thinking, *I never want to come back here again*, when I noticed the music that was playing—"O Solo Mio." The song has Christian lyrics that go, "Down from His glory. . .my God and Savior came." Suddenly I felt so ashamed.

What were a few mosquitoes and jet lag and shoving crowds? If the Lord could leave the glories of heaven to come to earth with all its sin and degradation, what right do I have to complain?

Most of us are so easily discouraged by even moderate discomfort and inconvenience. A sick child kept you up most of the night. When you finally catch a few winks, you wake up with a headache. The whole day continues to go wrong. You flip open your Bible hoping to get a little encouragement, and you read, "We are therefore Christ's ambassadors" (2 Corinthians 5:20). You think, *Me—Christ's ambassador? Not today!*

Yet, giving of yourself in difficult circumstances is exactly what Jesus did. Can we do less?

Watch your life and doctrine closely. Persevere in them,
because if you do, you will save both yourself and your hearers.

1 TIMOTHY 4:16

Why I Am in Christian Ministry

I was a preacher's kid. Now, the stereotype of a preacher's kid is a youngster who hates being dragged to church five times a week and being held up as an example to the congregation.

So people ask, "If you were a preacher's kid and knew how difficult that life can be, why did you decide to go into Christian ministry?" I can give you two reasons.

The first is because of the consistency I saw in the lives of my parents. What they preached in church, they lived at home. And that made a difference in my attitude.

The second reason I am in Christian ministry is because of a decision my mother made when I was a little girl. In those days, people had high expectations for the pastor's wife. She was counted on to be in charge of the children's activities and the music ministry, to entertain guests and teach Sunday school—all this, in addition to caring for her family and her home. Knowing that my dad would be busy with church responsibilities, she decided that I needed one parent who would be available. So she determined I would come first in her priorities—whether or not she did any of those ministries in the church.

I can't overemphasize the sense of security her decision gave me, knowing that if I needed her, she would be there for me. In actuality, she worked in many areas of ministry, but none was more important than being a mother.

So if you want to influence your kids, let me encourage you in these two areas. Be consistent in practicing what you preach. As Paul said, "Watch your life and doctrine closely" (1 Timothy 4:16). And be there for your kids. If you are, I can tell you from experience that you'll have a tremendous influence in their lives.

I am not saying this because I am in need, for I have learned to be content whatever the circumstances. I know what it is to be in need, and I know what it is to have plenty. I have learned the secret of being content in any and every situation, whether well fed or hungry, whether living in plenty or in want.

PHILIPPIANS 4:11–12

Contentment

Author Linda Dillow writes about a young bride who married a Marine, thinking that traveling the globe and living in foreign countries would be romantic and exciting. Two years later, she wrote her complaints to her mother. She said she had no friends. Worst of all, her husband was never home. She wrote, "I can't take this any longer. I'm coming home." Her wise mother's short reply:

> *Two women looked through prison bars*
> *One saw mud, the other saw stars.*[1]

Each of us has a choice. As Linda writes,

> *Every woman has circumstances that appear to be prison bars. God*
> *wants you and me to learn to be content in our circumstances, not*
> *when they improve.*[2]

Linda's observation follows the apostle Paul's example. He wrote, "I have learned to be content whatever the circumstances (Philippians 4:11–12).

Contentment is difficult to learn, but not impossible. The Bible teaches us: "In every situation, by prayer and petition, with thanksgiving, present your requests to God. And the peace of God, which transcends all understanding, will guard your hearts and your minds in Christ Jesus" (Philippians 4:6–7). That's how we learn contentment: We pray—and find God's peace.

[1] Linda Dillow, *Calm My Anxious Heart* (Colorado Springs, CO: NavPress, 1998), 25–26.

[2] Ibid., 26.

The disciples went and woke him, saying, "Master,
Master, we're going to drown!" He got up and rebuked the
wind and the raging waters; the storm subsided, and all was calm.

LUKE 8:24

(THE WHOLE STORY: LUKE 8:22–25)

The Storm Can't Sink Us

Liz was a new Christian who had been attending my Bible study group for several weeks. Although she hadn't had a relationship with Jesus Christ for very long, she contributed much to our discussions. Often she amazed me with her insights into scripture.

One week we were studying the incident in Luke 8 where some of the disciples were in a boat with Jesus, crossing the Sea of Galilee at night. When a sudden storm came up, Jesus was asleep in the boat. The disciples roused Him, asking, "Master, don't you care that we're sinking?" Jesus rebuked the storm, and immediately the sea was calm.

Our discussion question was, "Think about the most difficult situation you now face. What phrase in this passage brings comfort to you?" Most people in the group agreed that it was verse 24, where Jesus "rebuked the wind and the raging waters; the storm subsided, and all was calm." But Liz said that the part she liked best was when Jesus fell asleep. Curious, I asked why.

She replied, "Sometimes we feel God is asleep at the wheel of our lives—we can't sense Him doing anything about our problems. But His presence with us is enough. Whether we see Him doing anything about the storm or not, we know that when He is with us, the storm can't sink us!"

Do you have that confidence? If you have invited Jesus to be Lord of your life, He will be with you in the inevitable storms you'll experience. You can't sink when Jesus is in your boat.

Surely in vain I have kept my heart pure
and have washed my hands in innocence.

PSALM 73:13

(THE WHOLE STORY: PSALM 73:4–5, 12–13)

Perspective on Life

If I were to give a title to Psalm 73, I would call it "Perspective on Life." The writer of this psalm is so low, he's reaching up to touch bottom. Envying the prosperity of arrogant, immoral people, he says, "They have no struggles; their bodies are healthy and strong. They are free from common human burdens. . . . Always free of care, they go on amassing wealth. Surely in vain I have kept my heart pure" (v. 4–5, 12–13).

But is it true? Are evil people free from problems?

No, of course not. They experience sickness and struggles just like everyone else.

Then something happened that changed the psalmist's outlook: he entered the presence of God. When he did, he said, "Then I understood their final destiny" (v. 17).

When the writer spent time in God's presence, he realized the difference. He wrote, "You hold me by my right hand. You guide me with your counsel, and afterward you will take me into glory. . . . My flesh and my heart may fail, but God is the strength of my heart and my portion forever" (v. 23–24, 26). Wow, what a change in outlook!

Pastor Chuck Gerwig says, "Never develop your theology in the middle of a storm." Good advice, because your perspective is warped when you're going through hard times. It seems like everybody else has it better than you do.

Build your faith on what God's Word tells us about Him, instead of what you see happening to people around you. Spend time in God's presence; then the next time you face trouble, you'll find God truly is the strength of your heart. You'll have *His* perspective on life.

Selected verses from Psalm 86

Refreshing Words from Psalms

Our Source of joy is available all day long. Will you call on Him today to lift up your soul?

> ¹*Hear me, LORD, and answer me,*
>   *for I am poor and needy.*
> ³*Have mercy on me, Lord,*
>   *for I call to you all day long.*
> ⁴*Bring joy to your servant, Lord,*
>   *for I put my trust in you.*
> ⁵*You, Lord, are forgiving and good,*
>   *abounding in love to all who call to you.*
> ⁶*Hear my prayer, LORD;*
>   *listen to my cry for mercy.*
> ⁷*When I am in distress, I call to you,*
>   *because you answer me.*

Lord, You are aware of my needy condition. Forgive me for living so much of my life using my power, not Yours. Your joy does lift up my soul!

Then I heard a loud voice in heaven say: "Now have come the salvation and the power and the kingdom of our God, and the authority of his Messiah. For the accuser of our brothers and sisters, who accuses them before our God day and night, has been hurled down."

REVELATION 12:10

Confessing to the Devil

Does the following describe you? You know you've done something that God isn't happy about—let's be honest, it's sin. You also know that Christ died for your sins. So you've confessed this sin to God, and He has forgiven you, for the Bible says, "If we confess our sins, he is faithful and just and will forgive us our sins" (1 John 1:9). That clears your conscience, right?

Well, maybe not. When you open your eyes the next morning, possibly you still have nagging feelings of guilt. You don't *feel* forgiven. So you confess your sin and ask God to forgive you all over again. It becomes an ever-repeating cycle.

My dad, who was a minister, believed that it is the devil that makes us feel guilty for sins already forgiven because he lies to us. He is called "the accuser of our brothers and sisters, who accuses them before our God day and night" (Revelation 12:10). The apostle John describes the devil: "When he lies, he speaks his native language, for he is a liar and the father of lies" (John 8:44).

When God has forgiven you, He has forgotten your sins. He is not your accuser. The Bible says, "There is now no condemnation for those who are in Christ Jesus" (Romans 8:1). Who else is left to accuse us? Only the devil.

But there's good news. The Bible says that we can "demolish arguments and every pretension that sets itself up against the knowledge of God, and we take captive every thought to make it obedient to Christ" (2 Corinthians 10:5). Resist the devil's lies and accept the truth of God's forgiveness, then joy will replace your feelings of guilt.

"Even to your old age and gray hairs I am he, I am he who will sustain you. I have made you and I will carry you; I will sustain you and I will rescue you."

ISAIAH 46:4

How to Age Gracefully

Our culture today tends to value the new and discard the old.

But that is not God's perspective. He has great promises for our later years, for He says, "Even to your old age and gray hairs I am he, I am he who will sustain you. I have made you and I will carry you; I will sustain you and I will rescue you." (Isaiah 46:4).

Our goal as we age is to do so gracefully? That is, by the G-R-A-C-E of God!

G—Get rid of the emotional garbage. Give up your grudges. Deal with your past hurts and let them go.

R—Realize that your value in God's sight doesn't diminish with age. The Lord says that as believers, we're part of His Body. He says, "Those parts of the body that seem to be weaker are indispensable." (1 Corinthians 12:22).

A—Appreciate your own life experiences. Share what you have learned with younger people.

C—Continue to serve. Many look at retirement as a new life of leisure and self-indulgence, but Psalm 92:12, 14 says, "The righteous. . .will still bear fruit in old age." Look for opportunities to improve yourself and help others.

E—Expect God to honor His word. Has God been faithful to you so far? Rest assured that He will still be.

There you have it: G-R-A-C-E, God's grace, which is indispensable for our aging years.

"His eyes are on the ways of mortals;
he sees their every step."
JOB 34:21

God Knows Exactly Where You Are

When our son became serious about rock climbing and backcountry skiing, we, his parents, became very serious about doing all we could to ensure his safety. We bought him a GPS unit, a small handheld device that tells him his location.

GPS stands for Global Positioning System, a space-based radio navigation system consisting of satellites and a network of ground stations for monitoring and control. A minimum of twenty-four GPS satellites orbit the earth at an altitude of approximately eleven thousand miles. These provide users with accurate information on their location anywhere in the world, in all weather conditions.

In practical terms, this means that when my son begins one of his adventures, he can set the GPS unit to record his starting location. He can then always find his way back because the GPS unit can tell him exactly where he is and guide him back to his starting point.

God must smile at our scientific inventions—simple toys to Him who has all knowledge. The Bible says, "From heaven the LORD looks down and sees all mankind" (Psalm 33:13). "His eyes are on the ways of mortals; he sees their every step" (Job 34:21).

How wonderful to know that God *always* knows where we are. As helpful as a GPS unit is, if the battery inside does not work, the unit is worthless. But God is always aware of our exact location. The Bible says, "The LORD watches over all who love him" (Psalm 145:20) and "The LORD will guide you always" (Isaiah 58:11).

Let those promises assure you.

But you are a chosen people, a royal priesthood, a holy nation,
God's special possession, that you may declare the praises of
him who called you out of darkness into his wonderful light.

1 PETER 2:9

Chosen

Adopting a child is one of the most beautiful, loving acts in this often painful world. Here is a child who has no parent to care for him. But someone comes along who says to him, "I want you to be my child. I want to love you and provide for you. I want to be your mom (or dad)."

When a baby is born into a family, his parents have to take him whether they want to or not, right? But in adoption, a child is *chosen*. If you are a Christ follower, do you realize that means you have been adopted into the family of God? Yes, God has chosen you to be His. The apostle Peter says, "You are a chosen people. . .God's special possession, that you may declare the praises of him who called you out of darkness into his wonderful light" (1 Peter 2:9).

A mother explained adoption this way to her child: "Most babies come from their mommy's tummy, but you came from my heart." You, friend, came from the heart of God. Ephesians 1:5 says that we are predestined "for adoption to sonship through Jesus Christ, in accordance with his pleasure and will."

In New Testament days, an adopted son received the full rights and privileges of a natural-born son, even if previously he was a slave. He received a new name, inheriting the father's estate on equal terms with the natural-born children, never to be disinherited.

When you are God's child, you, too, receive the full rights of a natural-born child (Galatians 4:5). Thank Him that He has taken you into His family. Thank Him that you can call him "Father."

*"Listen carefully to my words;
let this be the consolation you give me."*

JOB 21:2

Comfort in Grief

When a friend loses a family member, perhaps tragically, most of us usually dread going to visit. We think, *What will I say?*

Job, known for his great patience in suffering, gives us ideas of what to say and what not to say.

The Bible says that when Job's friends came to visit, "They sat on the ground with him. . . . No one said a word to him, because they saw how great his suffering was" (Job 2:13). That's the best thing they could have done—just be there.

But then they started to talk, and they talked too much. They tried to explain to Job why he was suffering and gave him unsolicited counsel.

What did Job really need? First, encouragement. Job said, "Will your long-winded speeches never end? . . . If you were in my place. . .my mouth would encourage you; comfort from my lips would bring you relief" (Job 16:3–5). Job needed support and hope, not philosophical speculation.

Second, Job needed to be listened to. He said, "Listen carefully to my words; let this be the consolation you give me" (Job 21:2). One grieving father said, "It always helped me to be able to talk about my children after they died, and the people who were the biggest help were those who let me."

Listen to your grieving friend with undivided attention. Encourage him or her with a hug. With a simple heart of love, you can make a difference.

"Everyone who calls on the name of the Lord will be saved."
ROMANS 10:13

180-Degree Change

An English earl who was visiting the Fiji Islands remarked to an elderly chief, "You're a great leader, but it's a pity you've been taken in by those foreign missionaries. They only want to get rich through you. No one believes the Bible anymore."

The old chief's eyes flashed. "See that great rock over there? On it we smashed the heads of our victims. Notice the furnace next to it? In that oven we roasted their bodies. If it hadn't been for those good missionaries and the love of Jesus that changed us from cannibals into Christians, you'd never leave this place alive! You'd better thank the Lord for the Gospel."[1]

Today God still changes lives 180 degrees! Roy was hooked on alcohol and drugs and nearly died. Desperate, he was ready to try anything to get out of the pit he was in.

His younger sister went to church, so he asked her if maybe church would change him. She called an evangelist who told Roy how to accept Jesus as his Savior. Roy thought, *What have I got to lose?* and prayed for Jesus to come into his life.

The next morning, he awoke overflowing with love and joy. When he told his girlfriend he had no desire to drink or take drugs anymore, she said, "You couldn't have changed like this overnight. You're faking it!"

"You're right, I couldn't," he said, "but God changed me!" Roy adds, "You're never too far gone for God to forgive you and change your life. I know!"[2]

Romans 10:13 says, "Everyone who calls on the name of the Lord will be saved." Maybe you're ready for a 180-degree change! Let God transform you.

[1]M. R. DeHaan, "The Wonderful Change," *Our Daily Bread* (Grand Rapids, MI: Radio Bible Class, 1972,) August 3.

[2]http://www.webspawner.com/users/royecork/, accessed September 15, 2008.

Selected verses from Psalm 103

Refreshing Words from Psalms

Today's psalm expresses what we sometimes have trouble putting into words:
God's marvelous goodness shown to us.

> *¹Praise the LORD, my soul;*
>   *all my inmost being, praise his holy name.*
> *²Praise the LORD, my soul,*
>   *and forget not all his benefits—*
> *³who forgives all your sins*
>   *and heals all your diseases,*
> *⁴who redeems your life from the pit*
>   *and crowns you with love and compassion,*
> *⁵who satisfies your desires with good things*
>   *so that your youth is renewed like the eagle's.*

I praise You, my God, for Your forgiveness, healing, compassion, and love.
Thank You for filling my life with the good things that really matter.

"On that day a fountain will be opened to the house of David and the inhabitants of Jerusalem, to cleanse them from sin and impurity."
ZECHARIAH 13:1

The Fountain That Washes Away Guilt

You've no doubt heard the saying "Variety is the spice of life," but you may not know that it was written by a famous hymn writer and poet named William Cowper.

Cowper lived a very troubled life. Suffering from severe depression, he repeatedly attempted to take his life. John Newton, composer of the hymn "Amazing Grace," became concerned with Cowper's increasing melancholy. Hoping to lift Cowper's spirits by keeping him busy, Newton suggested that he and Cowper coauthor a book of 280 hymns, which they did.

After his first attack of deep depression, Cowper felt as if he had offended God so deeply that he could never be forgiven. Then Zechariah 13:1 spoke to his heart: "On that day a fountain will be opened to the house of David. . .to cleanse them from sin and impurity." Cowper realized God can erase the stain of any sin. From this experience he wrote one of his most famous hymns. The lyrics go:

There is a fountain filled with blood drawn from Emmanuel's veins;
And sinners plunged beneath that flood lose all their guilty stains.
The dying thief rejoiced to see that fountain in his day;
And there have I, though vile as he, washed all my sins away.

Cowper died in 1800. In Westminster Abbey, the first stained-glass window on the left is an image of William Cowper. Under it is the title of his famous hymn, "There Is a Fountain Filled with Blood."

Cowper's life celebrated the apostle Paul's declaration that "all are justified freely. . .through the redemption that came by Christ Jesus. . .through the shedding of his blood—to be received by faith" (Romans 3:24–25).

A wife of noble character who can find?
She is worth far more than rubies.

PROVERBS 31:10

Three Kinds of Wives

One of King Solomon's favorite topics in the book of Proverbs is women. And that's not surprising, because he had seven hundred wives and three hundred concubines. As you can imagine, all these women posed problems.

Scripture says, "King Solomon. . .loved many foreign women besides Pharaoh's daughter. . . . They were from nations about which the LORD had told the Israelites, 'You must not intermarry with them, because they will surely turn your hearts after their gods' " (1 Kings 11:1–4). Sure enough, as Solomon grew old, he turned to other gods because of his wives.

When I jotted down all the verses in Proverbs that talk about wives, I found they fit into three categories. The first is the wayward wife who has a smooth tongue (6:24), utters seductive words (7:5), and is like decay in her husband's bones (12:4). Solomon calls her "a narrow well" (23:27), meaning that in the long run, a relationship with her does not satisfy.

The next type of wife is the quarrelsome or ill-tempered wife. Solomon lived in a fantastic palace, but in his opinion, it was better to live on a corner of the roof or in a desert than to share a house with a nagging wife (25:24; 21:9). She is "like the dripping of a leaky roof in a rainstorm," he says (27:15).

But now we get to the good wife: the prudent or noble wife. Solomon says, "Houses and wealth are inherited from parents, but a prudent wife is from the LORD" (19:14). She is "her husband's crown" (12:4), "worth far more than rubies" (31:10). Which category do you find yourself in today?

"Martha, Martha," the Lord answered,
"you are worried and upset about many things."
LUKE 10:41

Who's Going to Remember?

Since I get uptight when guests are coming for dinner, my friend sent me the following advice:

When you start to have stressful feelings, just say one of the following:
"Oh, who cares anyway!" No one ever notices the things that bother
you, such as mismatched table napkins or overcooked fish.

"Big deal!" If someone notices that your bedroom is messy and
there is toothpaste on the mirror, just tell them that perhaps someone
used your room.

"Just forget it!" This one is appropriate when everything is all
set for your outdoor dinner party—until the doorbell rings and you
notice rain drizzling on your beautifully set table.

"In ten years, who's going to remember?" This one is handy
when on the day of your party, you have an allergy attack and break
out in hives.

What is really worth getting stressed about, anyway? A child with a fever—yes! Your shoes don't go with your outfit—no! Your husband losing his job—yes!

Jesus said to His hostess in Bethany, "Martha, Martha. . .you are worried and upset about many things" (Luke 10:41). Whatever frustrations you're dealing with right now, remember it's people who count most with God—and they should count most with us, too.

Sometimes we're like the bride who is so heartbroken that her wedding was not picture-perfect that she forgets she still has the groom. Big deal! Who cares anyway? In ten years, who's going to remember? Just forget the imperfections of daily life and hug the people you love.

*"Say that the Lord needs them,
and he will send them right away."*

MATTHEW 21:3
(THE WHOLE STORY: MATTHEW 21:1–3)

The Lord Needs It

It was springtime, and the man was richer because his donkey had given birth. The colt was promising, for it had survived the newborn mortality rate, and although it had not yet been ridden, it had reached the age of real value.

Then something happened. The owner was approached by two of Jesus' disciples. Jesus had instructed them: "Go to the village ahead of you, and at once you will find a donkey tied there, with her colt by her. Untie them and bring them to me. If anyone says anything to you, say that the Lord needs them, and he will send them right away" (Matthew 21:2–3).

What Jesus asked for was valuable. No explanation was given—only that the Lord needed them. No questions were asked—the owner immediately sent the donkey to Jesus and became a player in the drama of fulfilled prophecy. For the Old Testament prophet Zechariah had foretold: "Behold, your King is coming to you; He is just and having salvation, lowly and riding on a donkey, a colt, the foal of a donkey" (Zechariah 9:9 NKJV).

When Jesus rode that colt through the streets of Jerusalem, no animal had ever carried more valuable treasure. The colt was eventually returned to its owner—hallowed because God had used it and useful now that it was broken and ready to be ridden by others.

Has God asked you for something and you've been struggling with giving it to Him? Maybe your time, maybe money that you've been saving? Be quick to give Him what He asks, for you can be sure that whatever you give to God will be used to its highest potential for eternity.

You make known to me the path of life; you will fill me with joy in your presence, with eternal pleasures at your right hand.

PSALM 16:11

Pleasure That Lasts

Kids opening gifts at Christmas—what a picture of fun! But all too soon the special day is over. And the kids know it will be another whole year before Christmas comes again.

Hymn writer Frances Ridley Havergal shares,

> *You never had a pleasure that lasted. You look forward to a great pleasure, and it comes, and then, very soon it is gone, and you can only look back upon it. The very longest and pleasantest day you ever had came to an end.[1]*

However, the Bible says, "You will fill me with joy in your presence, with eternal pleasures at your right hand" (Psalm 16:11). Eternal pleasures! Found in God's presence! Ultimately, lasting pleasure is found only in an intimate relationship with God.

A poor Methodist woman of the eighteenth century wrote,

> *I do not know when I have had happier times in my soul, than when I have been sitting at work, with nothing before me but a candle and a white cloth, and. . .with God in my soul.*

Eternal pleasure comes when you're growing closer to the Lord, getting to know Him better each day. That's a privilege—and a pleasure worth pursuing!

[1]Frances Ridley Havergal, *Opened Treasures,* compiled by William J. Pell (Neptune, NJ: Loizeaux Brothers, 1962), February 7.

[2]Quoted by Mary W. Tileston, *Daily Strength for Daily Need* (Uhrichsville, OH: Barbour, 1990), 25.

> *"My food," said Jesus, "is to do the will of him who sent me and to finish his work."*
>
> JOHN 4:34

The Sin No One Criticizes

Someone has called busyness "the sin that no one criticizes." In fact, we usually think of a busy person as ambitious and important. We think of busyness as the opposite of laziness. And since none of us wants to be thought of as lazy, we're willing to be busier than we ought to be.

So how do you set priorities? Most of us grew up thinking that a Christian's priorities should be:

> *Jesus first,*
> *Others second,*
> *Myself last.*

But I don't believe that is truly biblical. If I understand scripture correctly, our priorities should all be on a horizontal line with God over all. Take a sheet of paper and pen, then write "God" at the top. Under that, draw a straight line all the way across the paper. On the line write all your responsibilities, including family times and recreation. All are important; it's a matter of deciding what God wants you to be doing at any point in your day.

If you put God "first" in your life, then after you've spent time with Him in the morning, you'll just check Him off your list for the day. If you put God only at the center of your life, He will have little impact on the many details of daily living. But if you put God over all of your life, you will find yourself checking with Him to see if you are doing what's best each moment of your day. Jesus said, "My food. . .is to do the will of him who sent me and to finish his work" (John 4:34).

If God has spoken to you today about priorities, take a definite step of obedience.

Selected verses from Psalm 108

Refreshing Words from Psalms

Let's get some perspective here. His love? Higher than the heavens. His faithfulness? Reaches to the skies. Your "enemies"? Not a problem for Him.

> *¹My heart, O God, is steadfast;*
> *I will sing and make music with all my soul.*
> *³I will praise you, LORD, among the nations;*
> *I will sing of you among the peoples.*
> *⁴For great is your love, higher than the heavens;*
> *your faithfulness reaches to the skies.*
> *⁶Save us and help us with your right hand,*
> *that those you love may be delivered.*
> *¹²Give us aid against the enemy,*
> *for human help is worthless.*
> *¹³With God we will gain the victory,*
> *and he will trample down our enemies.*

Lord, I ask You to please save me from those people and situations in my life that mean trouble for me. Thank You for Your help, Your deliverance, Your victory.

Each of you should use whatever gift you have received to serve others,
as faithful stewards of God's grace in its various forms.
1 PETER 4:10

A Friend Who Inspires Me

Some people are an inspiration—just thinking about them encourages you when the going is tough. Loana is such a friend. She has always been a joy to know, a faithful wife and mother of five. But when her husband died and she had to pick up the pieces of life and go on, I saw a depth in her that I had not known before.

Music has always been a big part of Loana's life. When her kids were young, the whole family sang together. She is one of the best piano accompanists I know, and she often accompanied her husband, Jim, when he sang in his rich tenor voice.

For years Loana and Jim had a Christmas tradition of inviting friends to their home for a carol sing-along, accompanied by great food. But after Jim died, she couldn't bring herself to do it. The memories were just too painful. Then one Christmas, I received an unexpected invitation to come to her home.

The house was fully decorated for Christmas, and beautiful china and crystal adorned the table. I had thought that we'd be eating a few snacks that evening, but Loana had prepared a delicious full dinner for us. Afterward, she sat down at the piano and led us in singing all our favorite carols.

The whole evening was special because of the gift that Loana gave to each of us—the gift of herself. The apostle Peter said, "Each of you should use whatever gift you have received to serve others, as faithful stewards of God's grace in its various forms" (1 Peter 4:10).

Thank you, Loana. You've done just that.

When I saw him, I fell at his feet as though dead. Then he placed his right hand on me and said: "Do not be afraid. I am the First and the Last. I am the Living One; I was dead, and now look, I am alive for ever and ever! And I hold the keys of death and Hades."

REVELATION 1:17–18

The Beginning, the End, and Everything in Between

In the last book of the Bible, Revelation, Jesus says, "Do not be afraid. I am the First and the Last. I am the Living One; I was dead, and now look, I am alive for ever and ever!" (Revelation 1:17–18).

I was privileged to grow up knowing that God was the beginning of everything. I learned early that there is nothing that predates God. He was and is the First. As I've gotten older, I'm glad to know that He is also the Last—nothing will ever come after Him. Another Bible translation, the King James Version, says He is Alpha and Omega—the first and last letters of the Greek alphabet.

God was there for my beginning years, bringing me through a difficult birth and a serious childhood infection. And I'm so glad to know He will be there for the ending years of my life as well.

Eventually there comes a time when your birthday seems to come around faster and faster, and the years begin to add up. You realize you've hit the peak of your career. You develop health problems. You wonder what the rest of your life holds. Be encouraged by remembering that Jesus is Alpha and Omega, the beginning *and* the end. He has a plan for your later years just as much as He did in your early years.

Whatever period of life you are in, Jesus is there for you. While it's true that He is Alpha and Omega, He is also all the letters in between. He wants to be your whole alphabet. Aren't you glad?

For who makes you different from anyone else?
What do you have that you did not receive? And if
you did receive it, why do you boast as though you did not?

1 CORINTHIANS 4:7

Humility

Did you hear about the guy who wrote a book he called *Humility and How I Attained It?*

You don't hear much about humility these days. You're more likely to read a magazine feature on self-confidence, self-assertion, or self-esteem. But is humility synonymous with low self-esteem? Absolutely not.

One of the humblest men I know is very accomplished. He speaks eight languages and fought with the Dutch underground movement in World War II. Later, he headed a large relief organization in Eastern Europe, which involved a great deal of responsibility. Yet if you met him, you would have a hard time finding out these things about him, for he would direct the conversation toward what was happening in your life. Quick to express appreciation for any small kindness, he could criticize an issue while maintaining a compassionate attitude toward the people involved. Humble? Yes. Lacking in self-esteem? No.

True humility comes by knowing Jesus and following Him. He said, "Take my yoke upon you and learn from me, for I am gentle and humble in heart" (Matthew 11:29). No one could ever accuse Jesus of being weak. But He was humble. He did not promote Himself but sought to exalt His Father in heaven.

When you get to the bottom line, what do you have that hasn't been given to you? Scripture asks, "If you did receive it, why do you boast as though you did not?" (1 Corinthians 4:7). When we realize that all we have has been given to us by God, our response will be humility.

On the first day of every week, each one of you should set aside
a sum of money in keeping with your income, saving it up,
so that when I come no collections will have to be made.

1 CORINTHIANS 16:2

How Much Should You Give?

How much of your money should you give away? That's a question worth thinking over because the Bible gives clear instructions on giving: "Each of you should give what you have decided in your heart to give, not reluctantly or under compulsion, for God loves a cheerful giver" (2 Corinthians 9:7).

Growing up as a preacher's kid, I sometimes sat by myself in church, with my dad leading the service and my mom playing the organ. One Sunday, one of the choir members left her purse on the seat next to mine so she could sit with me during the sermon. When offering time came, however, she was still seated in the choir loft, watching helplessly as, unprompted, I opened her purse and took out money for the offering—I have no memory of how much. She gave, but I don't know how cheerfully.

In the Old Testament, giving was to be a tithe—that is, 10 percent of your income for the Lord. But in the New Testament Paul wrote, "On the first day of every week, each one of you should set aside a sum of money *in keeping with your income*" (1 Corinthians 16:2, italics added).

Actually, tithing isn't totally fair. If a person makes $500 a month and gives $50 of it, it is a sacrifice. But if a rich man makes $50,000 a month and gives $5,000 of it, he still has $45,000 left to spend. That's why the Bible says our giving should be in keeping with our income.

The famous Bible teacher G. Campbell Morgan wrote, "Test all your giving by your own prosperity."[1] It's a good rule for deciding how much money you should give.

---

[1] G. Campbell Morgan, *The Corinthians Letters of Paul* (Westwood, NJ: Fleming H. Revell Company, 1946), 209.

*We are confident, I say, and would prefer to be away
from the body and at home with the Lord.*
2 CORINTHIANS 5:8

At Home

Of all the ways the apostle Paul could have described what heaven is like, he chose the phrase "at home with the Lord." He wrote, "We are confident, I say, and would prefer to be away from the body and at home with the Lord" (2 Corinthians 5:8).

The word *home* gives a feeling of peace. Home is the place where you can let your hair down and just be yourself. After all the struggles of the day, home is where you spend time with those you love most—eating a bowl of ice cream together while you watch a video, curling up in a big chair with your favorite book, or chatting with a friend over tea.

Paul could have described the grandeur of heaven—the thousands of angels, the gleaming golden streets or gates of pearl. He could have told how we will bow in worship to the King of kings and Lord of lords. Instead, he chose to describe heaven as "at home with the Lord," such a heartwarming image.

Heaven is the end of the battle, the place of ultimate peace. No more struggle with sin. No more sorrow. No more suffering. But more than the absence of all that is difficult, heaven is the *presence* of the Lord. Paul didn't just say, "We'll be at home." He said, ". . .at home with the Lord." We'll experience closeness with the Lord that goes beyond anything in this life. Let me add that if your home is not a "heaven on earth," all the more you can look forward to your heavenly home. There you will experience all that a home should be. Today, let that thought bring hope to your heart.

For you know the grace of our Lord Jesus Christ, that though
he was rich, yet for your sake he became poor, so that
you through his poverty might become rich.

2 CORINTHIANS 8:9

Grace

The apostle Paul so often began his writings to the New Testament churches with the greetings, "Grace and peace." Bible teacher G. Campbell Morgan says that in the Greek language, *grace* was, first of all, an intellectual and artistic word. It included the idea of "beauty as against ugliness, health as against disease, order as against chaos, all the realm of that which is beautiful."[1]

In time the word came to mean God's desire to impart order and beauty and life to us—a giving. A fuller meaning of grace, however, includes not merely the gifts and the desire to give those gifts, but also the activity that carries out the desire. "Grace," writes Morgan, "is ultimately the activity of God which puts at the disposal of sinful men and women all the things that give delight to Him."[2]

When a baby is born, the parents look at their little one and anticipate all the wonderful experiences they want to share with their child. Because they love their baby, they can hardly wait to give to him out of the joy in their hearts.

Is God so different? Out of His heart of love He has made us spiritually rich. "For you know the grace of our Lord Jesus Christ," wrote Paul, "that though he was rich, yet for your sake he became poor, so that you through his poverty might become rich" (2 Corinthians 8:9).

God's grace! We don't deserve it. Today, stop and say, "Thank You, Lord!"

[1]G. Campbell Morgan, *The Corinthian Letters of Paul* (Westwood, NJ: Fleming H. Revell Company, 1946), 14.

[2]Ibid.

Selected verses from Psalm 6

Refreshing Words from Psalms

God can handle even our deepest anguish, our cries of "How long, O Lord, how long is my pain going to go on?"

> ¹*LORD, do not rebuke me in your anger*
> *or discipline me in your wrath.*
> ²*Have mercy on me, LORD, for I am faint;*
> *heal me, LORD, for my bones are in agony.*
> ³*My soul is in deep anguish.*
> *How long, LORD, how long?*
> ⁴*Turn, LORD, and deliver me;*
> *save me because of your unfailing love.*
> ⁶*I am worn out from my groaning.*
> *All night long I flood my bed with weeping*
> *and drench my couch with tears.*
> ⁹*The LORD has heard my cry for mercy;*
> *the LORD accepts my prayer.*
> ¹⁰*All my enemies will be overwhelmed with shame and anguish;*
> *they will turn back and suddenly be put to shame.*

Lord, thank You for Your unfailing love—Your love that doesn't turn away, that hears my cries for mercy and answers my prayers.

"Watch and pray so that you will not fall into temptation.
The spirit is willing, but the flesh is weak."

MARK 14:38

"I Don't Wanna"

A young mom who was having a frustrating week wrote me, "I'm in a kicking-screaming-I-don't-wanna-do-it mood this week." I can certainly identify with her. Sometimes I go so far as to get my week totally organized, and then I look at the first item on my to-do list and think, *I don't want to do this—in fact, I'm not going to do it!*

In the Bible there's a word for this attitude—it's *disobedience.* Oh, I don't like to call it that. It sounds harsh. But doing God's will in the present moment is all-important because this is really the only moment I have. Joe Stowell says, "Followers [of Christ] can reduce all of life to the question, 'What is it that my Father in heaven wants for my life in this moment?'"[1] Doing what I ought to do when I ought to do it really means, "Do I love God enough to put His will above my own—right now?"

It's okay to tell God about the "I-don't-wanna" feelings you may have—in fact, it's a lot better than taking it out on everybody around you. If you don't face these feelings and instead suppress them, they may show themselves as an urge to waste time, eat junk food, watch too much TV, or get angry and depressed.

After we have told God how we feel, however, we still have to admit that the real issue is obedience. That's when we must settle it with Him.

Jesus said, "The spirit is willing, but the flesh is weak" (Mark 14:38). *You're right, Lord. Please help me. The spirit is willing, but oh, that body!*

[1]Joseph M. Stowell, *Following Christ* (Grand Rapids, MI: Zondervan Publishing House, 1966), page unknown.

"His master replied, 'Well done, good and faithful servant! You have been faithful with a few things; I will put you in charge of many things. Come and share your master's happiness!'"

MATTHEW 25:23

If I Just Had Enough Money

Finish this statement: "If I just had enough money, I would. . ." Would you change your lifestyle? Help stop HIV/AIDS? Relieve world hunger? Share the Gospel in massive ways?

I'm sure that some of the things we'd do if we had enough money would be selfish, while other things would make a tremendous difference in our world. Watching the news on TV, you may feel overwhelmed by the needs and suffering of so many. But God holds us responsible only for what we can do.

My husband tells the story about two boys who were walking along a beach where an unusually high tide had washed a lot of crabs onto the shore. If the crabs were not soon returned to the water, they could die. One of the boys started picking up crabs and hurling them back into the ocean as fast as he could. His friend said, "Why are you doing that? You can't save them all."

"No, I can't," replied the first boy, "but it makes a tremendous difference for the ones I do save."

When I was a kid, I heard a little rhyme that stuck with me:

> *It's not what you'd do with money,*
> *if riches should be your lot.*
> *It's what you're already doing with*
> *the dollar-and-a-quarter you've got.*

You and I have enough money to do whatever it is that God wants us to do, and what we do makes a difference for those we help. May we do what we can so that one day, we can hear the Master's words, "Well done, good and faithful servant!" (Matthew 25:23).

When pride comes, then comes disgrace,
but with humility comes wisdom.

PROVERBS 11:2

Sneaky Pride

Martin DeHaan, of Radio Bible Class (RBC) Ministries, describes pride when he writes,

> *I'm learning that [pride] is no fool. He flatters us. He defers to us.*
> *He encourages us to develop an exaggerated opinion of our own*
> *importance, while at the same time letting us think negative and*
> *self-destructive thoughts about ourselves. . . . He has hats for every*
> *occasion and masks for every emotion. He has a different voice for*
> *every decision.[1]*

It could be we are humble for no other reason than the fact that others are so proud! We all deal with pride in one form or another—we can even be proud of our humility! That's how sneaky pride is.

Pride can sneak up on us when we're not looking. A little success in our arena of endeavor can make us feel that we're better than we really are. Before we know it, we've become proud. It's dangerous because "pride goes before destruction, a haughty spirit before a fall" (Proverbs 16:18).

It's not pride to know what your talents, abilities, and gifts are, or what you're good at doing. Abilities are gifts from the Lord to be used for His glory. Pride comes only when we compare our gifts with those of others and think that ours are more valuable than theirs.

The Bible warns us, "God opposes the proud but shows favor to the humble" (James 4:6). Thank God for the gifts and abilities He has given you, and remember what Proverbs 11:2 says: "When pride comes, then comes disgrace, but with humility comes wisdom."

[1]Martin DeHaan, *A Great Imposter* (Grand Rapids, MI: RBC Ministries, February 2005).

"In any case, I must press on today and tomorrow and the next day—
for surely no prophet can die outside Jerusalem!"

LUKE 13:33

I Must Keep Going. . .

In the 1980s, while working in Deep Valley in South Africa, the lives of Heather Reynolds and her husband, Patrick, were forever changed when an orphaned Zulu girl walked onto their property, looking for work.

The girl was about fourteen, pregnant, hungry, and homeless. Though Heather knew that having a Zulu girl live with them would make their neighbors angry, she could not turn her away. Then as Heather explored Deep Valley further, she found thousands more young children in broken-down huts trying to care for even younger brothers and sisters. Many were starving. Heather was touched in ways that required her to act. What Heather had was heart, drive, and an enormous faith in God.

This was the humble beginning of a loving home for thousands of children with HIV/AIDS and those who had been orphaned by this dreaded killer. The Reynoldses outreach has since saved countless Zulu children. They call it God's Golden Acre.

Over the years that God's Golden Acre has existed, Heather has experienced times when there was no food for the children. She has shared her bed with critically ill babies and cried as they died in her arms. But she has never given up.

Whenever she feels low, Heather turns to a quote pinned to her office wall—"Obstacles are those frightful things you see when you take your eyes off the goal."[1] Heather demonstrates Jesus' words: "I must press on today and tomorrow and the next day" (Luke 13:33).

Oh for the determination, perseverance, and faith of Heather Reynolds!

[1]Dale le Vack, *God's Golden Acre* (Oxford, UK: Monarch Books, 2005), 262.

Love is patient, love is kind. . . . Love never fails.
1 CORINTHIANS 13:4, 8

True Love

I read the following on a wall plaque in a restaurant:

Love puts the fun in together,
The sad in apart,
The hope in tomorrow,
The joy in a heart.

I like that. It's true that love gives us joy in being together. When we can't be together with the ones we love, we're sad, for love always desires closeness. What exactly is love? It's hard to define, isn't it? More than just an emotion or passion, love is a commitment to care.

When two single people are attracted to each other, a spark ignites their relationship. This may be intense at first, but it can't truly be called love yet because they still don't know each other deeply. As they spend time together sharing their innermost selves, the attraction grows. They discover respect for each other's ideas, common life goals, and an ever-growing desire to spend the rest of their lives together.

More than the warm, happy feelings love gives us, love also drives us to sacrifice for each other. True love is unselfish. In fact, if you want a description of true love, you can do no better than that famous chapter in the Bible, 1 Corinthians 13. It says: "Love is patient and kind. Love is not jealous or boastful or proud or rude. It does not demand its own way. It is not irritable, and it keeps no record of being wronged. It does not rejoice about injustice but rejoices whenever the truth wins out. Love never gives up, never loses faith, is always hopeful, and endures through every circumstance. Prophecy and speaking in unknown languages and special knowledge will become useless. But love will last forever!" (1 Corinthians 13:4–8 NLT).

Now, *that's* true love.

"Now this is eternal life: that they know you, the only true God, and Jesus Christ, whom you have sent."

What Are Blessings?

Larry Crabb, author and psychologist, tells of the time when the doctor told him they had found a mass the size of a tennis ball near his stomach; it was likely malignant.

From his hospital window that evening he noticed a Starbucks café across the street. He imagined a Christian couple there sipping decaf lattes before they would drive home, snuggle in bed, and then get up the next morning for church. He thought, *They have the abundant life; I have cancer. It's not fair.*

Then God spoke to his heart. Larry shared,

> *I was more aware of my desires for health and good times. My eyes focused. I realized that I wanted God more than anything or anyone else, with my whole being. . . . That night I experienced the presence of God. What more—or less—could I want?[1]*

We think we're closest to God when everything is going well—that smooth sailing in our lives is a sign of God's blessing. What are God's blessings? Health? Good times? Have we lost sight of the fact that, as Larry discovered, the greatest blessing is knowing God? Larry said,

> *Every hard thing we endure can put us in touch with our desire for God, and every trial can strengthen that desire until it becomes the consuming passion of our life. Then comes the experience of God. . . . It's the source of our deepest joy, the real point of living.[2]*

Friend, if you still do not know God, "the source of our deepest joy" and "the real point of living," I pray that you will turn to Him. "Now this is eternal life: that [you] know. . .the only true God, and Jesus Christ, whom [God] sent" (John 17:3). Knowing Him is truly the greatest blessing of our lives.

[1]Larry Crabb, "When Life Begins," *Spirit of Revival*, date unknown, 4–6.

[2]Ibid.

Selected verses from Psalm 107

Refreshing Words from Psalms

We have a God who specializes in good things, wonderful deeds—and satisfaction for our souls. He made us, and He knows exactly what each of us needs.

> ¹*Give thanks to the LORD, for he is good;*
>   *his love endures forever.*
> ⁹*For he satisfies the thirsty*
>   *and fills the hungry with good things.*
> ²¹*Let them give thanks to the LORD for his unfailing love*
>   *and his wonderful deeds for mankind.*
> ⁴³*Let the one who is wise heed these things*
>   *and ponder the loving deeds of the LORD.*

Lord, thank You for always meeting my needs in exactly the right way and the right time. I give thanks to You!

Listen, you heavens, and I will speak; hear, you earth, the words of my mouth. Let my teaching fall like rain and my words descend like dew, like showers on new grass, like abundant rain on tender plants.

DEUTERONOMY 32:1–2

Words That Fall like Showers on New Grass

In my family, my father-in-law will always be remembered for saying, "When you're driving, never back up farther than you have to." He gave this advice to his sons, who told it to their sons. It is now being passed on to our grandsons as they, too, learn to drive. You, too, can probably recall a bit of wisdom someone gave you that has influenced your life. That person's spoken words continue to make a difference.

We are also influenced by the written word. Several years ago I wrote a little book called *Created for a Purpose*. A young woman who was on drugs bought the book at a truck stop in California when she was driving cross-country with a boyfriend who was abusing her. By the time she had read chapter 4, she stopped taking drugs and began to regain her confidence and self-esteem. Somewhere around chapter 6 and halfway across the United States, she jumped out of her boyfriend's truck and was picked up by a passerby, who brought her back home. When she wrote to me, she was reading chapter 7—and beginning a new life.

Now, in case you think it was my words that changed her, think again! It's what the Holy Spirit does with our words that changes people. Moses said, "Let my teaching fall like rain and my words descend like dew, like showers on new grass, like abundant rain on tender plants" (Deuteronomy 32:2). Because God can use what we say to make such a difference, pray that God will help you to speak helpful and nourishing words.

How beautiful on the mountains are the feet of those who bring good news,
who proclaim peace, who bring good tidings, who proclaim salvation,
who say to Zion, "Your God reigns!"

ISAIAH 52:7

A Beautiful Woman

Evelyn Harris was a well-off, beautiful woman. So beautiful was she that artists competed for the privilege of painting her portrait.

But with her husband, Jesse Brand, she left the luxuries of London to become a missionary among the hill people of India. There, she bore Paul, who at age nine went to England for schooling. During this time, Jesse died from fever, and Evelyn returned to London—a woman beaten by pain and grief. When Paul saw her again, he thought, *Could this bent, haggard woman possibly be my mother?*

Against all advice, Evelyn went back to India, nursing the sick, rearing orphans, pulling teeth, clearing jungle land, and preaching the Gospel. She traveled constantly, sleeping under a tiny mosquito net shelter. By this time, Paul had become a gifted doctor to the lepers of India. When his mother broke her hip at age seventy-five, Paul asked her, "Shouldn't you think about retiring?" But no argument could dissuade her.

"Paul, if I leave, who will help the village people? In any case, why preserve this old body if it's not going to be used where God needs me?" It was her final answer.

Paul wrote of her, "In old age Mother was thin and crippled, her face furrowed with deep wrinkles. And yet I can truly say that Evelyn Harris Brand was a beautiful woman, to the very end."

At ninety-five Evelyn died and was buried among her people.[1] As the Bible says, "How beautiful on the mountains are the feet of those. . .who proclaim salvation" (Isaiah 52:7).

---

[1]Dr. Paul Brand and Philip Yancey, *The Gift of Pain* (Manila, Philippines: OMF Literature Inc., 2000), 306–9.

"In the future, when your children ask you, 'What do these stones mean?' tell them that the flow of the Jordan was cut off before the ark of the covenant of the LORD."

JOSHUA 4:6–7
(THE WHOLE STORY: JOSHUA 4:1–9)

"What Do These Stones Mean?"

When Joshua was ready to lead the Israelites across the Jordan River to enter the land the Lord had promised them so many years before, God said to him, "Choose twelve men from among the people, one from each tribe, and tell them to take up twelve stones from the middle of the Jordan. . .and carry them over with you and put them down at the place where you stay tonight."

So Joshua called together the twelve and told them, "In the future, when your children ask you, 'What do these stones mean?' tell them that. . .these stones are to be a memorial." The Israelites set up the twelve stones, where they stood for many years as a memorial to God's fulfilled promise (Joshua 4:1–9, excerpted).

Perhaps you have a memento of something special God did for you. I once heard about a family who had survived a serious car accident and were so thankful that they were all still alive, they took pieces of the wreckage and formed them into a collage. They put it on their wall so that when people asked about it, they could tell of God's miraculous protection. That's a great idea!

Whether it's a gift someone gave you or a picture or plaque, it can be a reminder of God's faithfulness and a conversation starter for you to tell your story. Maybe one day your grandchildren will ask you, "What does this mean, Grandma?" And you'll be able to tell them how God answered your prayer.

I desire to depart and be with Christ, which is better by far.

PHILIPPIANS 1:23

What You Have to Be to Get There

A pastor was talking to a group of children about going to heaven. He asked, "Where do you want to go?"

"Heaven!" they all piped up.

Again, the pastor asked, "And what do you have to be to get there?"

"Dead!" one boy yelled.[1]

You'd think we didn't want to go to heaven, with the way we fight death and aging. Searching for the fountain of eternal youth, we seem to begrudge every grain of sand that passes through the hourglass of life. The apostle Paul's outlook was such a contrast to this attitude. His desire was that Christ would be exalted in his body, as he put it, "whether by life or by death. For to me, to live is Christ and to die is gain. . . . Yet what shall I choose? I do not know! I am torn between the two: I desire to depart and be with Christ, which is better by far" (Philippians 1:20–23).

Paul did not dread death because, as he wrote, "We. . .know that as long as we are at home in the body we are away from the Lord. . . . We are confident, I say, and would prefer to be away from the body and at home with the Lord" (2 Corinthians 5:6, 8).

Can you be sure that if you die today you'd go to heaven? You can. Because Jesus rose from the grave, we know that He has conquered death. As you ask for forgiveness for your sins and commit your life to Him, you will receive the confidence that Paul had. You can look forward to heaven. What a destination!

---

[1]Stan Toler, *Humor for a Mom's Heart* (West Monroe, LA: Howard Publishing Company, 2002), 166.

And not only that, but we also glory in tribulations,
knowing that tribulation produces perseverance.

ROMANS 5:3 NKJV

Old Word, But Up-to-Date Problem

Tribulation is a word that you probably don't use often, but you experience it nearly every day. Tribulation means trouble, problems, hardship, misery, difficulty, distress, ordeals, pain, and suffering.

You may think, *I'm an expert in tribulation!* Then you'll be interested in the origin of the word. When Rome ruled the world, grain was a precious commodity. Across the sheaves of cut grain, the Romans pulled a cart that had rollers instead of wheels. Sharp stones and rough bits of iron were attached to these rollers to separate the husks from the grain. This cart was called a *tribulum*. From *tribulum* we got our word *tribulation*—a fitting expression for how troubles grind us and put us under pressure.

A Roman farmer, however, did not use his tribulum to destroy grain—only to refine it. God also uses our troubles to make us stronger, for "tribulation produces perseverance" (Romans 5:3 NKJV).

The apostle Paul wrote that God "comforts us in all our tribulation" (2 Corinthians 1:4 NKJV). "Comfort" and "tribulation" go together. When we experience tribulation, we desperately need someone who will comfort us. How fortunate we are that we have the Holy Spirit, the Comforter (John 14:26 KJV).

Bible teacher G. Campbell Morgan says that *comfort* means more than reassurance or consolation. It is also reinforcing a person and sustaining him; it is coming to his side to help. God's comfort is no less than His strengthening companionship and upholding power.[1]

Experiencing tribulation? Ask God's help. The divine Comforter will strengthen you.

[1] G. Campbell Morgan, *The Corinthian Letters of Paul* (Grand Rapids, MI: Fleming H. Revell Company, 1946), 227.

We love because he first loved us.

1 JOHN 4:19

Telling God "I Love You"

Dr. Gary Chapman says there are five "love languages." Love languages are ways we express love, whether to a spouse, child, family, or friends. They are the languages of gifts, touch, acts of service, words, and quality time. Each of us has a primary love language that we use and respond to.

I believe these five love languages are also ways through which we can express love to our heavenly Father. Let's see how.

First, we can express love to God through gifts, such as a portion of our money. Love is to be the motive for all that we give to Him. Remember: God so loved us that He gave us His Son.

When it comes to touch, while we can't physically touch God, we can certainly touch Him in quiet, concentrated prayer.

An act of service for others is also a way of expressing love for God, for when we show kindness to people, Jesus said we're actually doing it to Him (Matthew 25:31–46).

What about words? It's easy to think, *Well, God knows everything, so He already knows I love Him. I don't need to tell Him.* But God longs to hear us say we love Him.

Then there's quality time. This is not just time for prayer; it is focusing our thoughts on God throughout the day. Thomas Merton, a Trappist monk, wrote: "Solitude is not turning one's back on the world; it is turning our face toward God."[1]

Have you expressed your love to God today? You have five ways to do it. John wrote, "We love because he first loved us" (1 John 4:19).

[1]Thomas Merton, *New Seeds of Contemplation* (New York: New Directions, 1962), 52–63.

Selected verses from Psalm 18

Refreshing Words from Psalms

In times of trouble, He hears our cry and offers refuge.

> *¹I love you, LORD, my strength.*
> *²The LORD is my rock, my fortress and my deliverer;*
>   *my God is my rock, in whom I take refuge,*
>   *my shield and the horn of my salvation, my stronghold.*
> *⁶In my distress I called to the LORD;*
>   *I cried to my God for help.*
> *From his temple he heard my voice;*
>   *my cry came before him, into his ears.*
> *¹⁶He reached down from on high and took hold of me;*
>   *he drew me out of deep waters.*
> *¹⁹He brought me out into a spacious place;*
>   *he rescued me because he delighted in me.*
> *²⁹With your help I can advance against a troop;*
>   *with my God I can scale a wall.*
> *³⁰As for God, his way is perfect:*
>   *The LORD's word is flawless;*
>   *he shields all who take refuge in him.*

Lord, thank You for offering me Your refuge, Your strength, and Your perfect way today!

The man of God replied, "The LORD can give you much more than that."
2 CHRONICLES 25:9

God Is Able to Give You Much More

Amaziah, the king of Judah, was headed to war with 300,000 soldiers. But he didn't think this was enough, so he hired another 100,000 from the nation of Israel, for which he paid a tidy sum that amounted to between three and four tons of silver.

About this time a man of God came along, and when he found out that Amaziah had hired troops from Israel, he told the king that God was not in this—that if he let the Israelite soldiers fight with their troops, they would be defeated.

"But," asked Amaziah, "what about the hundred talents I paid for these Israelite troops?" The man of God replied, "The LORD can give you much more than that" (2 Chronicles 25:9).

Amaziah hated to lose his money, but he obeyed the man of God, sent the Israelite troops home, and God gave him a great victory.

Aren't we all tempted at times to take shortcuts with God? Maybe you're tempted not to give money to missions because there is something else for which you think the money is needed. Remember, the Lord can give you much more than that. Maybe, like me, you're tempted to cut your prayer time short because there's something else you think you need to get done. You and I should remember that if we put Him first, God is able to give us much more efficiency in our day so that we accomplish much more.

We must simply do the right thing, trusting God at any cost for all the rest—because God is able to give us much more in return.

Dear friends, now we are children of God, and what we will be has not yet been made known. But we know that when Christ appears, we shall be like him, for we shall see him as he is.

1 JOHN 3:2

How to Be like Jesus

For years I've been fascinated by John's words in the Bible, where he wrote that when Jesus comes back to earth, we will be like Him, "for we shall see him as he is" (1 John 3:2).

Yes, for now we don't see Him physically, but we can "see" Him with our spiritual eyes, and that is how we become like Him.

I'm reminded of Moses' experience on Mount Sinai when he asked God to let him see His glory. The Lord said, "When my glory passes by, I will put you in a cleft in the rock and cover you with my hand until I have passed by. Then I will remove my hand and you will see my back" (Exodus 33:22–23).

After this experience, when Moses came down from the mountain, his face was always shining with the glory of God. He even put a veil over his face because of the radiance. But whenever he entered the Lord's presence to speak with Him, he removed the veil.

Referring to that event, Paul wrote, "And we all, who with unveiled faces contemplate the Lord's glory, are being transformed into his image with ever-increasing glory, which comes from the Lord" (2 Corinthians 3:18).

Wouldn't it be great to be like the Lord—as loving as He is, and patient and gracious? So let's just admit we can't be like the Lord in our own efforts. But the more we focus our attention on Him and spend time with Him in prayer and in reading His Word, the more He will transform us to be like Him. That's very exciting!

*For everything that was written in the past was written to teach us,
so that through the endurance taught in the Scriptures and the
encouragement they provide we might have hope. May the God
who gives endurance and encouragement give you the same attitude
of mind toward each other that Christ Jesus had.*

ROMANS 15:4–5

The God Who Gives Endurance and Encouragement

I like to read the bestseller list to see what kind of books people are buying. Many are fiction. Most deal with various issues of life in the twenty-first century. But there's one book on the bestseller list that dates back more than 4,000 years—yet people still read it today. Of course, it's the Bible. Amazing, isn't it, that people still read a book that was written so many years ago?

Most of us tend to read the New Testament more than we do the Old Testament. Some reason, "Why bother to read the Old Testament? Wasn't it replaced by the teachings of Jesus?" The Bible itself tells us why. In the book of Romans, Paul wrote, "For everything that was written in the past was written to teach us, so that through the endurance taught in the Scriptures and the encouragement they provide we might have hope" (Romans 15:4). The next verse calls God "the God who gives endurance and encouragement."

You see, when we read the Old Testament, we learn principles about God—about His character and how He deals with us human beings. Because the writing of the Old Testament covered a period of about 1,400 years, we see God's faithfulness over a long period of time. Over the centuries He kept His promises. He supplied the needs of His people. What He said would happen came true. This encourages us to keep trusting God with our problems.

Need a fresh injection of hope today? For a change, read the Old Testament. Perhaps Isaiah 41 would be an interesting place to start. You will see the God who gives endurance and encouragement—and hope.

Only be careful, and watch yourselves closely so that you do not forget the things your eyes have seen or let them fade from your heart as long as you live. Teach them to your children and to their children after them.

DEUTERONOMY 4:9

Don't Forget...

I hate to say it, but I tend to forget what I read, so I underscore meaningful thoughts, jotting down the page number and subject in the back of the book. Then when I finish the book, I type the quotes so that I have a collection of the author's significant ideas. It's extremely helpful to go back years later and reread these quotations.

For instance, years ago I read the book *Following Christ* by Dr. Joseph Stowell. Just this morning I reread the following excerpt I had typed from his book:

> *Following Christ is a relationship that drives and defines all we are and do. In fact, that's what I love about followership. It's not a project. It's a Person. It's a relationship to a Person who perfectly loves and cares for us.[1] Followers can reduce all of life to the question, "What is it that my Father in heaven wants for my life in this moment?"[2]*

Those are two thoughts I'd like to remember. First, following Christ is not a project but a relationship. And, second, life can be reduced to the question, "What does God want for me in this moment?"

It's no accident when God allows you to come across an inspirational book that speaks to your heart. Save those thoughts in a notebook or computer file so you can remember them in the future.

Now, don't forget. . . .

[1]Joseph M. Stowell, *Following Christ* (Grand Rapids, MI: Zondervan Publishing House, 1966), 17.

And he died for all, that those who live should no longer live for themselves but for him who died for them and was raised again.

2 CORINTHIANS 5:15

A Scary Prayer?

Sometimes when you're reading a book, a phrase jumps off the page and catches your attention. It happened to me this week. I was reading Jill Briscoe's book *The Deep Place Where Nobody Goes,* and the phrase that stood out was in the middle of a conversation that Jill was having with God. The phrase? Simply the words, "Spend me."[1]

I thought, *That's a very courageous request to pray to God—that phrase "Spend me." Who knows what God will ask a person to do who prays that? Do I really want God to "spend me"?* And yet, the idea is intriguing. What would God do with our lives if every day we truly offered every single part of them to Him to use as He wills? What if our only thought in the day was, *Lord, take this moment, this energy I have, and use it any way You wish?*

When you think about it, isn't it really a privilege to offer ourselves to God for Him to spend? The Bible says that Christ died for all "that those who live should no longer live for themselves but for him who died for them" (2 Corinthians 5:15).

It may be scary for you to think of praying, "Spend me." *That means I won't have any say over what happens in my life,* you reason. That's right, for God will be in charge. But don't think you'll be wiped out like a sentence the teacher erases off the chalkboard. If God spends your life, you'll achieve the purpose for which you were created. Nothing wasted. Nothing lost. Everything gained. *Yes, Lord, spend me!*

[1]Jill Briscoe, *The Deep Place Where Nobody Goes,* (Oxford, England: Monarch Books, 2005), p. 13.

Keep your lives free from the love of money and be content with what you have,
because God has said, "Never will I leave you; never will I forsake you."

HEBREWS 13:5

I Want That!

Do you enjoy watching home and garden television programs? I do. I enjoy the creativity of people who design beautiful landscaping and choose lovely colors and decor for their homes.

One of the programs, *I Want That!*, especially caught my attention. It features new inventions for the home—all the latest gizmos and appliances. I had to laugh when I first heard the name of the show because I recognized that the producers had latched on to a very human trait. We all tend to want the latest and the best of everything whether we need it or not. This reminded me of what Richard Foster wrote in his classic book *Freedom of Simplicity:*

> *When taken as a whole, the media commercials constitute a world*
> *view, a rival religious philosophy about what constitutes blessedness.*
> *We are told by television that the most idiotic things will make us*
> *insanely happy. The purpose of all this media bombardment is to*
> *increase desire. The plan is to change "That's extravagant!" into*
> *"That would be nice to have," and then into "I really need that,"*
> *and finally into "I've got to have it!"* [1]

Yes, like Eve, who saw the beautiful fruit on the tree, I find it easy to say, "I want that!" But a biblical writer reminds us, "Be content with what you have, because God has said, 'Never will I leave you; never will I forsake you' " (Hebrews 13:5).

When we know we have God and that He will never leave us, we have the most important possession in the world—the only one that matters.

[1] Richard Foster, *Freedom of Simplicity* (Aylesbury, Bucks, UK: Hazell Watson & Viney Ltd., 1981), 114–15.

Selected verses from Psalm 9

Refreshing Words from Psalms

Watch for the wonders He will work in your life today!

> ^{1}*I will give thanks to you, LORD, with all my heart;*
>   *I will tell of all your wonderful deeds.*
> ^{2}*I will be glad and rejoice in you;*
>   *I will sing the praises of your name, O Most High.*
> ^{9}*The LORD is a refuge for the oppressed,*
>   *a stronghold in times of trouble.*
> ^{10}*Those who know your name trust in you,*
>   *for you, LORD, have never forsaken those who seek you.*

Lord, I know Your name—help me to trust You with each hour today.

For those God foreknew he also predestined to be conformed to the image of his Son, that he might be the firstborn among many brothers and sisters.

ROMANS 8:29

When Life Isn't Fair

I was asked to speak to a group of women on how to live with infidelity, alcoholism, or abuse. I was unqualified to speak from personal experience, so my walking partner Terri came up with a plan: "Why don't I set you up to talk to some of my friends who have found God's strength to survive this kind of pain?" Terri did just that. So for a week I listened and took notes.

I'd like to share five of the principles Terri's friends gave me for women living with these serious problems.

1. *Don't blame yourself, but accept the responsibility to change the future.* If the situation is dangerous, don't hesitate to remove yourself and your children at least temporarily.
2. *Learn to speak the truth in love*—a principle found in Ephesians 4:15. Aim to be assertive—loving but firm, setting boundaries with consequences.
3. *Make God your source of self-esteem.* God's unconditional love saves us from despair.
4. *Find the support of other Christian women.* One woman found a prayer partner who would call her every morning and pray with her on the phone.
5. *Seek an intimate relationship with God.* A woman living with abuse came to a point where she totally abandoned her life to God. She would withdraw within her own heart to talk to God in prayer. By praying without ceasing she found strength to endure.

As you work toward a solution, be assured God will not waste your suffering but use it to make you more like Christ, conforming you "to the image of his Son" (Romans 8:29).

Whoever dwells in the shelter of the Most High will rest in the shadow of the Almighty. I will say of the LORD, "He is my refuge and my fortress, my God, in whom I trust." Surely he will save you from the fowler's snare and from the deadly pestilence. He will cover you with his feathers, and under his wings you will find refuge; his faithfulness will be your shield and rampart.

PSALM 91:1–4

Dark Days

I'm always fascinated to listen to people tell how God met them at a point of desperation. Take the Elegados, for instance. In the mining business during the Japanese occupation of the Philippines, Mr. Elegado had the only car allowed to enter sensitive areas; to pass checkpoints he had to have a Japanese sticker on the car.

Eventually, however, he was arrested by the Japanese and taken to prison. For months his wife left their children every weekend to search for him. She knew that if she did not find him he would die, for he could not survive on prison rations. Her heart cried out, "If there is a God—if You are really alive—help me."

At the end of eight months of searching, she found him and began to bring food to him. God preserved his life through two more years of imprisonment in that dark place, and ever since that time, she and her husband have been dedicated to the Lord.

There is a postscript to the story. The Japanese imprisonment, horrible as it was, saved Mr. Elegado's life. For immediately after he was arrested, the Filipino guerrillas sought to kill him for the Japanese sticker on his car. But Mr. Elegado was safe in prison.

When we are in a very dark place, perhaps the darkness is only the shadow of God's hand shielding us from greater danger. Psalm 91 says, "Whoever dwells in the shelter of the Most High will rest in the shadow of the Almighty. . . . He will cover you with his feathers, and under his wings you will find refuge" (v. 1, 4).

*"She did what she could. She poured perfume on my body
beforehand to prepare for my burial."*

MARK 14:8

Sister Freda

They call her Sister Freda, and she is an inspiration to me! A Kenyan nurse who
saw great need and did something about it, she started a medical clinic in an
area of great poverty.

The needs are overwhelming, but Sister Freda does what she can. When
she runs out of medicines, she prays—and God answers in miracles of timing.
If she needs a doctor, she convinces a doctor in the area to help. But she isn't
satisfied with just a clinic. She has established an inoculation program, a school,
and a feeding program for children. And until a few years ago, she did all of
this with no electricity except for a generator that pumped water and one that
serviced the operating room.

When I met Sister Freda, so great was her compassion that I immediately
felt the love and presence of Jesus. She does what she does with the simplest
of facilities and equipment. Can she help everyone? No. But for the ones she
helps, she makes all the difference in the world.

Sister Freda's life brings to mind a phrase in the Bible that Jesus said of
a woman who had done a kindness to Him, "She did what she could" (Mark
14:8). Too many of us want to wait until we can do something perfectly before
we do anything at all. Sister Freda is a reminder for us to do what we can and
let God take care of the results. For the ones we help, the difference will be
transforming.

Then God said, "Let us make mankind in our image, in our likeness,
so that they may rule over the fish in the sea and the birds in the sky,
over the livestock and all the wild animals, and over all the creatures that
move along the ground." So God created mankind in his own image,
in the image of God he created them; male and female he created them.

GENESIS 1:26–27

Image

Image is so important to a woman. Our appearance and the impression we make certainly extend the time we spend in front of the mirror beyond that of our male family members!

Now, we do feel better about ourselves when we look nice. Part of our self-esteem may come from our appearance, but I'm quick to say it's a pretty superficial kind of self-esteem.

Image is talked about in the Bible, too—but it's not the image of fashion. It's the image of God. We are all created in the image of no less than the eternal God Himself. In Genesis, the very first book in the Bible, we read that God said, "'Let us make mankind in our image, in our likeness. . . .' So God created mankind in his own image. . .male and female he created them" (Genesis 1:26–27).

Being made in God's image means that our bodies are valuable, but not for what they look like. Angie Conrad writes,

> *I have never read any verse in scripture spelling out what constitutes a*
> *perfect body image. There are no biblical specifications of how much*
> *we should weigh, what color our hair should be or the sizes of our*
> *noses, ears, or feet. God is concerned with the condition of our hearts,*
> *not our physical features. Although we may never fit in society's*
> *image, we are made in His image.[1]*

Made in the image of God! What a privilege! Today enjoy God's workmanship in you.

[1]Angie Conrad, "The Not-So-Perfect Image," *Tapestry Magazine*, January 2006, no page number.

"Come, follow me," Jesus said, "and I will send you out to fish for people."
At once they left their nets and followed him.

MARK 1:17–18
(THE WHOLE STORY: MARK 1:14–20)

You probably remember that some of Jesus' disciples were fishermen. In fact, several were fishing at the moment when Jesus called them. "'Come, follow me,' Jesus said, 'and I will send you out to fish for people.'" Do you remember what their response was? "At once they left their nets and followed him" (Mark 1:17–18).

Dr. Joseph Stowell, in his book *Following Christ*, points out that we, too, have "nets" we need to leave in order to follow Christ. Nets are anything in our lives that we value more than God. Sometimes we're so tangled in these nets that we find them hard to leave in order to follow Christ.

For instance, it's a bit of a silly example, but I find it very relaxing to do puzzles. Nothing wrong with that, right? But what if doing puzzles consumes so much time that I never get around to stopping by to visit my needy neighbor?

Dr. Stowell says,

> *Every time I refuse to drop a net—every time I refuse to. . .change a pattern of living because of something I treasure more—I tell Christ where He stands in my life.[1]*

Ouch! That really strikes home, doesn't it? We don't want to let go of anything. We want Jesus—and everything else in life as well. If we're really to follow Him, however, we have to make choices—how we use our time, our money, our energy. Truly following Christ means our lives will have the significance that they would otherwise never have.

Question: What nets do you need to drop in order to follow Christ?

[1]Joseph M. Stowell, *Following Christ* (Grand Rapids, MI: Zondervan Publishing House, 1966), 148.

They speak of the glorious splendor of your majesty—
and I will meditate on your wonderful works.

PSALM 145:5

Wonder—and Worship!

"Oh, Terri, just look at that gorgeous rose! See the delicate markings and shading? Just *look* at it!"

Terri, my walking partner, is getting used to my exclamations as we pass by lovely flowers. She knows I just *have* to exclaim about them. And she knows she might as well stop right where she is until I've had time to take a closer look.

Flowers don't catch her attention, but beautiful skies do. Several times we've taken a second loop to the top of a hill for another look at unusual cloud formations or the changing colors of the sunrise. Sometimes it seems we can peer into heaven itself.

I'm the same way about majestic mountains, multicolored tropical fish, or a new baby. Enjoying beauty takes me out of the doldrums and lifts my eyes and my heart from the muck I'm slogging through to the loveliness of God's handiwork—and ultimately to God Himself.

The created world tells us what God is like. The Bible says, "For since the creation of the world God's invisible qualities—his eternal power and divine nature—have been clearly seen, being understood from what has been made" (Romans 1:20).

King David said, "I will meditate on your wonderful works" (Psalm 145:5). Right now you can look out your window and see something God has created, even if it's only a scrap of blue sky or tiny blades of grass that have pushed their way through cracks in the concrete of a busy road.

Let the beauty you see lead you to worship the One who made it all. Go take a look.

Selected verses from Psalm 143

Refreshing Words from Psalms

What does the morning bring for you today? God longs to bring you His unfailing love and show you the way.

> *¹Lord, hear my prayer,*
>   *listen to my cry for mercy;*
> *in your faithfulness and righteousness*
>   *come to my relief.*
> *⁶I spread out my hands to you;*
>   *I thirst for you like a parched land.*
> *⁷Answer me quickly, Lord;*
>   *my spirit fails.*
> *Do not hide your face from me*
>   *or I will be like those who go down to the pit.*
> *⁸Let the morning bring me word of your unfailing love,*
>   *for I have put my trust in you.*
> *Show me the way I should go,*
>   *for to you I entrust my life.*

Lord, thank You for reminding me that while my spirit fails, You don't. I look to You for assurance of Your unfailing love.

*"Since you are precious and honored in my sight, and because I love you,
I will give people in exchange for you, nations in exchange for your life."*

ISAIAH 43:4

Precious

When I was growing up, a family friend had a dog she named Precious. My dad
would almost get ill whenever he heard her call the dog by that name. She was
a rather homely little animal and besides, he reasoned, "Precious" is much too
sentimental, gushy, and syrupy a name for any dog.

Believe it or not, that prompted me to look up the word *precious* in my Bible
concordance to see how the word is used in scripture. Not surprisingly, it is
used to describe jewels and rare metals, and in many other ways as well.

In the Old Testament, when Leah's sixth son was born, she said, "God has
presented me with a precious gift" (Genesis 30:20). Job said—and he knew this
from experience—that a smile in the time of trouble is precious (Job 29:24).
Life is also called "precious" (Psalm 22:20, 35:17), as is death, for the Bible
says, "Precious in the sight of the LORD is the death of his faithful servants"
(Psalm 116:15). Wisdom is more precious than rubies (Proverbs 3:15, 8:11).
God's words are "more precious. . .than much pure gold" (Psalm 19:10), and
so are His "very great and precious promises" (2 Peter 1:4).

It's not surprising that the blood of Christ is also called precious (1 Peter 1:19). In fact, Jesus Himself is called the "precious cornerstone" of the
Church, or Body of Christ (1 Peter 2:6–7). And last, Peter speaks of our faith
as being precious (2 Peter 1:1).

There's one more thing in scripture that God says is precious—you! God says,
"You are precious and honored in my sight. . .and. . .I love you" (Isaiah 43:4).

Take that thought with you today!

He determines the number of the stars and calls them each by name.

PSALM 147:4

Name a Star

Do you want to give someone a unique gift? You can name a star in your friend's honor. Several Internet sites offer to do just that.

Now, before you get too excited, let me say that only the International Astronomical Union can officially name celestial objects, and they use numbers. A star-naming website admits, "Naming a star is a symbolic gesture."[1]

Even though it's just symbolic, you will not have any problem running out of stars. Australian astronomers estimate that there are 70 sextillion stars![2]

Using two of the most powerful telescopes in the world, these scientists surveyed one strip of sky. Within this strip, some 10,000 galaxies were pinpointed and measurements of their brightness taken to calculate how many stars they contained. That number was multiplied by the number of similar-sized strips needed to cover the entire sky and then multiplied again, out to the edge of the visible universe.

Only God knows *exactly* how many stars there are. The Bible says, "He determines the number of the stars and calls them each by name" (Psalm 147:4). If God can keep track of the names of 70 sextillion stars, don't you think He can keep track of all the details of your life as well? Thank Him today that He is bigger than any task or problem you face. Then go about your work, trusting Him to guide you just as He guides the stars in the sky.

[1]Robert Roy Britt, "Name a Star? The Truth about Buying Your Place in Heaven," http://www.space.com/spacewatch/mystery_monday_030915.html, accessed September 16, 2003.

[2]"Star Survey Reaches 70 Sextillion," www.cnn.com/2003/TECH/space/07/22/stars.survey/ accessed September 16, 2008.

I will hasten and not delay to obey your commands.
PSALM 119:60

Procrastinating

The slogan on the T-shirt said "Procrastinators, Unite—Tomorrow."

Can you relate to that? Most of us are very good at putting off until tomorrow what we don't want to do today. Some of us even make lists of what we know we should do, carefully arranging the tasks in order of importance—and then totally forget about the list and do what we feel like doing. I know, because I'm a procrastinator.

Dr. John Perry, professor in Stanford University's philosophy department, says,

> *Procrastinating does not mean doing absolutely nothing.*
> *Procrastinators seldom do absolutely nothing; they do marginally*
> *useful things, like. . .sharpening pencils or making a diagram of how*
> *they will reorganize their files when they get around to it. Why does*
> *the procrastinator do these things? Because they are a way of not*
> *doing something more important.*[1]

For years I have admired the way my husband does the most important tasks first. In fact, if there is something he doesn't want to do, he does that first and gets it out of the way.

Today I found a verse in the Bible that spoke to my heart about putting things off. The writer of Psalm 119 says, "I will hasten and not delay to obey your commands" (v. 60). There's no wiggle room in that verse. Hasten—and not delay—well, if God wants me to do it, I'd better get to it. Good advice for a procrastinator like me!

[1]John Perry, "Structured Procrastination," http://www-csli.stanford.edu/~john/procrastination. html, 1995, accessed September 18, 2008.

Now it is required that those who have
been given a trust must prove faithful.
1 CORINTHIANS 4:2

Use Your Talent

George Washington Carver was an American botanist who became famous for discovering three hundred uses for the lowly peanut. The story goes that Carver asked the Lord,

> *"Lord, what is the universe?" The Lord said, "George, that's too big*
> *for your little head. Suppose you let me take care of the universe."*
> *Greatly humbled, the scientist asked, "Then, Lord, if the universe*
> *is too big for me to understand, please tell me, what is a peanut?"*
> *And then the Lord answered, "Now George, you've got something*
> *your own size. A peanut can understand a peanut; go to work on the*
> *peanut while I run the universe."* [1]

Carver discovered that growing peanuts would put necessary nitrogen back into nutrient-depleted soil. Then he worked to find practical uses for the crop; he made cheese, milk, butter, flour, ink, dyes, soap, stains, and many other products from peanuts.

The problems of the universe are too big for us to solve. But we can work on whatever opportunity the Lord has put in our path. He doesn't ask us to do what we cannot do. The talents, abilities, and interests God has given us are to be used for Him. The Bible says, "Now it is required that those who have been given a trust must prove faithful" (1 Corinthians 4:2).

Maybe He has given you motivational skills. Or artistic talents. Or computer abilities. Maybe the trust God has given you is the family you are raising. Whatever it is, know that you *can* fulfill the purpose for which God created you. Go for it!

[1] M. R. DeHaan, "Small Beginnings," *Our Daily Bread* (Grand Rapids, MI: RBC Ministries), October 27, 1962.

Not that I have already obtained all this,
or have already arrived at my goal, but I press on to
take hold of that for which Christ Jesus took hold of me.

PHILIPPIANS 3:12

Purpose

Much is being written these days about purpose—about finding the reason for your being on earth. What does God want you to do with your life?

The apostle Paul was concerned about purpose as well. He said that his desire was that he could take hold of that purpose for which Christ Jesus had took hold of him (Philippians 3:12).

You may remember that before he was a believer in Christ, Paul was on his way to Damascus to persecute Christians when God stopped him in his tracks with a blinding light and introduced him to His Son, Jesus. It's natural that Paul would want to know why God brought about such a drastic change in his life.

Although your conversion may not have been as dramatic as Paul's, your being chosen as God's child is just as miraculous. What is that purpose for which Christ Jesus laid hold of you?

To me, finding God's purpose is both a challenge and a comfort. It's a challenge because only God *fully* knows what that purpose is. I have many indications—what I'm good at, what I'm passionate about, what I'd be willing to do if I were never to be paid for it.

Endeavoring to fulfill God's purpose is also comforting because we don't have to fill anyone else's shoes. Although He stretches us at times, God seldom asks us to do what we're not good at. The way you fulfill God's purpose doesn't have to be important in the eyes of the world—just in God's eyes. His purpose for you is designed *just for you*. And He will reveal it one day at a time as you look to Him for guidance.

If you haven't done so already, ask God today to help you lay hold of His purpose for your life. Then get ready for a life of fulfillment.

He got up, rebuked the wind and said to the waves, "Quiet! Be still!"
Then the wind died down and it was completely calm.

MARK 4:39
(THE WHOLE STORY: MARK 4:35–39)

God Hears

Jesus was tired. He had taught large crowds of people gathered at the Sea of Galilee, and when evening came, He said to His disciples, "Let us go over to the other side." So they left the crowd behind and rode a boat across the lake. Jesus was so tired that He put His head on a cushion and went to sleep.

A strong squall came up and waves broke over the boat, so that it was nearly swamped. Jesus slept on. Finally the disciples woke Him. "Teacher, don't you care if we drown?" they asked. Immediately Jesus stood up, rebuked the wind, and said to the waves, "Quiet! Be still!" Then the wind died down and it was completely calm (Mark 4:35–39, excerpted).

To me, the remarkable truth from this story is not merely that the storm obeyed the command of Jesus. That is, of course, amazing! But the thought that comforts me is that although the howling of the wind and the splashing of the waves didn't waken Jesus, the cries of the men in trouble did.

Like a mother who at night can tune out the din of traffic outside but waken at the slightest whimper of her baby, the Lord responds to the needs, fears, and cries of His children.

Isn't that comforting? The psalmist said, "The righteous cry out, and the LORD hears them; he delivers them from all their troubles" (Psalm 34:17). The God of heaven hears when you call. If the storm in your life is about to swamp your boat, call the One who said to the wind and waves, "Quiet! Be still!"

Selected verses from Psalm 138

Refreshing Words from Psalms

Whose job is it anyway to bring about the fulfillment of God's purpose in my life?

> *¹I will praise you, LORD, with all my heart;*
>   *before the "gods" I will sing your praise.*
> *²I will bow down toward your holy temple*
>   *and will praise your name*
>   *for your unfailing love and your faithfulness,*
> *for you have so exalted your solemn decree*
>   *that it surpasses your fame.*
> *³When I called, you answered me;*
>   *you greatly emboldened me.*
> *⁶Though the LORD is exalted, he looks kindly on the lowly;*
>   *though lofty, he sees them from afar.*
> *⁷Though I walk in the midst of trouble,*
>   *you preserve my life.*
> *You stretch out your hand against the anger of my foes;*
>   *with your right hand you save me.*
> *⁸The LORD will vindicate me;*
>   *your love, LORD, endures forever—*
>   *do not abandon the works of your hands.*

Lord, I praise You for fulfilling Your purpose for me! Do not abandon the works of Your hands in my life, but have Your will in my life today.

So whether you eat or drink or whatever you do,
do it all for the glory of God.

1 CORINTHIANS 10:31

Stressssss!

Patricia Sprinkle, author of *Women Who Do Too Much*, writes,

> *Stress does not come from being busy. Stress comes from being busy*
> *about things we don't want to do, or from not being busy about things*
> *we do want to do.*[1]

I agree. I don't resent being busy—so long as I'm doing something I want to do. But tell me to do something I hate doing, and I immediately feel stress.

What about those times you want to do a task, but circumstances stand in your way like a concrete wall? No matter how you try to find time for what you want to do, you can't.

I believe these stressful feelings come to us for one of two reasons. Maybe what we want to do is not God's plan for us for this day. Perhaps we're trying to cram far too many tasks into one day.

A second common cause of stress is that we don't recognize God's purpose in common, ordinary tasks. There are times when washing dirty laundry is the most important thing to be done. Sometimes, it's making a phone call to settle a problem with a coworker. The secret to de-stressing these dreaded or boring tasks is to accept that they are God's will for you at that moment.

Paul wrote, "So whether you eat or drink or whatever you do, do it all for the glory of God" (1 Corinthians 10:31). Today, try doing that smallest or most difficult task for God's glory and from His perspective and see if your stress level doesn't go down.

[1]Quoted by Mary M. Byers, *How to Say No and Live to Tell About It* (Eugene, OR: Harvest House Publishers, 2006), 105.

Remember your Creator in the days of your youth,
before the days of trouble come.

ECCLESIASTES 12:1

Keep on Going

Have you ever read this pitifully sad description of old age that King Solomon gave us some three thousand years ago? He wrote: "Don't let the excitement of being young cause you to forget about your Creator. Honor him in your youth before the evil years come—when you'll no longer enjoy living. It will be too late then to try to remember him when the sun and light and moon and stars are dim to your old eyes, and there is no silver lining left among your clouds. For there will come a time when your limbs will tremble with age. . .and your teeth will be too few to do their work. . . . Then let your lips be tightly closed while eating when your teeth are gone! . . . You will waken at dawn with the first note of the birds; but you yourself will be deaf and tuneless, with quavering voice. You will be afraid of heights and of falling—a white-haired, withered old man, dragging himself along. . .standing at death's door, and nearing his everlasting home as the mourners go along the streets" (Ecclesiastes 12:1–5 TLB.)

What a gloomy description of old age! I can just see what a cartoonist would do with that! The truth is, our senior years are equally important to God as our youth. His will for us is in keeping with the stage of life we are in and the vitality He gives us.

No matter what your age, make the most of it. Honor God by never stopping the pursuit of His purpose for your life. As God gives you strength, keep on until the joyous day you stand before Him face-to-face.

*Each one of you also must love his wife as he loves himself,
and the wife must respect her husband.*

EPHESIANS 5:33

Men Are Not Easy to Train

A woman was considering marriage to a man who had reached his late forties without ever marrying. The man had some good points, but he also had some idiosyncrasies. A group of women were discussing whether or not she could "shape him up," so to speak, and ensure a good marriage. One of the gals sounded a warning when she commented, "Men are not easy to train!"

While everyone laughed at her remark, I began to think about the adjustments that come in every marriage. For instance, how long does it take, ladies, to train a man to know that when you tell him your problem, he doesn't have to solve it—he just has to listen with empathy; to know that you need time for recreational shopping as much as he needs time for watching sports on TV; and to know you like receiving flowers even though they die in three days? Yes, it takes time to train a man to know these things.

Paul told us, "Each one of you also must love his wife as he loves himself, and the wife must respect her husband" (Ephesians 5:33). If your husband's faults bother you, stop and think very hard before you give up on him. Think of all his good characteristics. Before you throw him out because of his imperfections, think of all the imperfections that *you* have that he has to deal with. Keeping in mind how long it would take you to "teach" another man to understand and know you, how about loving your husband as he is?

And if you are single but considering marriage, do remember you, too, will have adjustments to make.

"You may ask me for anything in my name, and I will do it."
Jᴏʜɴ 14:14

God Keeps His Word

Heather Reynolds, of a ministry called God's Golden Acre, has helped count-less orphaned Zulu children in South Africa. Here's a story about her that will inspire you.

God's Golden Acre desperately needed sand to complete the refurbishing of one of the center's buildings. A volunteer, who was an atheist, challenged Heather, "Why don't you ask your God to provide the sand if you have no money to buy some?"

Heather said to herself, *This young man is quite right. God, why don't You answer our prayers? Do You want me to beg?* She picked up the phone and called the local building supply—for the third time—asking for a load of sand as a donation. She was told, "No," and adamantly told not to call again.

About half an hour later, Heather was disturbed by loud laughter outside on the grounds.

"What's all this about?" asked Heather, going outside.

"It's your miracle," said the atheist volunteer. "You see that man walking through the gate over there? He's the driver of a ten-ton truck of sand, and his truck has just broken down on our driveway. He has asked our permission to tip all this sand so his company can tow the truck away." Ironically, it was the same company from which Heather had just asked for sand.[1]

One of Heather's favorite Bible promises is John 14:14: "You may ask me for anything in my name, and I will do it." Heather has proved that God keeps His word!

―――――――――

[1]Dale le Vack, *God's Golden Acre* (Oxford, UK: Monarch Books, 2005), 244–45.

*"But blessed is the one who trusts in the LORD,
whose confidence is in him."*

What Kind of Confidence?

I read a book where the author suggested that you replace negative, condemning thoughts about yourself with positive, encouraging thoughts to raise your self-esteem. She believes that by visualizing what you want your life to be, you can change it. I tried it, but I have found that thinking positively about myself is not enough. Too often I cannot live up to even my own expectations.

Another author, Deborah Smith Pegues, who has been successful in the corporate world, presents a different viewpoint:

> *For many years I was a staunch advocate of self-confidence. I embraced
> the teachings of secular motivational speakers who convinced me
> that if I believed in myself, the sky was the limit in. . .what I could
> accomplish. However, having faced several. . .situations that required
> greater skills, knowledge, and mental fortitude than I possessed, I
> began to realize that my self-confidence was woefully inadequate.[1]*

She explains that the core meaning of the word *confidence* is "with faith"; and that the focus of our faith should be God, not ourselves, since God says, "Apart from me you can do nothing" (John 15:5). She adds that, "The most detrimental quality we can have is self-confidence." Instead, we need to replace self-confidence with Supreme confidence—a personal confidence based on our confidence in God.

Do you have self-confidence or Supreme confidence? The Bible says, "Blessed is the one who trusts in the LORD, whose confidence is in him" (Jeremiah 17:7). His work in your life is the most positive thinking you can have.

[1]Deborah Smith Pegues, *Conquering Insecurity* (Eugene, OR: Harvest House Publishers, 2005), 122.

"So if the Son sets you free, you will be free indeed."
JOHN 8:36

Freedom!

Perhaps you think of the Bible as a book full of only rules and regulations. It tells you to stop doing what you want and insists that you start doing what you have no interest in doing.

I have good news for you. Yes, there are rules in the Bible. They were put there so that we would know what God's standards are. But God knew we could never keep all His laws. So God sent His Son to earth to die on the cross to pay for our sins. He offers us forgiveness for all that we have done wrong—yes, all of it. When we ask His forgiveness and place our faith in Him, He puts the Holy Spirit in our hearts to help us obey and live for Him. That's real freedom! No more need to put up with guilty feelings. No more fear that God is out to "get you" when you mess up.

If you have placed your faith in Jesus Christ to forgive your sins, you have freedom to come to God, who loves you deeply and will forgive you when you ask Him. Even people who already have a relationship with Jesus sometimes forget that they don't have to carry around a load of guilty feelings. Keep your conscience clean by confessing any known sin to the Lord.

Don't live another day as a slave to sin and guilt. Find the true freedom that comes from knowing you are totally forgiven. Jesus, the Son of God, said, "If the Son sets you free, you will be free indeed" (John 8:36).

Selected verses from Psalm 62

Refreshing Words from Psalms

In God is rest for your soul that no one else can give. Notice the words *rock, fortress, refuge.*

> *¹Truly my soul finds rest in God;*
> *my salvation comes from him.*
> *²Truly he is my rock and my salvation;*
> *he is my fortress, I will never be shaken.*
> *⁷My salvation and my honor depend on God;*
> *he is my mighty rock, my refuge.*
> *⁸Trust in him at all times, you people;*
> *pour out your hearts to him,*
> *for God is our refuge.*

Lord, be my rock, my refuge, my fortress in the demanding circumstances of my life.

He who began a good work in you will carry it on to
completion until the day of Christ Jesus.
PHILIPPIANS 1:6

Something Beautiful

An artist had in mind exactly what he wanted to paint when he began working on a canvas. He was busy painting the colors that were to make up the background when a friend came by to see him.

"I plan this to be the greatest work I have ever done!" the artist told his friend.

His friend could hardly suppress his laughter. "It looks like one big daub of gray paint," he responded.

"Ah," replied the artist, "you cannot see what is going to be there. I can."[1]

As you look at your life, you may not see much more than a drab splatter of paint. But the Divine Artist has an image in mind. God knows what He wants to paint on the canvas of your life.

It's not up to the canvas to become a valuable piece of art—it's up to the artist. The canvas itself isn't worth much. But when the artist transfers his vision to the canvas, then the work becomes beautiful and valuable.

There is no better way to live than to offer ourselves to God to create in us the masterpiece He has in mind. His plans are far greater than ours, for He says, "As the heavens are higher than the earth, so are my ways higher than your ways and my thoughts than your thoughts" (Isaiah 55:9).

Give yourself to the Lord, and He will make something truly beautiful of your life, for "He who began a good work in you will carry it on to completion until the day of Christ Jesus" (Philippians 1:6).

[1]Harry A. Ironside, *Notes on Philippians* (New York: L. B. Printing Co., Inc., 1943), 19–20.

Many are the plans in a person's heart,
but it is the LORD's purpose that prevails.

PROVERBS 19:21

Welcoming Interruptions?

Have you noticed that Jesus never seemed to mind being interrupted? He could accept delays in life because He saw time from an eternal perspective. Jesus knew the past, the present, and the future—all at the same time.

We can't know that, and that's why we get so frustrated when things don't go as planned. We have our schedule all arranged to accomplish things we feel are important. And then along comes an interruption. Nothing else is left to do but to trust God will work out His purposes in spite of the disruption in our day.

James O. Fraser, a missionary in China in the early 1900s, experienced this problem when he needed uninterrupted time for language study. He said,

> *It is a mistake to plan to get through a certain amount of work in a certain time. It ends in disappointment, besides not being the right way to go about it. . . . It makes one impatient of interruptions and delay. Just as you are nearly finishing—somebody comes along to sit with you and have a chat! I think it is well to cultivate an attitude of mind which will enable one to welcome him from the heart and at any time.[1]*

Why am I writing about interruptions today? Because I just had a four-hour interruption pop up that totally changed my plans. But Proverbs 19:21 assures me, "Many are the plans in a person's heart, but it is the LORD's purpose that prevails." If God sends the interruption, then it's a divine appointment!

[1]Quoted by Elisabeth Elliot in her online devotional "Gateway to Joy," November 3, 2005, www .backtothebible.org.

He said to them, "Go into all the world
and preach the gospel to all creation."

MARK 16:15

Should You Be a Missionary?

How do you know if you're meant to be a missionary? Do you wait until you hear an audible voice calling you to the mission field? Or do you sense an urge in your heart that won't just go away?

Jonathan Goforth, a missionary in China, tells how he was directed to missions: "Although I was clearly led to be a minister of the Gospel, I rejected all thought of being a foreign missionary."[1]

Then he heard Dr. G. L. Mackay, a pioneer missionary to Taiwan, tell of how he had traveled in Canada trying to persuade a young man to come to Formosa (now Taiwan) to help him, but failed. Goforth said,

> *As I listened to these words, I was overwhelmed with shame. Had the floor opened up and swallowed me out of sight, it would have been a relief. There was I, bought with the precious blood of Jesus Christ, daring to dispose of my life as I pleased. I heard the Lord's voice saying, "Who will go for us and whom shall we send?" And I answered, "Here am I; send me." From that hour I became a foreign missionary.[2]*

It is said that 13,000 Chinese came to faith in Christ as a result of Goforth's ministry. He spent forty-six of his seventy-seven years in China.

We'd better have a good excuse for *not* being missionaries because Jesus said, "Go into all the world and preach the gospel to all creation" (Mark 16:15). Because Jesus bought us from death with His precious blood, whatever our calling, we have no right to order our lives as we please without asking Him what He wants us to do. Think about it.

[1]Rosalind Goforth, *Goforth of China*, originally published in 1937.

[2]Ibid.

See what great love the Father has lavished on us, that we should be called children of God! And that is what we are! The reason the world does not know us is that it did not know him.

1 JOHN 3:1

The Retirement Years?

In a book I read about the various seasons of our lives, the author referred to our sixties as the decade for preparing for retirement. I couldn't help smiling as I thought, *That author has not yet experienced being in her sixties, or she would know that for most of us who are in this period of life, they are years filled with far more than preparing for retirement.*

I'm past seventy now, and so far, *retirement* is not in my vocabulary. Of course, I'm realistic enough to know that eventually I'll have to slow down. But right now my husband and I still carry a full load of travel, writing, radio broadcasts, seminars, and speaking at churches and conferences. It is truly a joy for us to continue what we so enjoy doing.

But what if we were hit with an injury or disabling disease that changed all this? What if we had to limit our outreach and stay home because we were not physically able to continue? Would we be less valuable to God? No, not at all. All of us are valuable to God because He loves us for who we are—His children, made in His image—not for what we accomplish.

The apostle John wrote, "See what great love the Father has lavished on us, that we should be called children of God!" (1 John 3:1). No matter what your age, no matter what you can do or are unable to do, if you are God's child, He loves you in a lavish way. What more could any of us ask?

*Those the LORD has rescued will return. They will enter Zion
with singing; everlasting joy will crown their heads. Gladness
and joy will overtake them, and sorrow and sighing will flee away.*

ISAIAH 35:10

Obsolete!

Was last night sleepless for you because you've recently lost someone dear to you? Weeks may have even passed since you said good-bye, but you've not been able to process the grief. You spend most nights crying, and even now, the tears are flowing.

If it seems to you that you will never get over your grief, I want to remind you there's a day coming when "sorrow and sighing will flee away" (Isaiah 35:10). Did that thought really sink into your heart—that one day the words *sorrow* and *sighing* will be forever gone from our vocabulary?

Famous London preacher Joseph Parker said that when you look through a dictionary, you will sometimes come across a word that is marked "obsolete." That means the word is outdated and no one uses it anymore. There will come a day, Parker said, when *sorrow* and *sighing* will be two words we will never use again.[1] Revelation 21:4 gives us four more words: "There will be no more *death* or *mourning* or *crying* or *pain*." All obsolete! Archaic! Forgotten!

In the meantime, know that the Lord is near you during this difficult time. He knows how you feel. When He was in the Garden of Gethsemane before He was crucified, the Bible says that He "offered up prayers and petitions with fervent cries and tears" (Hebrews 5:7). He understands. The Bible tells us, "The LORD is close to the brokenhearted and saves those who are crushed in spirit" (Psalm 34:18).

Come to Him. Let Him hold you close to His heart.

[1] R. W. DeHaan, *Our Daily Bread* (Grand Rapids, MI: Radio Bible Class, September 11, 1969).

All have turned away, all have become corrupt;
there is no one who does good, not even one.

PSALM 14:3

The Great Exchange

She sat across the table from my husband and me and, with tears in her eyes, said, "I'd like to have Jesus in my heart, but I don't think I can be good enough."

"I'm so glad you told us how you feel," we told her, "because there's good news. You don't have to be good enough. None of us can be. The Bible says, "There is no one who does good, not even one" (Psalm 14:3). That's exactly why Jesus came to this earth—to die for our sins. He did for us what we could not do for ourselves."

Yes, Jesus came to carry on an exchange; to say to us, as only a good God can say: "You give me your humanity and I will give you My divinity. You give Me your time and I will give you My eternity. You give Me your sin and I will give you My purity. You give Me your broken heart and I will give you My love. You give Me your nothingness and I will give you My all."

What an exchange! We give Him our brokenness, and He gives us His wholeness.

If we had to be good enough to deserve forgiveness and salvation, not one of us would qualify—not the kindest, most generous person in the world. But that's the beauty of God's exchange offer. We ask Him to take our sin, and in the greatest trade-in program in the world, He gives us His righteousness.

If you have not made that great exchange, you can do it right now. If you already have, pour out your gratitude to the Lord.

Selected verses from Psalm 91

Refreshing Words from Psalms

God promises He will rescue the one who loves Him. Seek shelter under His wings.

> ¹*Whoever dwells in the shelter of the Most High*
> *will rest in the shadow of the Almighty.*
> ²*I will say of the LORD, "He is my refuge and my fortress,*
> *my God, in whom I trust."*
> ⁴*He will cover you with his feathers,*
> *and under his wings you will find refuge;*
> *his faithfulness will be your shield and rampart.*
> ¹⁴*"Because he loves me," says the LORD, "I will rescue him;*
> *I will protect him, for he acknowledges my name.*
> ¹⁵*He will call on me, and I will answer him;*
> *I will be with him in trouble,*
> *I will deliver him and honor him.*
> ¹⁶*With long life I will satisfy him*
> *and show him my salvation."*

Your promises, Lord, encourage me today. I will rest under the shadow of Your protection.

God made him who had no sin to be sin for us,
so that in him we might become the righteousness of God.

2 CORINTHIANS 5:21

When God Could Not Look

For years, Dr. Margaret Brand served as a missionary eye surgeon in southern India. In the rural areas she would sometimes do a hundred cataract surgeries in a day.

In one instance where there was no electricity, a twelve-year-old boy was asked to hold a large flashlight so that its beam gave Dr. Brand enough light to operate. Dr. Brand doubted whether the boy would be able to endure the sight of eyes being sliced open and stitched. For the first five operations he did his job impressively. During the sixth, however, he faltered.

"Little brother, show the light properly," Dr. Brand instructed him. But she could see that he simply could not bear to look at the eye. When she asked him if he was feeling well, she saw that tears were running down his cheeks. "Oh, doctor, I cannot look," replied the lad. "This one, she is my mother."[1]

When Jesus was hanging on the cross, God the Father could not look. Jesus cried out, "My God, my God, why have you forsaken me?" (Matthew 27:46). A great shadow had come between Jesus and the Father. Jesus was lonely on that cross because of you and me.

God had to turn His eyes away from His Son in those moments because of our sin. You see, "God made him who had no sin to be sin for us, so that in him we might become the righteousness of God" through putting our faith in Him (2 Corinthians 5:21).

Have you thanked Him recently that He was willing to pay that price?

[1] Dr. Margaret E. Brand, *Vision for God,* with Dr. James L. Jost (Grand Rapids, MI: Discovery House Publishers, 2006), 121.

"If you, then, though you are evil, know how to give good gifts to your children, how much more will your Father in heaven give good gifts to those who ask him!"

MATTHEW 7:11

Two Important Words

Kay Warren, wife of pastor and author Rick Warren, says, "In parenting, if you don't insist on anything else, insist that your kids learn to obey two words: 'Come' and 'No.'"

She explains that if your children learn to come to you when you call them and to accept your "No" when you have to deny them something they want, they will learn to obey God when He uses those same words.

How do you respond to God when you hear Him say, "Come" and "No"? God calls us, saying, "Come to me, all you who are weary and burdened, and I will give you rest" (Matthew 11:28). But even though we're bone tired from carrying a heavy load, we tell ourselves that we have no time to come to the Lord. We're much too busy. So we stubbornly muddle through in our own strength. God says, "Come," and we say, "No."

Other times it's God who says "No" to us. "Don't do that. It's not good for you." But we interpret that to mean, "God just doesn't want me to have what I want." Or we consider it "unanswered prayer," thinking God didn't hear or doesn't care.

Jesus said, "If you, then, though you are evil, know how to give good gifts to your children, how much more will your Father in heaven give good gifts to those who ask him!" (Matthew 7:11). If we want the best for our own children, surely we can understand that God wants the best for us as well.

Teach your kids to obey those two key words, "Come" and "No." As adults, let's also learn to obey those same words ourselves when we hear them from our heavenly Father.

*L*ORD*, our Lord, how majestic is your name in all the earth!*
You have set your glory in the heavens.

PSALM 8:1

How Big?

As you know from reading this book, I get excited when I learn about the enormity of creation because I get a hint of how great our God is. Obviously, the person who makes something is greater than what he makes, so God is greater by far than the incredible size of any newly discovered object in space.

The heavens are the work of God's fingers. We can almost picture God deciding one day to do some arts and crafts, so He created the universe.

No wonder David cried out,

> *L*ORD*, our Lord,*
> *how majestic is your name in all the earth!*
> *You have set your glory*
> *above the heavens. . . .*
> *When I consider your heavens,*
> *the work of your fingers,*
> *the moon and the stars,*
> *which you have set in place,*
> *what is mankind that you are mindful of them,*
> *human beings that you care for them?*
> PSALM 8:1, 3–4

God does care. I don't know how big a problem you're dealing with today. But I can assure you of one thing: God is bigger—and He cares. Talk to Him about it now.

"Who among the gods is like you, LORD? Who is like you—
majestic in holiness, awesome in glory, working wonders?"

EXODUS 15:11

Renewed by Wonder

I've found a simple cure for the blues that works for me. Maybe it will work for you, too: just go outdoors and look at what God has made.

If you are a city dweller, you see more concrete than you do trees and stars. You probably spend most of your day looking at things that are man-made, and as great as some of those things are, they don't renew the spirit. So try going to a park or the beach.

I think you'll be amazed at what spending an entire day outdoors will do for your soul. In her book *When You're Running on Empty*, Cindi McMenamin writes,

> *As you. . .appreciate creation once again, you will enjoy life rather than feel drained by it. Your anxiety will be replaced with appreciation, and your busyness with rest. Engaging your imagination and sense of wonder with life will slow you down and cause you to smell the flowers.[1]*

Scripture says of the Lord, "Who is like you—majestic in holiness, awesome in glory, working wonders?" (Exodus 15:11) and "Many, LORD my God, are the wonders you have done" (Psalm 40:5).

Seeing God's handiwork is rejuvenating. Whether the area you live in is tropical, mountainous, desert, or by the sea, His creative wonders are there. As you admire God's creation, your tension will go and your faith will be renewed. As Cindi says, "To live with a sense of wonder is to believe God can do the incredible."[2]

Come on, you can do it. As soon as you can, schedule just one day outdoors from sunrise to sundown. You'll be renewed by wonder.

[1]Cindi McMenamin, *When You're Running on Empty* (Eugene, OR: Harvest House Publishers, 2006), 154.

[2]Ibid.

Be made new in the attitude of your minds.

EPHESIANS 4:23

Stuck in Pain

Is your life a bed of roses, free of problems? "Are you kidding?" I can hear you say. "Right now I can't even remember what a rose *smells* like!"

I've noticed through my own painful experiences that sometimes we get *stuck* in our pain. I mean, we take the attitude, "I refuse to feel better until this situation that can't be changed *is* changed." When we do this, we are stuffing ourselves in a tight corner with no one there but us and our pain.

When I am stuck in pain, no one else is responsible for my feelings except me. I may not be able to change the circumstances, but I can choose my attitude toward them.

Someone sent me a humorous e-mail called "Attitude Is Everything!" It is about a woman who woke up one morning and noticed she had only three hairs on her head.

"Well," she said, "I think I'll braid my hair today." She did and she had a wonderful day. The next day she woke up and saw that she had only two hairs on her head. "Hmm, I think I'll part my hair down the middle today." And she had a grand day. The next day she woke up and noticed that she had only one hair on her head. "Today I'm going to wear my hair in a pony-tail." And she had a great day. The fourth day she woke up and saw that there wasn't a single hair on her head. "Wonderful!" she exclaimed. "I don't have to fix my hair today!"

What a difference our attitude can make! The Bible says, "Be made new in the attitude of your minds" (Ephesians 4:23). That's good advice for all of us.

If only they were wise and would understand
this and discern what their end will be!

DEUTERONOMY 32:29

Mature Choices

When my husband speaks on "Ten Commandments for Parents of Teens," he points out that what teens want and what parents want for them are not the same thing. What teens want more than anything else is independence—the right to make their own decisions. On the other hand, what you want for your teens is maturity—the ability to make the *right* decisions.

God says to His people, "If only they were wise and would understand. . . and discern what their end will be!" (Deuteronomy 32:29). That verse is a great description of maturity—the ability to discern the possible results of our decisions. If a person can weigh a situation, looking down the road to see the possible result of each choice—and then choose the best one, he or she has true wisdom and understanding.

The popular poem "The Road Not Taken" by Robert Frost poignantly illustrates a man coming to a point in life where he is confronted with a choice:

> *Two roads diverged in a wood, and I—*
> *I took the one less traveled by,*
> *And that has made all the difference.*[1]

No doubt we want our teens to make the best choices. We can help them by talking to them less and listening more. If you have teens or are counseling teens who have to make decisions that will affect their future, spend plenty of time listening to their thinking. Ask pertinent questions. Resist the urge to tell them what to do. Get them to think about what the results will be for each of their choices. And then pray for them. You may be thankfully surprised at the mature choices they will make.

[1]http://www.bartleby.com/119/1.html, accessed September 17, 2008.

Selected verses from Psalm 46

Refreshing Words from Psalms

The only antidote to fear is trust in the ever-present help of God.

> *¹God is our refuge and strength,*
>   *an ever-present help in trouble.*
> *²Therefore we will not fear, though the earth give way*
>   *and the mountains fall into the heart of the sea,*
> *³though its waters roar and foam*
>   *and the mountains quake with their surging.*
> *¹¹The LORD Almighty is with us;*
>   *the God of Jacob is our fortress.*

Today I feel like the mountains have fallen, and I'm being tossed by the raging sea of circumstances. Lord, be my strength and fortress.

*[The Lord] satisfies your desires with good things
so that your youth is renewed like the eagle's.*

PSALM 103:5

Things We Like to Eat

Before we began eating our meal together, my dad bowed his head. I can still hear his deep voice as he prayed,

> *For things we like to eat,*
> *Thy loving gift of food,*
> *We thank Thee, Lord, today,*
> *For Thou art kind and good.*
> *Amen.*[1]

He was eighty-eight years old and still praying a prayer that he taught me when I was a little girl. We used to say it out loud together as a family. Recently, I came across the book from which that prayer was taken, and the memory came back.

Although I no longer pray those exact words, I realize how many times I still thank the Lord for food that I really like to eat. My husband and I travel a lot, and when we do, we eat some—well, let's say "unusual" foods. Most of them are good, but some are pretty strange to our taste. When I come back home after times like that, the prayer springs from my heart, "Thank You, Lord, for food that I *like* to eat. It tastes so good!"

Maybe you eat gourmet cuisine prepared by an outstanding chef. Maybe your food is simple fare—bread or rice and a bit of meat and vegetables. Regardless of how expensive or cheap our food may be, you'd probably agree that the best-tasting meals are those we really like. But let us not forget that our food is a gift from the Lord because He loves and cares for us.

The psalmist said God "satisfies your desires with good things so that your youth is renewed like the eagle's" (Psalm 103:5). Thank You, Lord, for good-tasting food!

[1]Mary Alice Jones, ed., *Prayers for Little Children* (Chicago: Rand McNally Company, 1937), 59.

"As for God, his way is perfect: The LORD's word is flawless;
he shields all who take refuge in him."

2 SAMUEL 22:31

The Committee That Lives in Your Head

Author and speaker Jan Johnson says that for a long time, she was plagued by what she calls "the committee that lives in my head."[1] She said there were four people on the committee who harassed her thoughts.

The first, "The Looking-Good Kid," always urged Jan to work hard to be admired. "Don't make any mistakes—and then I'll be proud of you," he said.

The second member was "The Rescuer." This person urged Jan to help others so they would feel obligated to her and love her. So Jan kept an impossible schedule.

Third was "The Attitude Police Officer." She was always evaluating Jan, who could never live up to her expectations.

The final member was "The Grouch," who told her others should be paying more attention to her. "You poor thing!" he would taunt.

Like Jan, you may have this committee in your head. It's utterly impossible to please. How different this committee is from God! "For he knows how we are formed, he remembers that we are dust" and cannot live up to the impossible expectations of others (Psalm 103:14).

Jan found relief when she confronted the committee with the truth that God is not interested in our performance but, rather, in a relationship with us.

When thoughts of inadequacy disturb you, replace them with Bible truth. "As for God, his way is perfect: The LORD's word is flawless; he shields all who take refuge in him" (2 Samuel 22:31). You aren't perfect, but you have a perfect Savior.

[1] Jan Johnson, "What Happens in Solitude?" in *Conversations,* (Atlanta, GA: vol. 1:2 2003), 68.

The LORD is my strength and my shield; my heart trusts in him, and he helps me. My heart leaps for joy, and with my song I praise him.

PSALM 28:7

The Lord Is My Strength

In his painting *The Helping Hand*, French artist Emile Renouf portrays an old fisherman seated in his rowboat with a little girl next to him. Both the old man and small child have their hands on the large oar as they make their way across the water. From the look on the little girl's face, you can see that she is intense in her efforts to help him row the boat, although, of course, the man's strong arms are really doing the work.

How like us in our efforts to accomplish what God has given us to do! We sometimes act as if it all depends on us, when really we're merely putting our hands on the oar.

Whether you are in Christian ministry or the secular workplace, God warns His people that after they have become successful, they may be tempted to say, " 'My power and the strength of my hands have produced this wealth for me.' But remember the LORD your God, for it is he who gives you the ability to produce wealth" (Deuteronomy 8:17–18).

Maybe you're in the middle of a big task. Your hands are on the oar—and you may even be getting blisters. Remember, God's strong hands are also there, and it's His help we need if we're ever going to finish the job. David said so many years ago, "The LORD is my strength and my shield; my heart trusts in him, and he helps me" (Psalm 28:7).

Keep on rowing, knowing that it's a privilege to work with God—and a blessing to be helped by Him.

That ye, being rooted and grounded in love, may be able to comprehend with all saints what is the breadth, and length, and depth, and height; and to know the love of Christ, which passeth knowledge.

EPHESIANS 3:17–19 KJV

Saints in Circulation

In the mid–1600s, England was running out of silver for making coins. So Oliver Cromwell, the Lord Protector, sent his soldiers to a local cathedral to look for silver. When they returned, they reported that the only silver they could find was in the statues of the saints standing in the church. "Good!" Lord Cromwell replied. "We'll melt down the saints and put them into circulation."[1]

Saints are not just silver statues; the Bible refers to all believers in Christ as "saints." Paul prays that the Ephesians "may be able to comprehend with all saints what is the breadth, and length, and depth, and height; and to know the love of Christ" (Ephesians 3:18–19 KJV). He urges them to "always keep on praying for all the saints" (Ephesians 6:18). He also speaks of "the riches of the glory of [God's] inheritance in the saints" (Ephesians 1:18 NKJV). In Colossians, Paul writes that the previously unknown reality of Christ literally dwelling within us has been disclosed to the saints (Colossians 1:26). Jude urged believers to "contend for the faith that was once for all entrusted to the saints" (Jude 1:3).

You may not think of yourself as a "saint," because your idea of a saint is someone "other-worldly" and, well, "perfect." In biblical terms, however, a saint is simply someone whose sins have been forgiven and whom Christ has made righteous.

If ever we needed "saints melted down and put into circulation," it is today: believers who will penetrate our culture in every area and demonstrate, by their lives and their love, the truth of the Gospel. Our world is looking not for perfection but authenticity.

[1]*God's Little Devotional Book on Prayer* (Tulsa, OK: Honor Books, Inc., 1997), 9.

Your path led through the sea, your way through the mighty waters,
though your footprints were not seen.

PSALM 77:19

Lord, Where Are Your Footprints?

You're confronted with a crucial decision, not knowing which way to go. You search your Bible, you pray, you look for God's direction, but you can't seem to find an answer. You cry out, "God, I was following You. Where did You go? Where do I go now?" The crisis you face is like a vast ocean in front of you—and you know there are no paths to follow in oceans!

Like you, the Israelites were in great need of deliverance and direction. When they left Egypt following those painful years of slave labor, it wasn't long before they, too, reached a crisis: Pharaoh's soldiers running after them and the Red Sea in front of them—with no bridge to cross. But God parted the Red Sea, and Moses led the people through on dry land!

Recently I noticed an interesting phrase in Psalm 77:19: "Your path led through the sea, your way through the mighty waters, though your footprints were not seen." The last part stood out to me: "Your footprints were not seen."

That's where you are now, right? You have to move forward but you can't see God's footprints to follow, as if you were blind. Well, here's a special promise:

> *I will lead the blind by ways they have not known,*
> *along unfamiliar paths I will guide them;*
> *I will turn the darkness into light before them*
> *and make the rough places smooth.*
> *These are the things I will do;*
> *I will not forsake them.*
> ISAIAH 42:16

What great assurance! You don't have to see ahead—just take the next step, and along unfamiliar paths He will guide you as He has promised!

But God demonstrates his own love for us in this:
While we were still sinners, Christ died for us.

ROMANS 5:8

Why Doesn't God Tell Us?

Many of the whys of life are totally beyond our comprehension: a toddler run over by a car, a jetliner crashing because birds flew into its engines, violent earthquakes. Animals don't ask, "Why?" They just endure. But God gave human beings the ability to ask, "Why?" Our difficulty is that we have a mind that asks questions, but we do not have enough insight to understand the answers.

I believe that God set life up this way as a test of faith. If we could understand the answers to all our whys, we would not have to trust Him. Someday we'll understand, because then we'll have the perspective of eternity. In the meantime, trusting God with the whys is the ultimate test of whether or not we believe He is trustworthy.

The cross is the ultimate "why?"—why would God send His Son to die for us? Romans 5:8 says, "But God demonstrates his own love for us in this: While we were still sinners, Christ died for us." God's love for us gives us the confidence that He has our ultimate good at heart.

Refreshing Words from Psalms

No matter how bad the disaster, God promises He will fulfill the purpose that He has for you.

> [1]Have mercy on me, my God, have mercy on me,
>   for in you I take refuge.
> I will take refuge in the shadow of your wings
>   until the disaster has passed.
> [2]I cry out to God Most High,
>   to God, who vindicates me.
> [3]He sends from heaven and saves me,
>   rebuking those who hotly pursue me—
>   God sends forth his love and his faithfulness.
> [10]For great is your love, reaching to the heavens;
>   your faithfulness reaches to the skies.

Thank You for Your great love and faithfulness, Lord. They bring courage to my heart.

To answer before listening—that is folly and shame.
PROVERBS 18:13

Listening and Talking

An old proverb goes, "He who answers before listening—that is folly and shame." Yet, how many of us do just that? When people are talking to us, we're watching for that split second when their lips clamp shut so we can give them the "benefit" of our great wisdom. In fact, sometimes we just interrupt. I guess that's because we think that what we want to say is so much more important than what they are saying, right?

Well, the fact is, that old proverb is from the Bible: Proverbs 18:13. And we would do well to recognize its truth. Many, if not most, of our problems in communication are the result of a failure to really listen to people.

Sometimes the reason we don't listen is that the other person has chosen the wrong time to talk. Preparing the time, place, and circumstances is critically important if you want someone to listen to you—not when your husband is watching his favorite sports program on TV or your teen has just crawled out of bed in the morning and hasn't quite entered the real world.

James wrote, "My dear brothers, take note of this: Everyone should be quick to listen, slow to speak and slow to become angry" (James 1:19). Truly listening to your husband, your teen, your coworker, or your friend is one of the best gifts you can give. Listening says, "I care about you and want to understand you."

Listening is the most important part of the communication process. The Living Bible puts Proverbs 18:13 quite bluntly: "What a shame—yes, how stupid!—to decide before knowing the facts!"

Are you listening?

Blessed is the one whose transgressions are forgiven,
whose sins are covered.

PSALM 32:1
(THE WHOLE STORY: PSALM 32:1–5)

Misery—and Relief!

Remember when you were a kid and you'd done something wrong? You knew when you got home you'd have to face your parents—and the consequences—so you took the longest route home, dragging your feet all the way. You were miserable.

Well, that doesn't happen only when you're a kid. When we've done something that we know displeases God, we're also miserable—until we come near to Him and settle it with Him.

King David experienced all of that. He knew he had done wrong, and for days he avoided dealing with it. He describes his misery in these poetic words: "When I kept silent, my bones wasted away through my groaning all day long. For day and night your hand was heavy upon me; my strength was sapped as in the heat of summer" (Psalm 32:3–4). Oh yes, David, that's what a guilty conscience feels like!

But David decided to deal with his wrongdoing. He tells us, "Then I acknowledged my sin to you and did not cover up my iniquity. I said, 'I will confess my transgressions to the LORD'—and you forgave the guilt of my sin" (v. 5). Relief at last!

Maybe right now you are as miserable as David was. You're not on speaking terms with God because there's an issue you and He need to settle—a barrier between you and Him. What are you waiting for? Quit dragging your feet. Right now, come home to the Father, confess your sin, and find His forgiveness and restoration, His comfort and closeness. Then, with David, you can say, "Blessed is the one whose transgressions are forgiven, whose sins are covered" (Psalm 32:1).

*"As long as it is day, we must do the works of him who sent me.
Night is coming, when no one can work."*

JOHN 9:4

Do It Now

I am told that the following anonymous letter was written by an eighty-three-year-old woman to her friend:

> *Dear Bertha,*
>
> *I'm reading more and dusting less [these days]. I'm sitting in the garden and admiring the view without fussing about the weeds. I'm spending more time with my family and friends.*
>
> *Life should be a pattern of experiences to savor. I'm trying to recognize these moments now and cherish them. I'm not "saving" anything; we use our good china and crystal for every special event, such as losing a pound, or the first rose blossom. I'm not saving my good perfume for special parties, but wearing it for clerks in the store and tellers at the bank.*
>
> *The phrase "one of these days" is losing its grip on my vocabulary. If it's worth seeing or hearing or doing, I want to see and hear and do it now.*
>
> *It's those little things left undone that would make me angry if I knew my hours were limited. Angry because I hadn't written certain letters that I intended to write. Sorry that I didn't tell my husband and parents often enough how much I truly love them. I'm trying very hard not to put off or hold back anything that would add laughter and luster to our lives.*
>
> *Life is short; we do not know the time or the hour. We must cherish every day, for every breath truly is a gift from God.*

Jesus Himself said, "As long as it is day, we must do the work of him who sent me. Night is coming, when no one can work" (John 9:4). Let's make the most of today.

He raises the poor from the dust
and lifts the needy from the ash heap.

PSALM 113:7

Idinide

A missionary noticed that in the Bible translation of the tribe she was working with, the word *idinide* had been used for the English word *Savior*. *Idinide* literally means "picker-upper." She thought, *This is not the right word!*[1]

Then one day a tribal woman gave birth to a child, and the missionary was asked to visit and be the idinide or the "picker-upper." She found the newborn baby on the jungle floor and the mother lying in a hammock above.

"What am I supposed to do?" she asked the mother.

"You pick up and wash the baby," the mother replied.

Getting water from a nearby stream, she cleaned him as best as she could, washing away the blood.

"Now what?" asked the missionary.

"Take the baby to the village and present him to his father," the mother responded. The missionary found the father and showed him his newborn son.

Suddenly she began to understand why the word *idinide* had been used for *Savior*. No finer word picture could be used to show what Jesus does when He finds you—sometimes in the gutter, sometimes in your loneliness, but always in your sin. He cleans you up, cuts the cord that bound you to your sinful life, and finally brings you to the heavenly Father, saying, "This is your new adopted child; I gave My life to bring him into Our family!"

The Bible says God "raises the poor from the dust and lifts the needy from the ash heap" (Psalm 113:7). "The LORD upholds all those who fall and lifts up all who are bowed down" (Psalm 145:14). Idinide! Savior!

[1]Karl Crowe, personal newsletter (New Tribes Mission, April 2000), 1.

Jesus then took the loaves, gave thanks, and distributed to those who
were seated as much as they wanted. He did the same with the fish.

JOHN 6:11

(THE WHOLE STORY: JOHN 6:1–15)

Fifty-Seven Cents

Hattie May Wiatt, who lived in the 1800s, wanted to go to Sunday school, but there was no room in the classroom. The next morning the pastor spotted the little girl walking to school and told her, "Hattie, we are going to have a larger Sunday school when we get the money—large enough for all the children."

Sadly, Hattie May became sick and died. After the funeral, her mother handed the pastor a small bag containing fifty-seven cents that Hattie had gathered. At church the pastor stated they had the first gift toward the new Sunday school building—Hattie May's fifty-seven cents. He then changed all the money into pennies and auctioned them off to raise money. After they were sold, fifty-four of those cents were returned to him by the people who bought them, so he had them framed where they could be seen. A society was formed and dedicated to making Hattie May's fifty-seven cents grow, and soon a nearby house was purchased with the money Hattie May's gift had produced.

But there's more. The church was too small, so the pastor went to the owner of a nearby lot and told him they had only fifty-four cents but that they would like to buy his lot. Incredibly, the owner took the remaining fifty-four cents as down payment.

One last thing. The Sunday school building, bought as the result of Hattie Mae's fifty-seven cents, later held the first classes of Temple University, which now enrolls more than 27,000 students.[1]

Like the little boy who gave his lunch to Jesus (John 6:1–15), Hattie May's gift was multiplied to bless thousands.

What do we have to give?

[1]http://www.truthorfiction.com/rumors/h/hattiemaywiatt.htm, accessed September 17, 2008.

What other nation is so great as to have their gods near them the way the LORD our God is near us whenever we pray to him?

DEUTERONOMY 4:7

Where Is God When We Pray?

When we pray, sometimes we strongly sense God's presence right with us. Other times God seems very far away. Somebody quipped, "If God seems far away, guess who moved!" But I don't think that is true. That's like saying, if you can't "feel" God's presence, then He must not be there. Feelings follow faith; they don't precede it.

The prophet Moses declared that God is *always* near us when we pray: "What other nation is so great as to have their gods near them the way the LORD our God is near us whenever we pray to him?" (Deuteronomy 4:7).

The vastness of space can make you feel that God must be beyond our universe—He must be a great distance from where you are when you pray. Don't believe this feeling for a moment. Our God is big enough to be everywhere at the same time.

When King David tried to think of a place where God is not, he gave up, saying,

> *Where can I go from your Spirit?*
> *Where can I flee from your presence?*
> *If I go up to the heavens, you are there;*
> *if I make my bed in the depths, you are there.*
> *If I rise on the wings of the dawn,*
> *if I settle on the far side of the sea,*
> *even there your hand will guide me,*
> *your right hand will hold me fast.*
> PSALM 139:7–10

So, when you pray, don't base whether or not God is listening on your feelings. As Moses said, "the LORD our God is near us whenever we pray to him," listening to every word.

Refreshing Words from Psalms

Compassionate, gracious, forgiving—that's what our God is. He loves you like the best father you can imagine—and more.

> *⁸The Lord is compassionate and gracious,*
> *slow to anger, abounding in love.*
> *¹⁰He does not treat us as our sins deserve*
> *or repay us according to our iniquities.*
> *¹¹For as high as the heavens are above the earth,*
> *so great is his love for those who fear him;*
> *¹²as far as the east is from the west,*
> *so far has he removed our transgressions from us.*
> *¹³As a father has compassion on his children,*
> *so the Lord has compassion on those who fear him.*

Lord, it's because You do not treat us as we deserve that we can come to You with all our needs. I humbly look to You for help, knowing that You love me.

*Jesus replied, "You do not realize now what I am doing,
but later you will understand."*

Later You Will Understand

Shortly before He gave His life on the cross, Jesus told Peter, "You do not realize now what I am doing, but later you will understand" (John 13:7).

Linda, our accountant at Guidelines Ministries, has had some of those experiences that you just can't understand—among them, cancer showing up in her body three times, requiring four surgeries and radiation that destroyed half of her thyroid. She's also had open heart surgery, as well as five angioplasties with numerous stents placed in her arteries.

In addition, because of tough problems in her daughter's life, Linda has raised her grandson since he was twenty-two months old. But the biggest blow was the tragic news that her daughter's life was taken. Her grandson now has neither a mother nor father.

Yet, if you met Linda, you'd never know the weight of her burdens. She exudes love to everyone she meets from a heart that is tender, not bitter. When I asked her how she has coped, she told me,

> *My prayer was just to live long enough to raise my grandson. God
> has granted that and more to me, for which I am grateful. Paul wrote,
> "For God has not given us a spirit of fear, but of power and of love
> and of a sound mind" (2 Timothy 1:7 NKJV). This promise has
> carried me through the difficulties without fear.*

Why did all of this happen to one person? I absolutely do not know. As Linda says, "God's ways are not ours." But one day we will understand. And in the meantime, Linda says, "Trust the One who knows."

"Remember these things, Jacob, for you, Israel, are my servant.
I have made you, you are my servant; Israel, I will not forget you."

ISAIAH 44:21

Forgotten? Not by God!

When the Romans banished the apostle John to the isle of Patmos, they must have thought he would soon be forgotten and his influence wiped out forever. Pastor Jack Hayford points out,

> *A small mountainous island with rocky soil in the Aegean Sea,*
> *Patmos should have remained an anonymous piece of land that*
> *people were sent to and never heard from again. . . . But God had*
> *other ideas.[1]*

In this most unlikely location, John wrote the last book of the New Testament, Revelation, which tells what must take place at the end times.

Today John would be astounded to see that Patmos is a vacation spot, where tourists flock to see the place where God revealed Himself to him in such an outstanding way.

If you're in a difficult-to-understand situation right now, take hope. Like John, you may feel you've been taken out of the mainstream of life—sidelined. Perhaps your life is consumed in caring for a loved one so severely disabled that he or she doesn't recognize who you are. Or maybe you've had to discontinue teaching a Bible study that was the joy of your life. Or maybe you feel exiled to a job you hate but can't quit because you need the money.

To His people God says, "I have made you. . .I will not forget you" (Isaiah 44:21).

Feel forgotten? Not by God! Wherever your "Patmos" is, remember that while you are there, God has you clearly in His sight. Someday He will bring blessing from your banishment.

[1]Jack Hayford, from an address at the twentieth anniversary commencement of Angelus Bible Institute, Los Angeles, CA, 2006.

*To proclaim the year of the LORD's favor. . .to comfort all who mourn, and
. . .to bestow on them a crown of beauty instead of ashes, the oil of joy
instead of mourning, and a garment of praise instead of a spirit of despair.*

ISAIAH 61:2–3

❀

Unnecessarily Beautiful

Missionary doctor Margaret Brand writes of the time when her young son, Christopher, was outside playing in the hill country of India toward sunset time: "He rushed in excitedly. . .and tried to drag me outside as he almost shouted, 'Come see the sky. It's unnecessarily beautiful!' . . . His words have stayed with me ever since."[1]

God created beauty beyond anything the human mind could have imagined—truly unnecessarily beautiful. Some of the loveliest places on earth are so remote that they have never been seen by anyone, yet God still made them beautiful.

But you don't have to go far to see beauty. Think of where you live. What beauty has God brought into your life? Something as simple as a rose? Spectacular lightning? A beautiful view of the ocean? Perhaps God's unnecessary beauty in your life is as basic as having food that you *like*, not just food that keeps you alive. I mean, did you ever thank God for chocolate?

The Old Testament prophet Isaiah foretold some seven hundred years before Jesus was born that He would be appointed "to comfort all who mourn . . .to bestow on them a crown of beauty instead of ashes, the oil of joy instead of mourning, and a garment of praise instead of a spirit of despair" (Isaiah 61:2–3).

These comforting words tell of the Lord's blessings far beyond anything we deserve. Take a moment to thank Him for some specific beauty that He has blessed you with—unnecessary, perhaps—above and beyond anything you expected.

[1]Dr. Margaret E. Brand *Vision for God,* with Dr. James L. Jost (Grand Rapids, MI: Discovery House Publishers, 2006), 108.

*The LORD will perfect that which concerneth me: thy mercy, O LORD,
endureth for ever: forsake not the works of thine own hands.*

PSALM 138:8 KJV

Created for a Purpose

Whenever I speak on the subject of every one of us being here on earth for a reason, these questions inevitably come up: "But what about people with disabilities? Does God have a purpose for them? Or did He make a mistake when He made them?"

Let me tell you about Dr. John and Christine Haggai's son, Johnny, who was born with severe cerebral palsy. He could not talk or walk or feed himself and required care twenty-four hours a day. He lived to be only twenty-four years old.

An intoxicated doctor's negligence caused Johnny to be born with these acute limitations. But his parents chose to accept his birth as God's divine design for them. They devoted countless hours to his care, seeing him as an incredible blessing. Dr. Haggai said,

> *Chris and I are thoroughly convinced that Johnny came to us in the
> sovereign and loving will of God. Johnny lived a significant life.
> Significant not just because there is worth in every person, as there
> surely is, but. . .[Johnny] had a role to fill, a destiny to realize.[1]*

Rather than being a burden, Johnny enhanced his parents' lives and inspired them to push on in Christian ministry.

Our culture strongly values perfection—the beautiful woman, the athletic man, the skillful artist or gifted musician. Yet clearly the Bible points to a purpose for each of us being here—even if we are what the world sees as "broken." Encouraging is Psalm 138:8 (KJV), which says, "The LORD will perfect that which concerneth me." Let Him use you—whatever your limitations—to bless someone today.

[1]John Edmund Haggai, *My Son Johnny* (Wheaton, IL: Tyndale House Publishers, Inc., 1978), 80.

Look on me and answer, LORD my God.
Give light to my eyes, or I will sleep in death.

PSALM 13:3

Really Seeing

A village boy about twelve years old was helping Dr. Margaret Brand, a missionary eye doctor in India, as she did cataract surgery. After an operation, the boy bounced up and down with excitement, for the patient was his own mother. Because the woman had gone blind before he was born, she has never seen her son.

"*Amma,* can you see me now?" the boy asked.

When the mother received her new glasses, it took several minutes for her to realize she could see again. "She gazed at her son for a long time, and then, breaking into a smile, said, 'My son, all these years I thought I knew you, but today I see you.' "

Dr. Brand writes,

> *So many times I think I know a person. I make up my mind about them, and my opinion is not always favorable. Then God has to stop me and say, "Now just a minute. Let me show you how I see that person." In those moments I have to admit my own blindness and let God open my eyes.[1]*

We're all a bit blind when it comes to judging people, especially when we bump against their rough exterior. For example, your husband may have been critical of you this morning, and you assumed he was displeased with something you had done. But if you could have seen into his mind, you would have found that he was really worried about his job.

The psalmist prayed, "Look on me and answer, LORD my God. Give light to my eyes" (Psalm 13:3). May this be our prayer, too. We need God's surgery to see others as they really are.

[1]Dr. Margaret E. Brand *Vision for God,* with Dr. James L. Jost (Grand Rapids, MI: Discovery House Publishers, 2006), 122.

Do not be yoked together with unbelievers. For what
do righteousness and wickedness have in common?
Or what fellowship can light have with darkness?

2 Corinthians 6:14

Guard Your Heart

Two young businesswomen who traveled a great deal for their company were talking.

"Do men ever hassle you?" one asked the other.

"Rarely," she replied.

"Wow," said the first, "You are so beautiful that I would think you would be approached often by men you really don't want to meet."

"No," the woman explained, "I just say five words and immediately I'm left alone."

"Five words? What are they?"

"I just ask them, 'Are you a born-again Christian?' If they say, 'Yes,' we have a good conversation because Jesus is part of it. And if they're not interested in a relationship with Him, they're outta here!"[1]

That's one way to handle the situation!

Is it okay to date nonbelieving men? We call it "evangelism dating"—dating a guy in order to lead him to the Lord. But usually this is merely an excuse to be together. Scripture says, "Do not be yoked together with unbelievers. . . . What fellowship can light have with darkness?" (2 Corinthians 6:14). That clearly rules out marriage between a believer and a nonbeliever. But *can* a young woman lead a man to a relationship with Jesus Christ? Yes, of course. You don't have to date him to do that, though. You can invite him to church, or share Christ with him in a group, or ask another Christian guy to share the Gospel with him. But be very careful, for it is easy to move from concern about his eternal destiny to concern about *your* destiny with him! The writer of Proverbs said, "Above all else, guard your heart, for everything you do flows from it" (Proverbs 4:23).

[1] *God's Little Devotional Book for Women* (Tulsa, OK: Honor Books, Inc., 1996), 219.

Selected verses from Psalm 17

Refreshing Words from Psalms

If our days are extra busy, all the more we need to call on God for help. He has the answers!

> [6] *I call on you, my God, for you will answer me;*
>   *turn your ear to me and hear my prayer.*
> [7] *Show me the wonders of your great love,*
>   *you who save by your right hand*
>   *those who take refuge in you from their foes.*
> [8] *Keep me as the apple of your eye;*
>   *hide me in the shadow of your wings.*
> [15] *As for me, I will be vindicated and will see your face;*
>   *when I awake, I will be satisfied with seeing your likeness.*

From the din and disorder of my day, I take refuge in You, Lord. Help me see the wonder of Your great love.

*"Greater love has no one than this:
to lay down one's life for one's friends."*

JOHN 15:13

No Greater Love

Robert McQuilken was serving as president of Columbia Bible College when his wife, Muriel, developed Alzheimer's disease. Becoming increasingly confused, at last she could form only one sentence. But she said it often: "I love you."

After Robert would leave for work, Muriel often would walk to where he was—a one-mile round trip that she would sometimes make ten times a day. At night, he would see that her feet were bruised and bloodied. Finally he decided that he could no longer keep his position and care for Muriel at the same time, so he resigned from the college, saying, "Had I not promised forty-two years before, 'in sickness and in health. . .till death do us part'?"[1]

McQuilken was criticized. Other people could take care of Muriel, his critics said, but not everyone could fill his shoes at the school. Soon she would not even know who he was, so why should he give up his ministry in order to care for her?

He answered them,

> *It's not that I have to, it's that I get to. I love her very dearly. . . . It's
> a great honor to care for such a wonderful person.[2] Muriel is the joy
> of my life.[3]*

Robert McQuilken's love and sacrifice for his wife draws us to reflect on Jesus' love for us. Jesus said, "Greater love has no one than this: to lay down one's life for one's friends" (John 15:13). That is exactly what He did for us. We're not always very lovable. In fact, sometimes we're downright difficult. Yet He loves us—not because He *has* to but because He *wants* to.

[1] John Tucker, http://www.milfordbaptist.co.nz/sermon_20041003.htm, accessed July 16, 2008.

[2] http://www.youtube.com/watch?v=f6pX1phIqug, accessed October 9, 2008

[3] Tucker, ibid.

*"My Father, who has given them to me, is greater than all;
no one can snatch them out of my Father's hand."*

JOHN 10:29

Safe in God's Hand

As Mildred Dillon and her husband were sailing to England for their new ministry assignment, a storm developed. Quite simply, Mildred was terrified.

Mildred's fear was understandable. A little more than a year before, she almost lost her life when a tornado had swept through Fort Wayne, Indiana. A brick smokestack collapsed on the building she was in, burying her. Her back was broken, and two vertebrae were floating loose. The doctors didn't think she'd live through the night, much less walk again.

Prayers went out as doctors waited for the swelling to subside before attempting surgery. Then, amazingly, preoperation X-rays showed that the vertebrae had returned to their positions! Surgery was no longer necessary. Her broken back only required a full-body cast, but she had to relearn to walk. And she did!

But now aboard the ship, another storm was threatening Mildred's life and faith. She was restless throughout the night. Finally, at 4:30 a.m., a song formed in her heart that has brought confidence to many. The lyrics go:

> *Safe am I. . .*
> *In the hollow of His hand,*
> *Sheltered o'er. . .*
> *With His love forevermore.*
> *No ill can harm me; No foe alarm me;*
> *For He keeps both day and night.*[1]

God reminded her that He had been with her in the tornado, and He was still with her in this storm. What better refuge is there than God's great hand, for Jesus said that "no one can snatch you out of [our] Father's hand" (John 10:29).

[1]Mildred Leightner Dillon, "Safe Am I," quoted in an e-mail from Pastor James Gross, 2008.

I can do all this through him who gives me strength.

PHILIPPIANS 4:13

Terri's Testimony

David was born with an underdeveloped nervous system. Everything over-stimulated him—especially touch. He had no ability to calm himself, so he cried day and night, sleeping for only twenty minutes at a time.

Terri, his mom, recalls those exhausting months: "We could not touch his feet, head, or hands because these places are where the nerve endings are located, and the slightest touch would cause him excruciating pain.

"His doctor told me to get help because I could possibly go psychotic and hurt my baby due to lack of sleep. On top of that, he warned that 70 percent of marriages with children like this end in divorce. Then he said to hang in there—that it would take 'only' two years for my son's nervous system to be completely normal." Terri wasn't sure she would live that long!

Bill and Terri defied the odds. Their marriage survived and even became stronger. "We gave each other grace for misspoken words and misunderstandings," Terri says. Bill also stepped down from his corporate job to spend more time with his family.

This couple held on ever so doggedly to Philippians 4:13, "I can do all this through [Christ] who gives me strength." These words were a life preserver to which they clung in desperation, and in faith.

Today, David is a normal young adult who loves the Lord and excels in what he does. "I would never wish to go through it again," Terri adds, "but I'm grateful the Lord used my son's physical problem to mature my relationship with Him and with my husband."

In your impossible situation, hold on to Christ. Terri will tell you, "Only He can give you strength to go on."

*He will swallow up death forever. The Sovereign L*ORD
*will wipe away the tears from all faces; he will remove his
people's disgrace from all the earth. The L*ORD *has spoken.*

ISAIAH 25:8

No More Tears

Joey O'Connor was exhausted. He had just come home from the memorial service for a close friend who had been killed in a freak boating accident. Worn out by grief, Joey flopped down on the bed to spend a few quiet moments with his three-year-old daughter, Janae. Immediately she began to ask questions about the accident and Joel's death.

"Where's heaven?"

"Well, I don't know exactly where heaven is," Joey admitted, "but I can tell you what heaven is like." Then he explained that the Bible promises heaven to be a place where we will live with God forever. That there's no death in heaven, no pain or ow-ees or scraped knees, and finally, that there are no tears because it is a wonderful, happy place with nothing to make us sad.

Suddenly the light came on for Janae. "Yeah," she responded, "heaven's *not* a crying place."[1]

You have it right, Janae. The prophet Isaiah tells us that in the life to come, God "will swallow up death forever. The Sovereign LORD will wipe away the tears from all faces." And then, like a signature to his statement, he adds, "The LORD has spoken" (Isaiah 25:8).

The book of Revelation tells us that God "will wipe every tear from their eyes. There will be no more death or mourning or crying or pain, for the old order of things has passed away" (Revelation 21:4).

On earth, tears are a God-given outlet for the pain that we experience, but heaven's "not a crying place." It's God's promise.

[1]Joey O'Connor, *Heaven's Not a Crying Place* (Grand Rapids, MI: Fleming H. Revell, 1997), 15–19.

"The LORD himself goes before you and will be with you; he will never leave you nor forsake you. Do not be afraid; do not be discouraged."

DEUTERONOMY 31:8

Discouragement and Fear

How's your day so far—has it been discouraging?

People in the Bible had discouraging days, too—they felt like giving up. One of the most familiar phrases in the Bible is "Do not be afraid; do not be discouraged," because God knew we'd need to hear that—often!

I found nine examples in the Old Testament where those phrases are used. Sometimes people were facing heavy leadership responsibilities. Others had been assigned a project that challenged every skill they had. Some had received news that invading armies were on their way. Others were leaving for war with the imminent possibility of death.

What I like is that right after the instruction not to be afraid or discouraged, God would often add more words of reassurance such as: "The LORD himself goes before you and will be with you; he will never leave you nor forsake you" (Deuteronomy 31:8); "The LORD your God will be with you wherever you go" (Joshua 1:9); "For the battle is not yours, but God's" (2 Chronicles 20:15); "Stand firm and see the deliverance the LORD will give you" (2 Chronicles 20:17).

Perhaps you have been given additional duties at work just when you thought you couldn't squeeze in another task. Or maybe you are in a sticky financial situation. Perhaps having several preschool children already, you are overwhelmed to learn that you are pregnant again.

Dear friend, "Do not be afraid; do not be discouraged." Just as God was with the fearful of the Old Testament, He is with you now. Call to Him; He is the Master of search and rescue!

My times are in your hands; deliver me from the
hands of my enemies, from those who pursue me.

PSALM 31:15

In the Nick of Time

She was desperate. Deciding that life wasn't worth living any longer, she climbed up to where she could loop a pair of panty hose over the rafters. Now she was ready to tie them around her neck and jump.

But her radio was on, and the speaker's words caught her attention. The message was only five minutes—*Guidelines*, a radio program that my husband has been producing for more than forty years. The topic that day was "What God Thinks of Suicide."

Instead of jumping, the woman called the radio station. The technician airing the program that day answered the call and in the next few moments, led her to faith in Christ. Since that time, she has visited the station, and it's been confirmed—she is a changed person!

Think of the timing of that incident. The program had been written several months earlier in order to meet programming deadlines. After the recording session, a Guidelines volunteer listened to be sure there were no grammatical errors or technical blips. Then a CD had to be produced and mailed to the station. Of course, there's the fact that the technician chose to air that program on that day. And the program went on the air at exactly the time the woman was about to end her life. No accident!

God makes no mistakes, for He is a God of precision. The psalmist wrote, "My times are in your hands" (Psalm 31:15). He can manage the timing in your life. Put your life in His hands and trust Him.

Selected verses from Psalm 30

Refreshing Words from Psalms

Take a moment to remember times when you have called on God for help and He gave you healing and renewed joy.

> ¹*I will exalt you, Lord,*
> *for you lifted me out of the depths*
> *and did not let my enemies gloat over me.*
> ²*Lord my God, I called to you for help,*
> *and you healed me.*
> ⁵*For his anger lasts only a moment,*
> *but his favor lasts a lifetime;*
> *weeping may stay for the night,*
> *but rejoicing comes in the morning.*
> ⁸*To you, Lord, I called;*
> *to the Lord I cried for mercy.*
> ¹¹*You turned my wailing into dancing;*
> *you removed my sackcloth and clothed me with joy,*
> ¹²*that my heart may sing your praises and not be silent.*
> *Lord my God, I will praise you forever.*

Yes, Lord, I truly want to give You thanks for the times You have brought me joy when my heart was heavy. Your faithfulness in the past gives me faith for the future.

What if he did this to make the riches of his glory known. . . ?
ROMANS 9:23

Perspective on Self

In recent years, we have learned much about the dimensions of space. For instance, telescopes in space send back faint infrared images of galaxies thirteen billion light-years away. Absolutely mind-boggling!

Author and preacher John Piper believes God must have created the vastness of space to give us some idea of the vastness of His glory. He says,

> *The untracked, unimaginable stretches of the created universe are a*
> *parable about the inexhaustible "riches of his glory" (Romans 9:23).*
> *The physical eye is meant to say to the spiritual eye, "Not this, but*
> *the Maker of this, is the Desire of your soul."[1]*

The created world is meant to draw us to the Creator—God Himself. "We are all starved for the glory of God, not self," writes Piper. He further says:

> *Indeed, what could be more ludicrous in a vast and glorious universe*
> *like this than a human being, on the speck called earth, standing in*
> *front of a mirror trying to find significance in his own self-image?"[2]*

Yes, in comparison with the almost inconceivable vastness of space, most of us live pretty self-centered lives. When I get down to the basics of life, what difference does it make what I think about myself compared to who God is? Most of us would do better to spend less time mulling over our own importance and spend more time considering the greatness of our God. I think it would change our perspective on life and our problems.

[1]John Piper, "Seeing and Savoring Jesus Christ," *Spirit of Revival November 2005*, 11.

[2]Ibid., 12.

"You have done a foolish thing," Samuel said.
"You have not kept the command the LORD your God gave you."

1 SAMUEL 13:13
(THE WHOLE STORY: 1 SAMUEL 13:1–15)

Waiting for God

The Philistines and Israelites were about to go to war, and Israel's King Saul and his troops were shaking with fear. They were waiting for their spiritual leader, Samuel, to come and plead for God's help. But Samuel hadn't come. So, against God's instructions that only a priest can offer the sacrifice, Saul offered up the burnt offering. Just as he finished, Samuel arrived.

"What have you done?" asked Samuel (v. 11). Then Saul explained. The men were scattering, Samuel had not come, and they could see the Philistines amassing their forces. "I felt compelled to offer the burnt offering," he said, justifying himself (v. 11). " 'You have done a foolish thing,' Samuel said. . . . 'The LORD has sought out a man after his own heart and appointed him ruler of his people, because you have not kept the LORD's command' " (1 Samuel 13:13–14).

Look at the steps to Saul's downfall. First, he focused on the circumstances rather than on God. Then he let those circumstances compel him to take matters into his own hands. Of course, since hindsight is 20/20, it's easy for us to see that Saul should have waited, trusting that God had everything under control.

Let's look at our own lives. When God doesn't bail us out when we think He should—when He doesn't meet our schedule—like Saul, don't we also tend to take matters into our own hands?

May God give us patience to wait for His divine timing in our lives. He will answer our prayers—if we will just wait on Him.

Be kind and compassionate to one another, forgiving each other,
just as in Christ God forgave you.

EPHESIANS 4:32

Freedom of Forgiveness

Author Ray Pritchard tells about an old monk and his young apprentice who were walking together along a trail. When they came to a river with a fast current, they saw an old woman weeping near the shoreline because she could not cross the river on her own. Their monastery had a rule forbidding all contact with women. Nevertheless, the older monk picked her up and, without a word, carried her to the other side.

The old woman went on her way, and the monk and his apprentice proceeded on their journey. Neither said a word, but on the inside, the young monk was seething. When he could stand it no longer, he blurted out, "My lord, why did you carry that woman across the river? You know that we are not supposed to touch a woman." The wise old monk looked down at the young man and said, "I put her down hours ago. Why are you still carrying her?"[1]

Like the young monk, you, too, may be carrying a burden from your past. Someone wounded you deeply; they were wrong and you were right, yet you are still carrying the load of your unforgiveness. Alan Paton said, "When a deep injury is done to us, we never recover until we forgive."[2] Physical, emotional, and even spiritual problems will continue to plague us until we forgive. Even though the person who wronged us has done nothing to deserve our forgiveness, the Bible says we should "be kind and compassionate to one another, forgiving each other, just as in Christ God forgave you" (Ephesians 4:32).

If Jesus could hang on the cross and pray, "Father, forgive them," can we do less?

[1]Ray Pritchard, *The Healing Power of Forgiveness* (Eugene, OR: Harvest House Publishers, 2005), 138.

[2]Ibid., 129.

After the earthquake came a fire, but the LORD was not in the fire.
And after the fire came a gentle whisper.

1 KINGS 19:12

That's God

A friend sent me this e-mail by an unknown author:

> *Have you ever been just sitting there, and, all of a sudden, you feel like doing something nice for someone you care for?*
> *THAT'S GOD talking to you through the Holy Spirit.*
> *Have you ever been down and out and nobody seems to be around for you to talk to?*
> *THAT'S GOD wanting you to talk to Him.*
> *Have you ever been thinking about somebody that you haven't seen in a long time and then next thing you know, you see him or receive a phone call from him?*
> *THAT [TOO IS] GOD.*
> *Have you ever received something wonderful that you didn't even ask for, like money in the mail, a debt that had been mysteriously cleared, or a coupon [for something] you needed but couldn't afford?*
> *THAT'S GOD knowing the desires of your heart.*

There is really no such thing as coincidence—only God working in our lives.

Of course, God speaks to us most clearly and dependably through His Word, the Bible. But sometimes He speaks loudly to us through our pain. Other times we trace His hand in the way circumstances inexplicably fall together. Often the Holy Spirit simply gives a quiet impression in our hearts to guide and direct us.

Today, be sensitive to how God is speaking to you.

Then those who feared the LORD talked with each other, and the LORD listened and heard. A scroll of remembrance was written in his presence concerning those who feared the LORD and honored his name.

MALACHI 3:16

Talking to a Friend Can Be Prayer

Talking is something most women enjoy. Because women value relationships, we relish time to share our thoughts and feelings with others. But because of our fast pace of living these days, talking with friends is something most of us now do by cell phone, texting, blogs, and e-mail, rather than face-to-face.

Yet conversation with people can be a form of prayer. No, I didn't make that up. It's in the Bible, in Malachi 3:16: "Then those who feared the LORD talked with each other, and the LORD listened and heard. A scroll of remembrance was written in his presence concerning those who feared the LORD and honored his name."

Think about that for a moment. When you get together with others who also love the Lord, you talk about what's happening in your lives—your jobs, your activities, your families. And God hears. When we talk with friends, we can know that God is listening. He takes note of what we talk about, especially when we speak of His goodness to us. The "scroll of remembrance" mentioned here shows us that God will remember those who love, honor, and respect Him.

Have you talked with a friend lately about spiritual matters—something in the Bible that encouraged you, or the spiritual struggles you have? As friends, do you hold each other accountable to keeping your relationship with God right? Do you praise Him for all the good things He has brought into your life? When you do, you're praying and He's listening!

"Be perfect, therefore, as your heavenly Father is perfect."
MATTHEW 5:48

Stolen Identity

I hope you have never opened your mail and had to say, "I certainly didn't buy those items with my credit card!" If that happened to you, you were the victim of identity theft. Someone used your name and personal information to commit fraud.

Identity theft can happen anywhere to anyone. If it occurs, you spend hundreds of hours cleaning up your credit and getting back your good name.

But what about your personal identity—not just what you own, but who you are? That's the most important identity of all. Author Kendry Smiley asks,

> *Where is your identity? Is it in your purse or in your family or in your speaking or writing? Is it in your achievements or awards or titles or accolades? If it is, someone can steal it! If your identity is in the Lord, it can never be stolen.*[1]

No matter how successful you may be, remember that your achievements— whether measured by how wonderful your children turned out, or how successful your career is, or how much cash and jewelry you own—have been possible only by God's grace. God is the one who has given you the talent, the intelligence, the health, and the opportunities to be who you are.

Jesus said, "Be perfect, therefore, as your heavenly Father is perfect" (Matthew 5:48). The word *perfect* means "complete." I like the way *The Message* translation of the verse puts it: "Live out your God-created identity. Live generously and graciously toward others, the way God lives toward you." God-created identity can never be stolen.

Be who you are with your whole heart—for God's glory.

[1]Kendry Smiley, quoted in *The Woman behind the Mask* by Jan Coleman (Grand Rapids, MI: Kregel Publications, 2005), 105.

Selected verses from Psalm 66

Refreshing Words from Psalms

Some days we overflow with gratitude for God's goodness. Other days praise is an act of faith. But always God responds to a thankful heart.

> *¹ Shout for joy to God, all the earth!*
> *² Sing the glory of his name;*
> *make his praise glorious.*
> *⁵ Come and see what God has done,*
> *his awesome deeds for mankind!*
> *²⁰ Praise be to God,*
> *who has not rejected my prayer*
> *or withheld his love from me!*

I praise You, Lord, for Your marvelous creative power. How wonderful, awesome, and all-powerful You are. You love me and listen to my prayers!

"Do not worship any other god, for the LORD,
whose name is Jealous, is a jealous God."

EXODUS 34:14

❀

When Jealousy Isn't Sin

We usually think of jealousy as a bad thing—a sin. On the contrary, you may be surprised to know that the Bible says God Himself is jealous. But He's jealous for the right reasons. You see, God loves deeply, and when you love someone intensely, you are jealous of anything or anyone who would steal from you the one you love.

God warned Moses, "Do not worship any other god, for the LORD, whose name is Jealous, is a jealous God" (Exodus 34:14). If I love anything—any person, any activity, any idea—more than I love God, He sees this as infidelity or unfaithfulness. God says, "I have been grieved by their adulterous hearts" (Ezekiel 6:9)—hearts that prefer something or someone else to Him.

Bible teacher G. Campbell Morgan says *jealousy* is a word that is similar to the word *zealous*.[1] Another synonym is *passionate*—the opposite of being apathetic or indifferent. In the vernacular we say God is "crazy about us."

Jealousy can be a good thing. I'm glad to know my husband is jealous of my love—that is, he doesn't want to share my love with anyone else. God is that way, too. His heart is pleased when our love for Him is fervent, real, and passionate! Not love that evaporates when difficulty heats up or the events of the day take precedence.

It's hard to admit that sometimes we do prefer someone or something else to God. Maybe if we reflect on that as infidelity, we'll think twice before choosing something instead of our God. Think about it.

[1] G. Campbell Morgan, *The Corinthian Letters of Paul* (Westwood, NJ: Fleming H. Revell Company, 1946), 130.

*The LORD replied, "My Presence will go with you,
and I will give you rest." Then Moses said to him, "If your
Presence does not go with us, do not send us up from here."*

EXODUS 33:14–15

When You Face a Move

Some of us cope well with change and some don't. For some, a move to a new location is an exciting challenge; they can hardly wait to see what is around the next corner. For others, moving is a frightening experience, tearing them loose from all that is familiar and secure.

When I looked up verses in the Bible on this subject, I was amazed how many verses promise comfort and encourage people who face a big move ahead. For instance, when Joshua was about to lead the Israelites into the promised land, God said, "Have I not commanded you? Be strong and courageous. Do not be afraid; do not be discouraged, for the LORD your God will be with you wherever you go" (Joshua 1:9). God encourages His people, "For I am the LORD, your God, who takes hold of your right hand and says to you, Do not fear; I will help you" (Isaiah 41:13).

If you are worrying about your move, remember that you are not alone in feeling that way. When Moses was at Mount Sinai in the desert with the thousands of Israelites he was leading to the promised land, he became concerned. God reassured him, "'My Presence will go with you, and I will give you rest.' Then Moses said to him, 'If your Presence does not go with us, do not send us up from here'" (Exodus 33:14–15). You don't have to make your move without God either! The God who has been your security where you are now will be with you in your new location, too.

After Paul had seen the vision, we got ready at once to leave for Macedonia,
concluding that God had called us to preach the gospel to them.

ACTS 16:10

Disappointment—or God's Appointment?

In the early 1800s, Barnabas Shaw made plans to go to Ceylon as a missionary. But instead he was sent to Cape Town, South Africa. There the governor banned him from preaching. Shaw and his wife had met frustration twice in a matter of months.

Not knowing what else to do, the Shaws purchased oxen and a cart, loaded up their possessions, and headed for the interior. After twenty-seven days, they were met by a group of Hottentots who were on their way to Cape Town looking for a missionary who, they believed, was being sent to teach them the Word of God. Amazingly, their paths had crossed in the dense jungle. The Hottentots led them further inland, where the Shaws eventually established a teaching center and helped spread the Gospel to the surrounding areas. The Shaws' disappointments were actually God's appointments for what He wanted to do.[1]

The apostle Paul had a similar experience. When Paul's plans to go to Asia and Bithynia were frustrated, he and his companions went to Troas, where Paul had a vision of a Macedonian man begging him to come and help. Acts 16:10 says, "We got ready at once to leave for Macedonia, concluding that God had called us to preach the gospel to them." In the capital city of Philippi, Paul established a strong church. Because of this trip, we have the book of Philippians, the beautiful letter Paul wrote to the church at Philippi.

Dealing with disappointments? Just wait. The next chapter of your journey hasn't unfolded yet. Your disappointment may be God's appointment to accomplish something outstanding.

[1]H.G.B., "Disappointment—His Appointment" (Grand Rapids, MI: Our Daily Bread, October 20, 1972).

Praise be to the God and Father of our Lord Jesus Christ,
the Father of compassion and the God of all comfort.

2 CORINTHIANS 1:3

The Comforter

After our grandson Christian was born, I gave his mother, Cheryl, a soft and cozy robe to wear when she got up at night to care for him.

Within a few months, however, Christian had decided that her new robe was what he would like to hold when he needed comfort. The robe was floor-length, so Cheryl simply cut twelve inches or so off the bottom for Christian to enjoy, still leaving her a robe to wear—or so she thought. The problem was that while Christian was okay with having "little robe" with him in the car, he wanted "big robe" when he went to sleep at night. Being the grandma, my solution was to buy Cheryl another robe.

As adults, we'd get some strange looks if we carried around a robe with us for comfort. But what—or who—can we hold on to when we need comforting? No less than God Himself—"the Father of compassion and the God of all comfort" (2 Corinthians 1:3). He welcomes us when circumstances are more than we can handle. All we have to do is put aside our high and mighty independence, come to God, and ask Him for His help. The beloved hymn "What a Friend We Have in Jesus" says,

> *O what peace we often forfeit,*
> *O what needless pain we bear,*
> *All because we do not carry*
> *Everything to God in prayer![1]*

Don't be ashamed to call on God for comfort when your heart is aching. He waits for you with open arms. Run to Him and let Him hold you close to His heart.

[1]Joseph M. Scriven, *The Hymnal for Worship & Celebration* (Waco, TX: Word Music, 1986), 435.

*Each of you should give what you have decided in your heart to give,
not reluctantly or under compulsion, for God loves a cheerful giver.*

2 CORINTHIANS 9:7

A Priceless Gift

Every Sunday night, Pastor Eric Denton takes a "Jackets for Jesus" team to the streets of Los Angeles to feed homeless people a hot meal and share the love of Jesus with them. Oh, and yes, if they're cold, they get a good, previously owned jacket as well.

Not too long ago, Pastor Eric invited them to bring a well-deserved birthday card the next Sunday for Jodi, the woman who for over a decade has been in charge of preparing the meals they serve each week. One homeless woman stopped and, placing her hand on Jodi's shoulder, told her she wouldn't be able to be with her for her birthday. She pulled out three filthy, crumpled one-dollar bills and pushed them into Jodi's protesting hands. They were all she had—a gift from the heart.

Looking at the grimy bills, Pastor Eric thought, "I wonder how many people have ever received the gift of a person's entire fortune given in thanksgiving?"

The Bible instructs, "Each of you should give what you have decided in your heart to give, not reluctantly or under compulsion, for God loves a cheerful giver" (2 Corinthians 9:7). A small gift is large in God's sight, if given in gratitude.

Pastor Eric writes, "Last week God turned $3 into a priceless birthday gift, never to be forgotten."[1] We each have the opportunity to give. Do it out of a heart of thanksgiving!

[1]Pastor Eric Denton, from *Jackets for Jesus Update* e-newsletter August 13, 2007, Jackets for Jesus, 5623 Arlington Ave., Riverside, CA, 92504.

Those who know your name trust in you, for you,
LORD, have never forsaken those who seek you.

PSALM 9:10

Never Forsaken

Chris Haggai was feeding Johnny, her adult son who had cerebral palsy, when a visitor arrived. The woman had come to take a look at a refrigerator the Haggais had just purchased because she was thinking of buying one like it. Chris had to continue feeding Johnny but told the visitor she could look at the refrigerator. The woman, however, became curious about Johnny.

"How do you ever cope?" the visitor asked.

"With Johnny? He's a darling!" Chris gave Johnny a loving pinch on the cheek. Just then, Johnny choked up some of his food—something that happened at least once a day. Chris hurried to make him comfortable.

"He must take hours of your day," the visitor said.

"God permits things for a purpose in our lives," Chris told her. "If I'm faithful, God will bless me for that faithfulness. If I refuse to accept what God permits, I'll be the loser."

After a few moments, Chris turned and found her visitor at the point of tears. "My husband died six months ago of a heart attack," the woman said. "I've been blaming God for taking my husband away from me."[1]

Chris shared deeply from her experiences and from the Bible about acceptance and trusting God. Before the visitor left, she had committed her life to Christ and began to understand that she could trust God to bring good from even the most painful experiences of life.

The psalmist wrote, "Those who know your name trust in you, for you, LORD, have never forsaken those who seek you" (Psalm 9:10). Wonderful assurance!

[1]John Edmund Haggai, *My Son Johnny* (Wheaton, IL: Tyndale House Publishers, Inc. 1978), 109–11.

Selected verses from Psalm 146

Refreshing Words from Psalms

Do you sing to the Lord? You know, don't you, that He doesn't care whether or not you can carry a tune? His delight is in the praise of your heart.

> *¹Praise the LORD.*
> *Praise the LORD, my soul.*
> *²I will praise the LORD all my life;*
> *I will sing praise to my God as long as I live.*
> *⁵Blessed are those whose help is the God of Jacob,*
> *whose hope is in the LORD their God.*
> *⁶He is the Maker of heaven and earth,*
> *the sea, and everything in them—*
> *he remains faithful forever.*
> *⁷He upholds the cause of the oppressed*
> *and gives food to the hungry.*
> *The LORD sets prisoners free.*
> *⁹The LORD watches over the foreigner*
> *and sustains the fatherless and the widow,*
> *but he frustrates the ways of the wicked.*
> *¹⁰The LORD reigns forever,*
> *your God, O Zion, for all generations.*
> *Praise the LORD.*

My hope, Lord, is ever in You. All my life I will praise You!

The words of a gossip are like choice morsels;
they go down to the inmost parts.

PROVERBS 18:8

Gossip

"The words of a gossip are like choice morsels," said King Solomon. The Living Bible puts it this way: "What dainty morsels rumors are. They are eaten with great relish!"(Proverbs 18:8). Come on now. Have you *never* been a bit excited to hear some salacious tidbit about a person you didn't like anyway?

We Christians can be so self-righteous! My daughter says, "Christians don't gossip; they just share prayer requests." I'm afraid that all too often she's right. When we sit in a circle to pray together, we often spend more time talking about the people who need prayer than praying for them.

God hates gossip. Romans 1:29 describes the godless, sinful person by saying that "they have become filled with every kind of wickedness, evil, greed and depravity. . .envy, murder, strife, deceit and malice." And the next three words are: "They are gossips."

You and I can do something to end gossip. Proverbs 26:20 says, "Without wood a fire goes out." So make it the rule of your life to be the stopping point of rumor and scandal.

If you're tempted to add fuel to the fire by passing on gossip you have just heard, write Ephesians 4:29 on a Post-it note and keep it where you can see it often. That's the verse where the apostle Paul instructs us, "Do not let any unwholesome talk come out of your mouths, but only what is helpful for building others up according to their needs, that it may benefit those who listen."

Let's ask God to help us squelch words that would hurt.

This is what the LORD says. . . . "If only you had paid
attention to my commands, your peace would have been
like a river, your well-being like the waves of the sea."

ISAIAH 48:17–18

If Only. . .

A young woman in her twenties told me that she really has no choice but to obey God because when she doesn't, she is the loser. At a young age she has figured out the very important principle that God's will, as difficult as it may sometimes be, is always the best for us.

God longs to bring good into our lives. In Isaiah we read,

> *This is what the LORD says—*
>   *your Redeemer, the Holy One of Israel:*
> *"I am the LORD your God,*
>   *who teaches you what is best for you,*
>   *who directs you in the way you should go.*
> *If only you had paid attention to my commands,*
>   *your peace would have been like a river,*
>   *your well-being like the waves of the sea."*
>   ISAIAH 48:17–18

"If only. . ." God says. If only you had not married that guy who doesn't share your faith. . . . If only you had pursued God's will for your life when you still had the chance to choose the direction your life would go. . . . If only you had shown more patience and tenderness toward your kids while they were still living at home. . . .

Well, we can't go back and unscramble scrambled eggs. What's done is done. But you can make a decision that, from this point on, with His help, you will obey God and choose to do His will.

Remember that He is the Lord your God, who "teaches you what is best for you, who directs you in the way you should go." Look to Him for guidance. Obey Him and find peace.

For since the beginning of the world men have not heard nor
perceived by the ear, nor has the eye seen any God besides You,
who acts for the one who waits for Him.

ISAIAH 64:4 NKJV

The God Who Acts on Our Behalf

Some people say, "All roads lead to God, so it doesn't matter which religion you follow as long as you're seeking God." But a wise prophet in Old Testament times strongly disagreed. He declared that the God of the Bible is different from all other gods. Isaiah said: "For since the beginning of the world men have not heard nor perceived by the ear, nor has the eye seen any God besides You, who acts for the one who waits for Him" (Isaiah 64:4 NKJV).

Isaiah asserted that other gods don't do anything to help their followers. They don't answer their prayers. On the contrary, these gods *demand* much from their followers, requiring sacrificial offerings, good works in order to achieve higher ranking, and sometimes even their very lives. But the one true God as revealed in the Bible cares about those who put their trust in Him and acts on their behalf.

Our God has power over everything in the universe, over the gods people worship—and over your problems as well. I like the perspective of the person who said, "Don't tell God how big your troubles are—tell your troubles *how big your God is.*"

Yes, if your God is the God of the Bible, you can count on Him to help. Just be patient a little longer. Keep waiting on God for His answer to your dilemma. Make these words your guide: "But as for me, I watch in hope for the LORD, I wait for God my Savior; my God will hear me" (Micah 7:7). The God of the universe, the God of the Bible, will answer your prayers if you expectantly and patiently wait for Him.

Godly men buried Stephen and mourned deeply for him.

ACTS 8:2

Is It Unspiritual to Grieve?

"Is it wrong for a Christian to grieve?" author Daisy Catchings asks. "Or is faith supposed to eradicate tears?"[1]

Well, in the Bible, even men of faith grieved. Abraham wept when Sarah died. David shed many tears when his son Absalom was buried. Even Jesus wept when Lazarus was in the tomb.

To me, the most remarkable incidence of grieving in the Bible occurred among believers when Stephen was stoned to death for preaching the Gospel. Since Jesus' resurrection had taken place just weeks before, the truth that all believers will be resurrected was fresh in the minds of the early Christians. Stephen had even seen a vision of Jesus just before his death. Yet we read that "Godly men buried Stephen and mourned deeply for him" (Acts 8:2). Knowing they would one day be reunited with Stephen didn't wipe out the reality that they were heartbroken because he was no longer with them.

The apostle Paul told the early Church that he did not want them to "grieve like the rest of mankind, who have no hope" (1 Thessalonians 4:13). He didn't say, "Don't grieve"; he said not to grieve the same way people grieve who have no hope of ever seeing their loved ones again.

Psychologists will tell you that the person who suffers a great loss but does not grieve faces the dangers of mental and emotional problems. Pent-up emotions will take their toll in one way or another.

Thank the Lord that He who gave us laughter to express happiness also gave us tears as an outlet for our grief, until the day when He will wipe all tears from our eyes.

[1]Daisy Catchings, *Under God's Umbrella* (Palm Springs, CA: Umbrella Ministries, 1999), 105.

But no human being can tame the tongue.
It is a restless evil, full of deadly poison.

JAMES 3:8

Keep Your Mouth Shut

Author and motivational speaker Sue Augustine writes, "I had to chuckle when I read what Elisabeth Elliot said about our words: 'Never pass up an opportunity to keep your mouth shut!' "[1] Sue continues,

> *Over the years, I have learned to pray, "Lord, walk beside me with one hand on my shoulder and the other over my mouth!" On days when my emotions threaten to rage out of control, my family members often overhear my hollering, "Oh, Lord—please shut my mouth before I say what's on my mind!"*[2]

Can you relate? Scripture says, "We all stumble in many ways. Anyone who is never at fault in what they say is perfect, able to keep their whole body in check" (James 3:2). I have yet to meet that perfect person who never says something she shouldn't.

That's why we need the Holy Spirit to control our lives. Sometimes preachers deliver a series of sermons on the fruit of the Spirit—the nine qualities listed in Galatians 5—as if they were separate fruits that we could grow in our lives. But I believe the fruit of the Spirit is nine descriptions of *one work* God's Spirit will do in our lives if He is in charge. Controlling what you say is the last to go, for self-control is number nine. As James 3:8 says, "No human being can tame the tongue"—only God can.

"Like a city whose walls are broken through is a person who lacks self-control," said King Solomon (Proverbs 25:28). When you ask God's Spirit to be in charge of all of your life, He will help you control what you say.

---

[1] Sue Augustine, *When Your Past Is Hurting Your Present* (Eugene, OR: Harvest House Publishers, 2005), 143.

[2] Ibid.

*Let us draw near to God with a sincere heart and
with the full assurance that faith brings.*

HEBREWS 10:22

God's Salad Bowl

Years ago a preacher advertised his sermon topic as "God's Salad Bowl." *What on earth is he going to talk about?* I thought. He spoke about the many times the phrase "Let us. . ." is used in the New Testament, such as "Let us stop passing judgment on one another" (Romans 14:13) and "Let us be awake and sober" (1 Thessalonians 5:6).

The sermon title might be corny and simplistic to us today, but the content remains relevant. Thirty-one times in the New Testament we're told to do something beginning with the words "Let us. . . ."

In the book of Hebrews, the phrase occurs five times in four verses in the original edition of the New International Version: "Let us draw near to God with a sincere heart in full assurance of faith. . . . Let us hold unswervingly to the hope we profess. . . . And let us consider how we may spur one another on toward love and good deeds. Let us not give up meeting together. . .let us encourage one another" (Hebrews 10:22–25).

The writer of Hebrews doesn't say, "Now, all of you out there, here's what I want you to do." No, he includes himself—"Let us" do these things, he says.

We'd be more effective in getting other people to do what they should be doing if we took a gentler approach. If you want members of your family to make changes, be willing to make changes yourself as well. If you want your employees to arrive on time, make sure you're never late.

"Let us not become weary in doing good" (Galatians 6:9)—all of us. We're all in this together.

Selected verses from Psalm 32

Refreshing Words from Psalms

Truly, the one who knows her sins are forgiven is blessed—happy!

> *¹Blessed is the one*
>   *whose transgressions are forgiven,*
>   *whose sins are covered.*
> *²Blessed is the one*
>   *whose sin the LORD does not count against them*
>   *and in whose spirit is no deceit.*
> *⁵Then I acknowledged my sin to you*
>   *and did not cover up my iniquity.*
> *I said, "I will confess*
>   *my transgressions to the LORD."*
> *And you forgave*
>   *the guilt of my sin.*
> *⁷You are my hiding place;*
>   *you will protect me from trouble*
>   *and surround me with songs of deliverance.*
> *¹⁰Many are the woes of the wicked,*
>   *but the LORD's unfailing love*
>   *surrounds the one who trusts in him.*

Even when I sin, Lord, Your unfailing love surrounds me. Just knowing that makes me want to love You more.

Do not take revenge, my dear friends, but leave room for God's wrath,
for it is written: "It is mine to avenge; I will repay," says the Lord.

ROMANS 12:19

Leave Room for God

In Robert Morgan's small but very practical book called *The Red Sea Rules,* he tells about a time when he was exceptionally worried about a situation. While reading his Bible, he came upon the phrase "leave room for God's wrath" (Romans 12:19). The context of the phrase is that we shouldn't try to get even when someone harms us, but instead leave room for God to settle the score.

If we can leave room for God's anger, Morgan reasoned, "Can we not, when facing other challenges, leave room for His other attributes? For His power? For His grace? For His intervention?" Morgan relates, "I underlined the words *leave room for God* and have leaned on them ever since."[1]

In the epic movie *The Ten Commandments,* the most famous scene is when the Israelites were facing the Red Sea, trapped by mountains on both sides, with the Egyptian army in pursuit. God parted the Red Sea so that the Israelites could cross on dry land to safety.

Like the Israelites, you may be trapped by your circumstances. The Red Sea of Sure Disaster is in front of you. The Mountains of Impossibility shut you in on both sides, and Certain Calamity is pursuing closer and closer. Friend, leave room for God. He still knows how to part the Red Sea.

Today may be the very day God rescues you. Moses told the Israelites, "Do not be afraid. Stand firm and you will see the deliverance the LORD will bring you today. . . . The LORD will fight for you; you need only to be still" (Exodus 14:13–14).

Just wait a little longer. Leave room for God to act.

[1]Robert J. Morgan, *The Red Sea Rules* (Nashville, TN: Thomas Nelson, Inc., 2001), 50.

*I will give thanks to you, L*ORD*, with all my heart;*
I will tell of all your wonderful deeds.

All of Me

A pastor tells about the time his young son burst into his office after the church's preschool. "Here, Dad, this is for you," the son said as he thrust a sheet of photographs into his hand. It was a pane of eight identical student photos—enough for everyone in the family.

"These are great, son," his dad responded, reaching for the scissors so he could snip one off to keep.

"No, Dad," his son stopped him. "Don't cut them. I want you to have *all* of me."

How like our heavenly Father, thought the pastor, as he slipped the whole sheet of photos under the glass that covered his desk. How He must long for us to run into His presence and declare, "Lord, I want You to have *all* of me!" Not offering Him 10 percent of our money, or one day a week, or some of our abilities, but throwing ourselves into His arms just as a little child does because we love Him so much.

Hymn writer Frances Ridley Havergal penned these words 150 years ago:

> *Take my love; my Lord, I pour*
> *at thy feet its treasure store;*
> *take my self, and I will be*
> *ever, only, all for thee.*[1]

That's the kind of outpouring of love that brings joy to our heavenly Father's heart.

[1]Frances Ridley Havergal, "Take My Life, and Let It Be," *Triumphant Service Songs* (Winona Lake, IN: The Rodeheaver Hall-Mack Co., 1934), 255.

But if we hope for what we do not yet have,
we wait for it patiently.

ROMANS 8:25

❦

Waiting and Patience

Waiting and *patience* are two words we don't like because they run counter to how we want to live. If you were to define *waiting,* you might say that it is "doing nothing until something happens." And you might define *patience* as "being willing to do nothing until something happens."

Yet these words are actually active words, not passive. A lot of faith is required to wait patiently, trusting that God's promises are true and His timing is best. You have to believe that ultimately you will achieve your goal if you stay the course. Otherwise, you will be very uptight, unhappy, and difficult to live with. The apostle Paul said, "If we hope for what we do not yet have, we wait for it patiently" (Romans 8:25).

In the book he wrote, James, in his always-practical way, uses farming as an illustration. "Be patient, then," he says. "See how the farmer waits for the land to yield its valuable crop, patiently waiting for the autumn and spring rains" (James 5:7). It takes faith to sow seed and patience to wait for the harvest.

So, the next time you have to wait—for your turn in a doctor's office, or for a promotion in the company, or for your child to grow out of the "terrible twos"—think of it not as a waste of time but as part of God's plan. Yes, you will have to do it by faith. By trusting Him, you can make *patience* and *waiting* active words in your vocabulary. In time, you can echo what the psalmist said: "I waited patiently for the LORD; he turned to me and heard my cry" (Psalm 40:1).

*There will be no more night. They will not need the light of
a lamp or the light of the sun, for the Lord God will
give them light. And they will reign for ever and ever.*

REVELATION 22:5

I Need Shades

Strolling through the mall, I caught sight of a T-shirt with the catchy slogan "The future is so bright, I need shades."

I couldn't help smiling. In fact, as I continued walking, my whole attitude lightened. Jesus is my Savior and heaven is my home. No matter how gloomy the present is, the future is bright—very bright. One day, when all the problems of this life are over, I'll spend forever with the Lord. What could be more hopeful?

I'm sure that if we could get even a glimpse into heaven, our human eyes would need heavy-duty sunglasses because of the light. The last book of the Bible tells us, "There will be no more night. They will not need the light of a lamp or the light of the sun, for the Lord God will give them light" (Revelation 22:5).

But instead of focusing on the bright future, I tend to focus on the depressing problem I'm dealing with right now. I need to put on the sunglasses of faith and look forward to the future with expectancy.

Jesus mastered that principle. He Himself exemplified forward-looking faith. The Bible tells us "for the joy set before him [Jesus] endured the cross (Hebrews 12:2). He bore the darkness of Calvary and its excruciating pain because He knew the light that awaited Him in His Father's presence. We can keep going the same way—enduring pain because of joy ahead.

If life is bleak, turn to Jesus, the Light of the world. Then look ahead, for the future is as bright as the promises of God. You may even want to get yourself one of those T-shirts.

For we know that our old self was crucified with him so that the body ruled by sin might be done away with, that we should no longer be slaves to sin.

ROMANS 6:6

A Brand-New Beginning

Is your past keeping you from being your best right now, in the present? Past sins do that, you know. David Eckman writes,

> *Sin walks us into a huge warehouse filled with video clips of us and says, "This is your life. We have thousands of clips of your failures. Many of them are so embarrassing. . . . That is all you are, and we have the record of it. So you might as well surrender to sin within, because you can't be better than this. You are these [video] clips—and nothing else."*[1]

Perhaps you are convinced that your past is who you are, and you can't change. There's good news: "Jesus has burned the warehouse!"[2]

The Bible tells us, "For we know that our old self was crucified with him so that the body ruled by sin might be done away with, that we should no longer be slaves to sin—because anyone who has died has been set free from sin. . . . In the same way, count yourselves dead to sin but alive to God in Christ Jesus" (Romans 6:6–7, 11).

Those video clips are a true picture of your past, no doubt about it. But Jesus paid the penalty that justice demands for your sins. When you accept God's forgiveness, it's as if you died and rose again to a new life. And that's where God wants you to live—in the present, not the past.

As a Christian, you are not the sum total of your past. You are a brand-new person with a brand-new beginning.

[1]David Eckman, *Becoming Who God Intended* (Eugene, OR: Harvest House Publishers, 2005), 153.

[2]Ibid.

*My flesh and my heart may fail, but God is
the strength of my heart and my portion forever.*

PSALM 73:26

When Your Hut's on Fire

The scraggly man had been washed ashore a small, uninhabited island—the sole survivor of a shipwreck. Every day he prayed feverishly for God to rescue him. And every day he scanned the horizon for help, but to no avail. Eventually he managed to build a little hut out of driftwood where he stored his few possessions and got some protection from the sun. At least now he had a place to call "home."

One day, after scavenging for food, he arrived back to find his little hut in flames, smoke rolling up to the sky. Stunned with disbelief and anger, he lifted his face to the sky and cried, "God! How could You do this to me?"

After a fitful sleep on the sand, he was awakened by the sound of a ship that had come to rescue him.

"How did you know I was here?" the weary man asked his rescuers.

"We saw your smoke signal," they replied.[1] You, too, may be distraught with the way things are going in your life. Shipwrecked, with your hut burning, everything you treasure seems gone. Your source of security—whether possessions or a person you depend on—has been taken from you. But, friend, remember you still have God. And He knows where you are. Don't lose heart. Your "burning hut" may be used by Him to signal help from a source you never thought would come to your rescue.

Many times the writer of the psalms despaired of any human help. Yet he knew he could count on God. He wrote, "My flesh and my heart may fail, but God is the strength of my heart and my portion forever" (Psalm 73:26). Hang on until help comes.

[1]http://intentional-christian.org/?p=221, accessed May 1, 2008.

Selected verses from Psalm 51

Refreshing Words from Psalms

If you have unconfessed sin in your life, hurry to God, acknowledge your wrongdoing, confess it, and receive His forgiveness.

> ¹*Have mercy on me, O God,*
>   *according to your unfailing love;*
> *according to your great compassion*
>   *blot out my transgressions.*
> ²*Wash away all my iniquity*
>   *and cleanse me from my sin.*
> ³*For I know my transgressions,*
>   *and my sin is always before me.*
> ⁴*Against you, you only, have I sinned*
>   *and done what is evil in your sight;*
> *so you are right in your verdict*
>   *and justified when you judge.*
> ⁷*Cleanse me with hyssop, and I will be clean;*
>   *wash me, and I will be whiter than snow.*
> ¹⁰*Create in me a pure heart, O God,*
>   *and renew a steadfast spirit within me.*
> ¹⁷*My sacrifice, O God, is a broken spirit;*
>   *a broken and contrite heart*
>   *you, God, will not despise.*

Lord, I shall stop covering up my sin and confess it now to You, recognizing that I need Your forgiveness. Thank You, thank You for removing my guilt. Renew a steadfast spirit within me.

Out those who hope in the LORD will renew their strength.
They will soar on wings like eagles; they will run and not
grow weary, they will walk and not be faint.

ISAIAH 40:31

Farther Than You Can See

For years in my mother's *Better Homes and Gardens* magazine, I looked forward each month to reading Bill Vaughan's column under the pen name Burton Hillis. In one of his witty observations of everyday life, he wrote:

> *"It is only a little farther," my father used to say when I was a little*
> *boy, winded and leg weary, out on the long Sunday afternoon walks*
> *that we used to take together. So I would brace up and struggle on*
> *a little longer, looking for the first familiar landmarks that would*
> *indicate we were back in our own neighborhood.[1]*

One day Burton asked his father how far "a little farther" really was. "It is farther than you can see," he replied, "but not as far as you can go."[2]

Like the walks Burton's father planned, the destination God sets before us is often beyond our sight. We can't see over the ridge or around the bend, nor do we know how much farther we have to go before we reach home.

But we can know that we are never without direction and strength for our journey. Isaiah wrote, "Whether you turn to the right or to the left, your ears will hear a voice behind you, saying, 'This is the way; walk in it'" (Isaiah 30:21) and "Those who hope in the LORD. . .will walk and not be faint" (Isaiah 40:31).

Perhaps the goal you've been working toward seems far away, and you wonder if you will *ever* get there. Keep going a little farther—perhaps farther than you can see, but not as far as you can go—with your hand in God's.

[1] Burton Hillis, *Better Homes and Gardens,* volume and date unknown.

[2] Ibid.

In Joppa there was a disciple named Tabitha (in Greek her name
is Dorcas); she was always doing good and helping the poor.
ACTS 9:36

Dorcas Had a Needle

She lived in Joppa, on the edge of the sparkling Mediterranean Sea. Day after day she picked up her needle to sew coats and garments she had envisioned in her mind. Her name was Dorcas, and she "was always doing good and helping the poor" (Acts 9:36). We don't know if she made clothing for the poor or sold her handiwork to help them. But we know she was called a "disciple." And probably she was a widow, for when she died, the widows of the area came to mourn her death. Dorcas was terribly missed.

The apostle Peter was sent for, and a miracle happened. Through God's astonishing power, Dorcas was raised back to life to continue her ministry of sewing. "This became known all over Joppa, and many people believed in the Lord" (Acts 9:42). All Dorcas had was a needle, but she used it for God's glory.

You may be all thumbs when it comes to sewing, but you're excellent at bookkeeping. Use your pencil for God.

Maybe you wouldn't know what to do with an artist's brush, but you're a wonderful cook. Use your ladle for God.

Perhaps you could never be a nurse because you can't stand the sight of blood. But given a couple of flowers and some leaves, you can create a lovely arrangement. Use your floral skills for Him.

Whether it's a camera or a pen or a gardening trowel, use it to serve God and bless needy people around you. You'll have far more joy than you would ever find using these tools only for yourself.

And we know that in all things God works for the good of those who love him, who have been called according to his purpose.

ROMANS 8:28

Chocolate Cake

My dad is in heaven now, but people still talk about his sermon illustrations. As people walked into church one Sunday morning, they saw a small table next to the pulpit. On it were some small food cartons, a bowl, a measuring cup, and a large spoon. What was all this doing in church?

As my dad began his sermon, he held up the measuring cup and a package of flour. As he poured the flour into the cup, he asked: "Who would volunteer to come up here and eat these two cups of flour?" No one responded. He teased them a little: "Why, everyone knows that many delicious things contain flour. This is the best flour. Someone come." Still no one responded.

Then he poured cocoa into the cup. "Well, will someone come and eat this good cocoa?" Again, no volunteers—not even the children.

Next he offered shortening. No takers. "How about a couple teaspoons of vanilla?" Still no response.

His scripture text for the morning's sermon was Romans 8:28: "We know that in all things God works for the good of those who love him, who have been called according to his purpose."

Often, things happen to us which, when viewed by themselves, just don't make sense—and sometimes don't "taste" too good. But when mixed together—well, just wait! At this point, my mom walked onto the platform carrying a scrumptious-looking chocolate cake. Delicious!

So, don't just focus on one unpleasant incident in your life. Look at it against the bigger picture. If you are God's child, you can be sure He will work your situation together with other circumstances for your good—and God knows how to make wonderful chocolate cakes!

"Very truly I tell you, unless a kernel of wheat falls to the ground and dies, it remains only a single seed. But if it dies, it produces many seeds."

JOHN 12:24

When a Kernel of Wheat Dies

"Why did Dennis have to die?" The question screamed in church worker Jean Galang's mind. This fourteen-year-old boy had all his life ahead of him. But during the church's summer camp, of all places, Dennis had drowned in the swimming pool. In a daze of disbelief and heartbreak, the camp was shut down and everyone went home.

"I could not stop struggling with [God's] method of bringing about His purposes,"[1] Jean recalls. As the weeks went by, she thought a great deal about what had happened. She said:

> *We took pride in coming up with a great camp to teach our young people some valuable lessons in life. Instead, God came up with His own plan to teach all of us through the life of His precious child, Dennis. . . . The incident made an impact on all of our lives far greater than a four-day camp would have.*

Jesus said, "Very truly I tell you, unless a kernel of wheat falls to the ground and dies, it remains only a single seed. But if it dies, it produces many seeds" (John 12:24). Dennis was, no doubt, a kernel of wheat. Although his life on earth was cut short, the effectiveness of his life was multiplied in the lives of camp students and staff alike. Never will he be forgotten.

Most of us think of a long life as a successful life. But God may have other plans. What matters most is your life's influence in light of eternity.

[1]Jean Galang, "Unless a Kernel of Wheat Falls," in *Women on the Journey: Defining Moments*, compiled and edited by Michelle Ocampo-Joaquin (Makati City, Philippines: Church Strengthening Ministry, Inc., 2004), 127.

*But I have calmed and quieted myself, I am like a weaned
child with its mother; like a weaned child I am content.*

PSALM 131:2

Satisfied

For a long time now I've been fascinated with Psalm 131:2—"I have calmed
and quieted myself, I am like a weaned child with its mother; like a weaned
child I am content." Why did the psalmist choose the comparison of a
weaned child to the peace and quiet he was experiencing in his heart?

I found the answer when I thought about my three kids. When they were
tiny babies, they were eager to be near me when they were hungry. But by the
time they were toddlers, they would just sit quietly on my lap because they had
been weaned.

Many of us are like needy newborn babies. Every time we pray, we want
something from God, immediately. Of course, He doesn't mind us drawing
near to Him. But I can't help thinking He would be pleased if sometimes we
would come into His presence just for the joy of closeness.

Wawa Ponce came to God with a need. She wanted a husband. Sad that
God had not yet met that yearning, her deep longing was almost a physical
pain. Then God led her to Psalm 131:2 and the image of a young child peace-
fully cradled in her mother's arms—so quiet, so still. Wawa wrote:

> *I want to be that child. No, I need to be that child. I need God to
> wean me from what I want, to prepare me for what He wants for me.
> I need to be still in His arms knowing that He would take care of
> my needs—even my wants.[1]*

Then she concluded with a prayer of acceptance: "Lord, I will wait and be
satisfied with Your answer." And peace came.

Have you quieted your soul? You can find peace and satisfaction in God's
arms.

[1]Wawa Ponce, "Weaning Love," in *Women on the Journey: Defining Moments*, compiled and edited
by Michelle Ocampo-Joaquin (Makati City, Philippines: Church Strengthening Ministry, Inc.,
2004), 173.

*I instruct you in the way of wisdom and lead you along
straight paths. When you walk, your steps will not
be hampered; when you run, you will not stumble.*

PROVERBS 4:11–12

Should I Say Yes or No?

Someone asked me, "How do you decide which ministry opportunities to accept and which to say no to?" The question is fair enough. Because my husband and I receive many invitations to minister—more than we can fulfill—we have to make hard decisions. These principles that help us determine God's will can help you as well:

1. Is this opportunity in line with your gifts and abilities?
2. Does the opportunity fit in with the schedule you've already committed to? Someone said that as the gears of a fine car work smoothly, "God's will is 'synchromeshed'—you don't have to grind your gears to do what He wants you to do."
3. Don't make a decision based merely on the size of the opportunity. Remember, Jesus ministered to individuals as well as to large crowds.
4. Can you honestly fulfill this opportunity and still meet the needs of your family and your own as well?
5. Pray until you have peace in your heart about your decision.

When you're in a Christian leadership position, if the devil can't get you to sin, he'll just drive you to work yourself to death. Either way you're of no use to God. So, just because something needs to be done doesn't automatically mean you're the one to do it. A need and a call to meet that need are not necessarily synonymous. You must determine if the Lord wants you to say, "Yes."

God promises, "I instruct you in the way of wisdom and lead you along straight paths. When you walk, your steps will not be hampered; when you run, you will not stumble" (Proverbs 4:11–12). Trust Him to do just that.

Selected verses from Psalm 19

Refreshing Words from Psalms

Skies, clouds, stars, sun, and moon—all speak to us of God's might and power. No matter where we live, we can look up and see God's handiwork in the skies above us.

> ¹*The heavens declare the glory of God;*
>   *the skies proclaim the work of his hands.*
> ²*Day after day they pour forth speech;*
>   *night after night they reveal knowledge.*
> ³*They have no speech, they use no words;*
>   *no sound is heard from them.*
> ⁴*Yet their voice goes out into all the earth,*
>   *their words to the ends of the world.*
> *In the heavens God has pitched a tent for the sun.*
> ⁷*The law of the* LORD *is perfect,*
>   *refreshing the soul.*
> *The statutes of the* LORD *are trustworthy,*
>   *making wise the simple.*
> ⁸*The precepts of the* LORD *are right,*
>   *giving joy to the heart.*
> *The commands of the* LORD *are radiant,*
>   *giving light to the eyes.*
> ¹⁴*May these words of my mouth and this meditation of my heart*
>   *be pleasing in your sight,*
>   LORD, *my Rock and my Redeemer.*

Lord, I bow in Your presence—You who created the skies and all they contain. I humbly acknowledge that You are able to take care of my needs today. May my words and thoughts please You.

"Go to the lake and throw out your line. Take the first fish
you catch; open its mouth and you will find a four-drachma coin.
Take it and give it to them for my tax and yours."

MATTHEW 17:27
(THE WHOLE STORY: MATTHEW 17:24–27)

Doing What You Can Do

In Bible days, Jewish men twenty years old and above were expected to contribute a two-drachma tax every year for the upkeep of the temple in Jerusalem.

The apostle Matthew, who himself was a tax collector, related that when Jesus and His disciples arrived in the region of Lake Galilee, collectors of the two-drachma tax asked Peter, "Doesn't your teacher pay the temple tax?"

Actually, the tax was several months overdue at this point because Jesus had not been in the area to pay it.

"Yes, He does," Peter replied, perhaps a bit presumptuously, for he had no money. Then Peter went to Jesus.

Jesus instructed him: "Go to the lake and throw out your line. Take the first fish you catch; open its mouth and you will find a four-drachma coin. Take it and give it to them for my tax and yours" (Matthew 17:24–27, excerpted).

What struck me is that Jesus didn't ask Peter to do something he couldn't do. What He asked, Peter knew how to do probably better than anything else—fish. That had been his vocation for years before Jesus called him as a disciple. When Peter did what he could, God miraculously provided what Peter lacked.

Jesus never asks us to do the impossible. He simply says, "Follow Me; do what I tell you, and I will do the rest."

Maybe *your* taxes are overdue—or you have some other pressing need. Listen to God's voice. Do what He tells you, and God will provide for you—even through a miracle.

Be very careful, then, how you live—not as unwise but as wise.

EPHESIANS 5:15

Be Careful How You Live

T-shirts with holes, jeans, and flip-flops were Bill's wardrobe for literally his entire time in college. A nonconformist, Bill had, nonetheless, become a Christian while attending college.[1]

Across the street from Bill's campus was a conservative church where people dressed up when they attended. The church wanted to develop a ministry to students but was not sure how to go about it.

One Sunday Bill decided to attend the service—in his usual attire. When he entered the packed church, people watched uncomfortably as he proceeded down the aisle and, not finding a seat, finally sat down on the carpet at the front. Tension in the air was thick.

Then the minister noticed a church deacon slowly making his way toward Bill. The silver-haired gentleman in his eighties was wearing a fine suit—very elegant, very dignified. Everyone was saying to themselves, "You can't blame him. How can you expect a man of his age and background to understand some college kid on the floor?"

In astonishment, the congregation watched as, without a word, the elderly man, with great difficulty, lowered himself and sat down next to Bill so Bill wouldn't be alone.

Softly, the minister began his sermon, "What I'm about to preach, you probably will never remember. What you have just seen, you will never forget. My sermon text this morning is Ephesians 5:15: 'Be very careful, then, how you live—not as unwise but as wise.'" And then he added, "You may be the only Bible some people will ever read."

---

[1]Story related to author by e-mail, February 12, 2005.

*"Come to me, all you who are weary and burdened,
and I will give you rest."*

MATTHEW 11:28

Living at High Speed

A fighter jet pilot flying upside down at tremendous speed became disoriented and pulled the flight stick in the wrong direction. A few moments later, the jet was only a flaming piece of wreckage.

Commenting on the tragedy, writer Del Fehsenfeld points out that most of us are in danger of making the same mistake—traveling so fast in life that we become mixed up about what is most important. Fehsenfeld observes,

> *Disorientation at a high rate of speed is a deadly combination for all of us. Capacity for discernment is diminished. . . . The result is a high risk of careening in wrong directions.*[1]

Yet for many of us, living at full throttle is normal. What we need is a pause in our activities and "room to listen and linger. Room to receive and reorient. Room to 'be still and know' that there is a God—and we aren't Him!"[2]

We live as if we, not God, are the ones who make things happen in life. We work as if everything depends on us. Consequently, most of us are running on nearly depleted physical, emotional, and spiritual fuel.

How do we balance our lives? "Come to me," Jesus said, very simply (Matthew 11:28). The reality is that when most of us come to the Lord, we want to do all the talking rather than just listen to Him. We need to pause long enough to come to Him and be quiet.

If your life has become a racetrack, stop. Retreat to a quiet corner and tell God, "Lord, I give up. I'm coming to You to realign my priorities and refill my fuel tank."

[1]Del Fehsenfeld III, editorial. *Spirit of Revival*, 2008, 4.

[2]Ibid.

*Though my father and mother forsake me,
the LORD will receive me.*

PSALM 27:10

Abandoned? Never Again!

Did you grow up in a one-parent home? Maybe your father turned his back on your mother, and your home was torn apart. You may have thought you're not worth very much or surely your dad would have stayed with your family.

Because of this, you may have difficulty thinking of God as your heavenly Father. A friend of mine whose father abandoned the family said that what helped her was studying the characteristics of God as our heavenly Father as found in the Bible. She learned what kind of a Father God is and then told herself, "That's the way a human father *should* be, even though my dad certainly was not."

The least likely people in the world to abandon you are your parents. Parents will believe their child when everyone else gives up. Sadly, however, some parents have done the unthinkable—they have forsaken their children.

The word *forsake* is not one we use frequently nowadays. We commonly just use its synonyms: *abandon, desert, leave, disown, relinquish,* or *give up.* You can rest assured that God will never do any of those things to you. Psalm 27:10 says, "Though my father and mother forsake me, the LORD will receive me." In Psalm 9:10 the writer David said, "You, LORD, have never forsaken those who seek you." When you become God's child, He puts His Spirit within you so that He literally never, never leaves you.

Today, thank God that He has taken you into His family. He is a Father you can count on, always.

Cast all your anxiety on him because he cares for you.

1 PETER 5:7

Practical Atheism

Once, Jesus said to a busy woman, "Martha, Martha, you are anxious and troubled about many things" (Luke 10:41 ESV). I can certainly relate to Martha. If you're like most women, you don't worry about just one thing. Because we're good at multitasking, we're usually anxious about a *collection* of things.

I did a search in the New Testament on the word *anxious* and discovered that every time the word is used, it's connected to our concern with what *we* are going to do about a situation—what we're going to say or do or wear or eat or whatever. I don't worry about whether the earth is going to keep turning on its axis. I worry about me—my needs, my health, my family, my work.

Are you worried? What do you think about this statement: "All anxiety is practical atheism"? I find it startling, because it means that when we are anxious and worried, we're living as if there were no God.

You may believe there is a God, but maybe you think solving your problems is *your* responsibility—you got yourself into this mess, so it's up to you to get yourself out of it. Or perhaps God seems remote, and you ask, "Does He really care about me?" So you carry a heart-heavy load of anxiety.

What we need to do when we're anxious is to stop being "practical atheists" and turn to the Lord. God is big enough to solve any problem. Peter tells us, "Cast all your anxiety on him because he cares for you" (1 Peter 5:7).

Do not merely listen to the word, and so deceive yourselves.
Do what it says.

JAMES 1:22

When God Speaks

John's phone rang. His teenaged daughter had been in a car accident. Would he come?

A short time later John was sitting on the curb with his daughter, waiting for the police to write a report on the accident, which, fortunately, had wrecked the car but caused no physical harm. All at once though, John began to seethe inside. Why had his daughter not been more careful? Did she not realize how serious this could have been? The more he thought about it, the angrier he became.

Then something caught his attention—a piece of paper floating in the gutter. As he looked more closely, he saw that it was the outline of last Sunday's sermon at his church. The title of the message was "Defusing Your Anger."

Picking up the outline, John had to smile. He thought, *God can really get creative when He speaks to us.*

Yes, He speaks to us in many ways—sometimes as we read the Bible, sometimes through a scripture verse we memorized years ago as a child, sometimes through a friend's biblical advice. Other times God speaks in our hearts with a quiet but insistent voice. If He wants to, He can even float His message to us in a gutter.

The question is, are you listening? God once said to His people, "I called but you did not answer, I spoke but you did not listen" (Isaiah 65:12). How sad! James 1:19 says, "Everyone should be quick to listen, slow to speak and slow to become angry." Yes, quick to listen to one another and also to God's voice speaking to us. Then he adds, "Do not merely listen to the word. . . . Do what it says" (v. 22).

Selected verses from Psalm 43

Refreshing Words from Psalms

We get discouraged when we focus more on our problems than on God. Stop long enough today to lift your eyes and your heart to Him. Your perspective will be readjusted.

> *⁵Why, my soul, are you downcast?*
>   *Why so disturbed within me?*
> *Put your hope in God,*
>   *for I will yet praise him,*
>   *my Savior and my God.*

I get downcast and disturbed, Lord, because I take my eyes off You. Right now, by faith, I renew my hope in You, trusting that You will bring me through this problem.

*"Do not be afraid of them, for I am with you
and will rescue you," declares the* LORD.

JEREMIAH 1:8

The Snake

Pastor Glenn Burris tells that one time when he hauled their large garbage
containers out to the street for pickup, the task took on an unexpected twist.

> *I had just rolled out the third can when I noticed. . .the snake. It
> was about five or six feet long and was lying in some grass just off
> our driveway. My heart was racing as I grabbed my cell phone and
> called [my wife] Debbie, who was inside the house. . . . I didn't want
> to leave in case the snake crawled away, because then I would worry
> about where it might go.*
>
> *When Debbie answered her phone, I quickly got to the point:
> "Grab the shovel and meet me at the street near the driveway. There's
> a humongous snake in our yard!"*
>
> *"I'll be glad to bring the shovel, but the snake is already dead," she
> said. "The gardener. . .killed it and left it in the yard for the crows to take."*
>
> *In just about fifteen seconds, my whole perspective changed. The
> source of fear that had gripped me so strongly just minutes before was now
> easily explained.[1]*

Often what we fear poses only an empty threat or never takes place at all.
Like Pastor Glenn, we worry about "dead snakes."

Because God knows fear is a natural reaction, in the Bible He tells us
repeatedly, "Don't be afraid." You can find instances of people who thought
they were going to starve, drown, be killed in war, die in childbirth, or be mur-
dered. But God brought them through safely.

So before you panic about your situation, look again. The snake may not
even be alive.

[1]Rev. Glenn Burris Jr., e-newsletter, June 2008.

Since we live by the Spirit, let us keep in step with the Spirit.
GALATIANS 5:25

A Sensitive Heart

Sometimes we are so busy we do not hear God's quiet voice telling us to do something special for someone who is hurting—a loving touch, comforting words, or just a short prayer.

Sister Freda Robinson, an example of someone who takes time to care, is one of my heroes. The outstanding work she does among the poor of Kitale, Kenya, greatly inspires me. Early in her career, before she had her own hospital and outreach, she was the head nurse at the best private hospital in the city.

One day Sister Freda had finished her work at the hospital and returned home. But no sooner had she entered the doorway when she felt an unmistakable urge to return to the hospital. Not able to brush it aside, she turned and went back.

Re-entering the hospital, Sister Freda quickly strode down the hallway. Passing by the prenatal care ward, she peeked in at the babies, because children always have a soft spot in Sister Freda's heart. Suddenly she stopped. One baby caught her well-trained eye. The boy didn't appear to be breathing. Rushing to the incubator, she snatched him up and massaged his heart, giving him mouth-to-mouth resuscitation.

"I felt the guiding hand of God that day," recalls Sister Freda. "As I worked with him, he gasped once. I gave him oxygen, and he began to breathe normally. Today Mr. Korir is an attorney in Kitale."

Galatians 5:25 says, "Since we live by the Spirit, let us keep in step with the Spirit." May God help us, too, be sensitive and responsive to His gentle voice.

Oh, the depth of the riches of the wisdom and knowledge of God!

ROMANS 11:33

(THE WHOLE STORY: ROMANS 11:33–36)

Questioning or Trusting

When life throws at us circumstances we can't understand, we either question God or trust Him. Lisa Beamer learned that lesson—twice.

Lisa is the wife of 9/11 hero Todd Beamer, who, with other passengers on United Airlines Flight 93, took control of their plane long enough to crash it to the ground, preventing an attack on the US Capitol.

After the crash, Lisa remembered when her father died quite suddenly when she was fifteen. At the time she had wrestled with the thought, *God, You could have prevented this if You had wanted to! Why didn't You?* Then one day a college administrator confronted her with the reality that it was time to accept that, for whatever reason, God had allowed her father's death.[1]

Bible verses Lisa had read came back to her:

> *Oh, the depth of the riches of the wisdom and knowledge of God!*
>   *How unsearchable his judgments,*
>   *and his paths beyond tracing out!*
> *"Who has known the mind of the Lord?*
>   *Or who has been his counselor?" . . .*
> *For from him and through him and for him are all things.*
>   *To him be the glory forever!*
>   ROMANS 11:33–34, 36

Lisa thought to herself, *Who are you to question God? You think you deserve a happy life and get angry when it doesn't always happen.* She decided to stop questioning God and start trusting Him, not knowing that she would need to lean on that decision again—with her husband's death.

No, we don't understand all that happens. But deciding to trust God is the only way to peace.

---

[1]Lisa Beamer, *Let's Roll*, with Ken Abraham (Wheaton, IL: Tyndale House, 2002), 82–83.

"Forget the former things; do not dwell on the past."

ISAIAH 43:18

The Pain of the Past

Too many people who have had a wrong done to them have "built a memorial to the event and placed it smack dab in the center of the living room of their life, going there every day to worship," so says a retired minister.[1] A memorial to a wrong done in the past! I had never thought of it that way, but I think he's right.

Memory can be a tremendous blessing as we recall happy days from the past. But memory can also be tremendously painful. What is it about the human mind that we tend to pull up wounding events from the past and relive them over and over again? When we do this, we are not survivors but perpetual victims.

One such victim came to my husband for counsel, bringing with him a file about three inches thick. Years ago someone had wronged him, and ever since he had been collecting evidence of that injustice.

It's time to break down that monument you've erected to the hurts in your past. I know you cannot easily erase them from your memory. But you can refuse to make them into a worship center in your life. Each time that painful memory comes to mind, bring it to the Lord and "dump" it on Him. God doesn't mind. In fact, He says, "Forget the former things; do not dwell on the past" (Isaiah 43:18).

Today is the only day we have. Yesterday is gone, and whether we ever have a tomorrow is unknown. Let's honor today by leaving the past with God.

[1] Quoted by Dr. Laura Schlessinger and Rabbi Stewart Vogel, *The Ten Commandments* (New York Cliff Street Books, an imprint of HarperCollins Publishers, 1998), 44.

"Before long, the world will not see me anymore,
but you will see me. Because I live, you also will live."
JOHN 14:19

The Land of the Dying

In his later years, pastor and Christian statesman Dr. D. James Kennedy wrote:

> *I know that someday I am going to come to what some people will*
> *say is the end of this life. . . . I don't want them to cry. I want them*
> *to begin the [memorial] service with the Doxology and end with the*
> *Hallelujah chorus, because. . .I am not going to be dead. I will be*
> *more alive than I have ever been in my life, and I will be looking*
> *down upon you poor people who are still in the land of the dying and*
> *have not yet joined me in the land of the living. And I will be alive*
> *forevermore.[1]*

Life on earth is often referred to as the "land of the living," but as Dr. Kennedy says, it's really the "land of the dying." If you are God's child, one day you will be in heaven, the true "land of the living." It was Jesus Himself who, after He was resurrected, said, "Because I live, you also will live" (John 14:19).

Are you certain that someday you're going to be in heaven? You can be. Romans 10:9 tells us, "If you declare with your mouth, 'Jesus is Lord,' and believe in your heart that God raised him from the dead, you will be saved."

When you take those two steps—confess Jesus as Lord and believe He rose from the dead, the Spirit of God comes to live within you. Then you know where you'll spend eternity.

Someday we'll say good-bye to the "land of the dying" and start Life with a capital *L* in the "land of the living." Meet me there.

[1] D. James Kennedy, Ph.D., "Christian Forums," http://65.240.226.104:8080/accessed 10-23-2016.

*"No one is greater in this house than I am. My master has withheld
nothing from me except you, because you are his wife. How then
could I do such a wicked thing and sin against God?"*

GENESIS 39:9

Temptation

Temptation comes to all of us. Who has not felt an intense desire to do something you really know you shouldn't?

One of the best descriptions I've ever read of temptation was by Wawa Ponce. I have to warn you: it's very graphic. She says, "Temptation is a luscious, chocolate-coated morsel that conceals a dozen wriggling maggots inside."[1] (Hey, I warned you!)

Temptation looks good on the outside, and giving in to it brings pleasure. Even the Bible speaks of the "pleasures of sin" (Hebrews 11:25). But after you've given in, the results are pretty disgusting.

It's easy to think, *Well, I'm not bothered by temptation—I never wanted to murder anyone or to cheat big-time.* But what about the temptation to ignore God? To get revenge? To pretend to be something you're not? To want what someone else has?

The good news is that we don't have to give in to temptation. 1 Corinthians 10:13 says, "No temptation has overtaken you except what is common to mankind. And God is faithful; he will not let you be tempted beyond what you can bear. But when you are tempted, he will also provide a way out so that you can endure it."

To keep from giving in to temptation, let's keep in mind that God is the one we are sinning against if we concede. When Joseph was tempted by Potiphar's wife to commit adultery, he turned from her, responding, "How. . .could I do such a wicked thing and sin against God?" (Genesis 39:9). Ask yourself this question the next time temptation strikes.

[1]Wawa Ponce, "Putrid Desserts," in *Women on the Journey: Defining Moments,* compiled and edited by Michelle Ocampo-Joaquin (Makati City, Philippines: Church Strengthening Ministry, Inc., 2004), 50.

Selected verses from Psalm 113

Refreshing Words from Psalms

Although enthroned in heaven, God stoops down to see the needs of us here on earth—the poor, the needy, the barren. He sees your needs—and cares.

> *⁵Who is like the L*ORD *our God,*
>   *the One who sits enthroned on high,*
> *⁶who stoops down to look*
>   *on the heavens and the earth?*
> *⁷He raises the poor from the dust*
>   *and lifts the needy from the ash heap.*
> *⁹He settles the childless woman in her home*
>   *as a happy mother of children.*
> *Praise the L*ORD.

Lord, I'm so glad that from heaven You see ordinary people, not just the "high and mighty" on earth—the VIPs. And You don't just observe—You reach down and "raise" and "lift" and "settle" us according to our needs. Thank You.

Who is wise and understanding among you? Let them show it by
their good life, by deeds done in the humility that comes from wisdom.
JAMES 3:13

Showing Jesus in Our Lives

How do we know what God is like? If you say the primary source for knowing God is the Bible, you're right. In the New Testament we learn what He is like by how Jesus, God's Son, lived right here where we live, on planet Earth. We read how, just like us, He experienced joy and pain, temptation and fatigue—the whole spectrum of life.

But people around us who don't read the Bible look at Christians to see what God is like. Kind of scary, isn't it? In fact, many people never read the Bible. They just judge God by us, who say we know Him.

You may be thinking, *That's a lot of pressure. I'm so far from perfect that the thought of others looking at me to find out what Jesus is like makes me uncomfortable.* But I don't think that when people look at our lives they're looking for perfection. They're looking for authenticity. They're looking for integration between what we say and what we do. They want to know if our walk matches our talk. They're looking to see if we have something they don't have—a reality that they would want for themselves. Does the presence of Christ in our lives make us more caring? Or do our lives convey the message that we think we're better than people who don't know Jesus?

James, the half brother of Jesus, asked, "Who is wise and understanding among you? Let them show it by their good life, by deeds done in the humility that comes from wisdom" (James 3:13).

Let's ask God to help us demonstrate Jesus to our world.

About midnight Paul and Silas were praying and singing hymns to God,
and the other prisoners were listening to them. Suddenly there was such
a violent earthquake that the foundations of the prison were shaken.
At once all the prison doors flew open, and everyone's chains came loose.

ACTS 16:25–26
(THE WHOLE STORY: ACTS 16:16–34)

Singing in the Dark

Dark periods in life come to us all, times when we feel as if we are in a prison cell and all we know about God is put to the test. The apostle Paul had an experience like that when he and Silas arrived in Philippi. As a result of casting an evil spirit out of a slave girl so that she could no longer foretell the future and make money for her owners, the two were severely beaten and put in prison.

So here they are, chained to a wall in total darkness with bloody, stinging backs. But instead of wallowing in self-pity, they rejoiced. "About midnight Paul and Silas were praying and singing hymns to God" (Acts 16:25). Amazing!

Then another amazing thing happened. A violent earthquake shook the prison so strongly that all the prison doors flew open and the prisoners' chains came loose. In the next few hours, Paul and Silas led their jailer to faith in Jesus. The jailer washed their wounds and fed them in his home. Afterward Paul and Silas baptized him, along with all his family.

Do your circumstances feel like a prison cell from which there is no escape? Does darkness surround you and you're in pain? Hold on to the unshakable truths about God—He is all-powerful, all-knowing, and all-loving. Do what Paul and Silas did—pray and sing hymns and worship songs to the Lord in the dark until He sends the earthquake that will release you from your cell. As Pastor Buddy Owens puts it, "Don't allow prison to shake your faith; let faith shake your prison."

Your beauty. . .should be that of your inner self, the unfading beauty of a gentle and quiet spirit, which is of great worth in God's sight.

1 PETER 3:3–4

Quiet Time

Author Elizabeth George writes,

> *If someone asked you to describe the quiet time you had this morning, what would you say? This is exactly the question Dawson Trotman, founder of The Navigators ministry organization, used to ask men and women applying for missions work. . . . He spent a half hour with each one, asking specifically about their devotional life. Sadly, only one person out of twenty-nine interviewed said his devotional life was a constant in his life.[1]*

You may be thinking, *Of course, people in full-time Christian ministry should be having a quiet time.* But you might be surprised to learn how few people in ministry regularly do take time not only to talk to God, but to let God talk to them. Before we get too critical of them, let's evaluate our own quiet time.

Many of us think we're doing God a favor by talking to Him, when it's really incredible we have that privilege at all. We're the losers if we carry a load of worry instead of bringing it to our Savior, who loves us so. I like the way Corrie ten Boom puts it: "As a camel kneels before his master to have him remove his burden, so kneel and let the Master take your burden."[2] It's worth giving up some sleep to have intimate time with Him.

Quiet time with the Lord will give us a quiet spirit, which is an "unfading beauty. . .of great worth in God's sight" (1 Peter 3:4). Don't miss this special time. It's better for us than any trip to the spa!

[1] Elizabeth George, *A Woman After God's Own Heart* (Eugene, OR: Harvest House Publishers, 1997), 30.

[2] Corrie ten Boom, *Don't Wrestle, Just Nestle* (Old Tappan, NJ: Revell, 1978), 79.

— DAY 312 —

We have different gifts, according to the grace given to each of us. . . .
If it is to encourage, then give encouragement.

ROMANS 12:6, 8

The Beauty of Encouragement

Yesterday I met a friend I haven't seen in a long time. She's a beautiful lady—one of those people who is slender and dresses impeccably. But she has another characteristic that I think is the true secret to her attractiveness. She always makes the person she is talking to feel special. Whenever I meet her, I go away from talking with her feeling that *I am* special, too.

Author and Bible teacher Anne Ortlund says,

> *There are two kinds of personalities in this world, and you are one of the two. People can tell which, as soon as you walk into a room: Your attitude says either, "Here I am" or "There you are."*[1]

Pastor Jim George advises,

> *With every encounter, make it your aim that people are better off for having been in your presence. Try in every encounter to give something to the other person.*[2]

At least three times in the New Testament we're reminded to "encourage one another." Okay, let's get practical. What words of encouragement can you give today to a family member? Or your coworker? Or maybe words won't be the way you encourage that person who needs a lift. A handful of flowers would brighten her day. Or a short note saying how special she is. Or a hug. You can do it—I know you can!

[1]Anne Ortlund, *The Disciplines of the Beautiful Woman* (Waco, TX: Word Incorporated, 1977), 96.

[2]Elizabeth George, *A Woman After God's Own Heart* (Eugene, OR: Harvest House Publishers, 1997), 205.

*The righteous perish, and no one takes it to heart; the devout
are taken away, and no one understands that the righteous
are taken away to be spared from evil. Those who walk
uprightly enter into peace; they find rest as they lie in death.*

Isaiah 57:1–2

Spared from Evil

Why do good people die while evil men continue to live and thrive? For example, why is a fine Christian killed in an auto accident while the drunk who hit him walks away uninjured?

I found a verse in the Bible that gives insight: "The righteous perish, and no one takes it to heart; the devout are taken away, and no one understands that the righteous are taken away to be spared from evil" (Isaiah 57:1). That means when a Christian dies, perhaps at a young age, it may be because God took him home to spare him from a difficult situation he would have had to face if he had lived longer.

My parents lived to be eighty-nine and ninety-two—long, full lives. After my dad went to be with the Lord, the last church where he was pastor veered from the direction of his leadership and big problems developed. The congregation dwindled drastically. Many a time I prayed, "Thank You, thank You, Lord, for taking him home so that he didn't have to see this happening." It would have broken his heart, for he truly loved the people in his congregation. It was at that point that I understood that God had taken my dad away "to be spared from evil."

I'm so glad believers in heaven don't know the sad things that happen on earth, for the Bible tells us God wipes "every tear from their eyes. There will be no more death or mourning or crying or pain" (Revelation 21:4), and "Those who walk uprightly enter into peace; they find rest as they lie in death" (Isaiah 57:2)—spared at last from all evil. *Thank You, Lord!*

We will tell the next generation the praiseworthy deeds of
the LORD, his power, and the wonders he has done. . .
so the next generation would know them, even the children
yet to be born, and they in turn would tell their children.

PSALM 78:4, 6

A Godly Heritage

Over one hundred years ago a baby girl named Audrey was born in Saskatch-ewan, Canada. She grew up on the Canadian prairie, learning at an early age to churn butter and bake bread in a woodstove.

Audrey was my mother. Raised in a Christian home, she accepted Christ as her Savior at a special church meeting in her town. Then she met a young pastor named Guy who began to show a singular interest in her. A favorite family story is, how after spending the evening at her parents' home, he took home one of her shoes—which, of course, gave him a good excuse to see her again the next day when he brought it back. I'm not sure he realized they were her *only* pair of shoes!

Eventually Audrey's family moved to British Columbia, where, coinciden-tally, Guy conducted special services in her church. She was asked to play the piano for the meetings—which again brought her to the attention of the young minister. To make a long story short(er), on July 3, 1935, they were married.

I'm so thankful for a Christian mother and grandmother on both sides of my family. What a heritage! Now our three children also love the Lord—and our eight grandchildren are being raised to know Him well.

If you are a parent or have children under your care, mark these verses in your Bible: "We will tell the next generation the praiseworthy deeds of the LORD, his power, and the wonders he has done. . .so the next generation would know them, even the children yet to be born, and they in turn would tell their children" (Psalm 78:4, 6).

Selected verses from Psalm 92

Refreshing Words from Psalms

We have no need to fear aging, for scripture says when we reach that period of life, we will still be productive—"fresh and green."

> ¹ *It is good to praise the L*ORD
>   *and make music to your name, O Most High,*
> ² *proclaiming your love in the morning*
>   *and your faithfulness at night.*
> ⁴ *For you make me glad by your deeds, L*ORD*;*
>   *I sing for joy at what your hands have done.*
> ¹² *The righteous will flourish like a palm tree,*
>   *they will grow like a cedar of Lebanon;*
> ¹³ *planted in the house of the L*ORD*,*
>   *they will flourish in the courts of our God.*
> ¹⁴ *They will still bear fruit in old age,*
>   *they will stay fresh and green,*
> ¹⁵ *proclaiming, "The L*ORD *is upright;*
>   *he is my Rock, and there is no wickedness in him."*

I admit, Lord, that I don't like to think about aging. Thank You for Your assurance that You will still have plans for me especially in "old age."

He will cover you with his feathers, and under his wings you will find refuge; his faithfulness will be your shield and rampart.

PSALM 91:4

When You Feel like Hiding

Sometimes I just want to be invisible. I don't want to hear anyone call my name, or ask me a question, or expect anything from me. I just want to hide somewhere where no one can find me. Do you know the feeling? Do you ever wish you could just stay in bed and pull the covers over your head for the entire day?

Few of us have that luxury. People are depending on us. Husbands and children need our care. We can't risk losing our jobs or neglecting our households. So we keep going.

There is one place, however, where we *can* go to hide. We can run to God, as a baby bird runs to its mother. Psalm 91:4 tells us: "He will cover you with his feathers, and under his wings you will find refuge."

For a baby bird, being under its mother's wings is being close to the one who takes care of its needs. For us, being under God's wings means safety, comfort, and provision.

If you're feeling tired and overstretched, may these verses give you rest:

- The psalmist David wrote, "In peace I will lie down and sleep, for you alone, LORD, make me dwell in safety" (Psalm 4:8).
- God says, "As a mother comforts her child, so will I comfort you" (Isaiah 66:13).
- The apostle Paul wrote, "And God is able to bless you abundantly, so that in all things at all times, having all that you need, you will abound in every good work" (2 Corinthians 9:8).

Under God's wings we know He comforts and protects us. Run to Him when you feel like hiding.

But now he has reconciled you by Christ's physical body through death to present you holy in his sight, without blemish and free from accusation.

COLOSSIANS 1:22

He Wants Us

Imagine being able to have anything you want—anything. You could just "speak it" and it would be in existence. That's how it is with God. He can create anything He desires. And He did.

What amazes me is that He created *us*, knowing that the free will He gave us would result in our rejecting Him and choosing our own way. Why? As incredible as it may be, God created us because He wants to have a relationship with us.

But there was a tremendous cost to this plan. God would have to redeem us from our fallen, or sinful, condition so that He—a holy God—could have fellowship with us. The price was the death of His Son, Jesus, on the cross. The Bible tells us, "But now he has reconciled you by Christ's physical body through death to present you holy in his sight, without blemish and free from accusation" (Colossians 1:22). What a price for God! What a miracle for us!

He did all this because He wants us for Himself.

> *But now, this is what the LORD says—*
> *he who created you, Jacob,*
> *he who formed you, Israel:*
> *"Do not fear, for I have redeemed you;*
> *I have summoned you by name; you are mine."*
> ISAIAH 43:1

We are His! He wants us! In spite of all our "warts" and imperfections and limitations, He wants us! What a magnificent truth! *Thank You, thank You, Lord!*

*But the LORD has become my fortress,
and my God the rock in whom I take refuge.*

PSALM 94:22

Saying Good-Bye

When my uncle Phil passed away with cancer, it was very difficult for my aunt, Margaret, for they had been so happily married for nearly sixty years. They had done everything together.

The following year, Margaret's friend watched her husband also lose the battle to cancer. Knowing the agony of losing one's spouse, Margaret wrote to her:

> *I remember those days. They are hard. You know what is happening, but it seems unreal because you are still living daily life. And you survive by doing just that—living daily life.*
>
> *While Ralph is here, give and receive lots of hugs and kisses, remember together lots of good experiences, say everything you need to say. [Phil and I] always knew we were good partners and we spoke of it often, thanking God. Now I wish I had looked him in the eyes a few more times and said very clearly to him, "You have been a wonderful husband."*
>
> *Before he died, twice Phil asked me if I would be okay. I replied, "I won't like it one bit. But I will be okay. The Lord and the girls will take care of me." And that has proven to be true.*
>
> *I will be praying as you offer your precious one to the Lord with thanksgiving and praise. It is just one step at a time. A cup of tea or coffee. A pat on the cheek. A kiss. A smile and a tease. Just live now. Don't think about what is next. When you get to "next," God will still be there.*

Margaret has come to realize that even though the person closest to her heart is gone, the Lord is still with her.

*Always giving thanks to God the Father for everything,
in the name of our Lord Jesus Christ.*
EPHESIANS 5:20

Remember to Say Thank You

*My little girl went out the door;
I hugged and squeezed her just once more,
Reminding her as oft before,
"Remember to say thank you."*

*And then the thought occurred to me,
I'd better check again to see
How long since I on bended knee
Remembered to say thank you.*[1]
AN ANONYMOUS MOTHER

It's easy to forget to say "thank you." Yet a word of thanks can do wonders. Pastor Mike Coppersmith tells about a man severely depressed who went to a small diner for breakfast. He hunched over the counter, stirring his coffee.

In one of the booths was a young mother with a little girl. They had just been served their food when the girl broke the silence by saying, "Mama, why don't we say our prayers here?" The waitress interrupted, "Sure, honey, we can pray. Will you say the prayer for us?" Turning to the rest of the people in the restaurant, the girl instructed, "Bow your heads."

One by one, the heads went down. The little girl then folded her hands and said, "God is great, God is good, and we thank Him for our food. Amen." Immediately the atmosphere in the restaurant got warmer. The despondent man said, "All of a sudden, my whole frame of mind started to improve. From that little girl's example, I started to thank God for all that I did have and stopped majoring in all that I didn't have. I started to be grateful."

[1]Eugene L. Clark, *My Hope* (Lincoln, NE: Back to the Bible Publication, 1979), 119.

"Such is the destiny of all who forget God; so perishes the hope of the godless. What they trust in is fragile; what they rely on is a spider's web. They lean on the web, but it gives way; they cling to it, but it does not hold."

Job 8:13–15

Relying on a Spider's Web

The book of Job includes a very interesting picture of the person who forgets God in his life.

> *Such is the destiny of all who forget God. . . .*
> *What they trust in is fragile;*
> *   what they rely on is a spider's web.*
> *They lean on the web, but it gives way;*
> *   they cling to it, but it does not hold.*
> Job 8:13–15

No security there! While a spider's web is actually very strong for a spider's weight, it is no match for the weight of a human being. Neither is anything else worth relying on except God. Nothing else will hold up.

Paul learned this. Telling of the hardships he experienced in Asia, he wrote: "We were under great pressure, far beyond our ability to endure, so that we despaired of life itself. Indeed, we felt we had received the sentence of death. But this happened that we might not rely on ourselves but on God, who raises the dead. He has delivered us from such a deadly peril, and he will deliver us again. On him we have set our hope that he will continue to deliver us" (2 Corinthians 1:8–10).

No spider webs for Paul! Because of his intense circumstances, he knew he needed to rely on God. And so do we.

The God we can rely on is no weak, frail God. Moses exclaimed, "Sovereign Lord. . .what god is there in heaven or on earth who can do the deeds and mighty works you do?" (Deuteronomy 3:24). When the winds are raging in your life, hold on to Him. Much stronger than a spider's web, God's arms will never let you down.

*When the perishable has been clothed with the imperishable,
and the mortal with immortality, then the saying that is written
will come true: "Death has been swallowed up in victory."*

1 CORINTHIANS 15:54
(THE WHOLE STORY: 1 CORINTHIANS 15:51–58)

Hope out of Tragedy

I attended my grandson's high school graduation, where diplomas were presented to the seniors by their parents. Since this was a homeschool group, emotions ran high as each set of parents spoke a few words expressing their thoughts to their children, for they had not only nurtured them but spent countless hours educating them as well.

I was impressed that every senior was accompanied to the microphone by two parents—so unusual in today's world of broken families. All, except Kristen. Her mom, Carol, would so much have wanted to be there for this moment. But her life had been cruelly taken three years earlier by a man who went on a rampage, pistol-whipping three members of the family. Kristen's two siblings survived, but her mom did not. Kristen's dad bravely presented the diploma to his daughter—alone.

The whole tragedy seemed so senseless. Why had God not prevented this? Yet the reality of life is that hard things happen to Christ believer and unbeliever alike. The difference is that we who have faith in Jesus Christ are not without hope. To go through a tragedy without hope is to despair. To go through Kristen's situation with the Lord is to have the assurance we will one day be reunited. That knowledge brings comfort that the unbeliever does not have.

The Bible says, "Listen, I tell you a mystery: We will not all sleep, but we will all be changed—in a flash, in the twinkling of an eye, at the last trumpet. For the trumpet will sound, the dead will be raised imperishable, and we will be changed. . . . Therefore, my dear brothers and sisters, stand firm. Let nothing move you" (1 Corinthians 15:51–52, 58).

Kristen's family is awaiting that glorious reunion.

Selected verses from Psalm 89

Refreshing Words from Psalms

Who is like our God? Absolutely no one! He is supreme. What a reason to praise Him!

> ¹*I will sing of the* L*ORD's great love forever;*
>   *with my mouth I will make your faithfulness known*
>   *through all generations.*
> ²*I will declare that your love stands firm forever,*
>   *that you have established your faithfulness in heaven itself.*
> ⁸*Who is like you,* L*ORD God Almighty?*
>   *You,* L*ORD, are mighty, and your faithfulness surrounds you.*
> ¹¹*The heavens are yours, and yours also the earth;*
>   *you founded the world and all that is in it.*
> ¹³*Your arm is endowed with power;*
>   *your hand is strong, your right hand exalted.*
> ¹⁴*Righteousness and justice are the foundation of your throne;*
>   *love and faithfulness go before you.*
> ⁵²*Praise be to the* L*ORD forever!*
> *Amen and Amen.*

Today, Lord, I don't want to ask You for anything. I just want to acknowledge how great You are. I praise You for Your love, Your faithfulness, and Your strong hand of help!

It is good to praise the LORD and make music to your name, O Most High,
proclaiming your love in the morning and your faithfulness at night.
PSALM 92:1–2

Praise: A.M. and P.M.

Did you notice these verses tell us how to pray in the morning and how to pray at night?

A.M.: Start your day by declaring His love. Doing this will put your day in perspective. I, for one, need that first thing in the morning. When we think about how much God loves us, we want to use the day wisely. The Bible says, "He died for all, that those who live should no longer live for themselves but for him who died for them" (2 Corinthians 5:15). Living for Christ is life in its highest form. Living for ourselves brings neither happiness nor significance.

Remembering how much God loves you will help you whether the day goes as you planned or is total chaos. If your boss questions your work, you still know that the Lord loves you and values you. If your teen ignores you, you still know God cares.

P.M.: Thank Him for His faithfulness—another day of good health, money to pay the bills, safety as you went to work. If your day held pain and disappointment, thank Him still, for He was faithful and got you through the day. Even Jesus said, "I must press on today and tomorrow and the next day" (Luke 13:33).

Not a day goes by that we have nothing for which to praise the Lord. The psalmist David said, "Every day I will praise you and extol your name for ever and ever" (Psalm 145:2).

One of them, when he saw he was healed, came back, praising God in a loud voice. He threw himself at Jesus' feet and thanked him.
LUKE 17:15–16

The Best Way to Say Thank You

When my husband and I lived in Asia, I was always surprised when we gave someone a gift and the person did not say, "Thank you." Since saying "thank you" is such an automatic response in the West, I was uncomfortable when I didn't hear those words. Did the person not like the gift? Did I choose the wrong time to give the gift? Was it wrapped in the wrong color paper?

As I learned more about Asian culture, I discovered that to an Asian, merely saying the words *thank you* is a rather inferior way of showing appreciation. After all, saying "thank you" costs nothing. If the person really wants to show appreciation, he or she will respond at a later time by giving you a gift in return, or doing you a special favor. Now, *that's* real appreciation because it costs something.

I couldn't help wondering if God feels the same way. Oh yes, He appreciates our gratitude expressed in words. But when God does something special for us, is there a more meaningful way we could show our appreciation than a cursory "thank you," giving God a quick nod and going back to life as usual?

Perhaps you remember the time Jesus healed ten lepers. Luke tells us, "One of them, when he saw he was healed, came back, praising God in a loud voice. He threw himself at Jesus' feet and thanked him" (Luke 17:15–16).

Bowing at His feet in full commitment—giving ourselves to Him—is, I think, the best way to tell Him "Thank You."

This is love: not that we loved God, but that he loved us
and sent his Son as an atoning sacrifice for our sins.

1 JOHN 4:10

The Disciple Whom Jesus Loved[1]

Five times in the New Testament, John is called "the disciple whom Jesus loved." Five times ought to be enough to convince anyone that Jesus really did love this man, right? What is interesting is that all five occur in one of the books John himself wrote, the Gospel of John. In other words, John described himself.

Did Jesus love him? Certainly He did; He loved all of His disciples. Do you think He loved John more than the other disciples? No, there is no indication of that in the Bible. So was it wrong for John to call himself the disciple whom Jesus loved? I don't think so. The only thing in which he boasted was the fact that Jesus loved him.

Jesus loved John—and He also loves you. Then aren't you, too, the disciple whom Jesus loves? Did you ever think of yourself as "the disciple whom Jesus loves"?

We know what love is because God first loved us. "This is love: not that we loved God, but that he loved us and sent his Son as an atoning sacrifice for our sins" (1 John 4:10).

Jesus died for us. That is how much He loves us! Karl Barth, the Swiss theologian, was asked about the most profound thing he had learned in his theological studies. He replied, "Jesus loves me, this I know, for the Bible tells me so."

The next time you stand in front of a mirror, look right into your own eyes and say, "I am the disciple whom Jesus loves." And then thank Him for that truth.

---

[1]I'm indebted to my dad, Dr. Guy Duffield, for this selection. These thoughts are from what people tell me was their favorite sermon he preached in his eighty-nine years.

For when we came into Macedonia, we had no rest, but we were
harassed at every turn—conflicts on the outside, fears within.

2 CORINTHIANS 7:5

How Much Is Too Much?

Life gets more complex—and more stressful. One reason is that we have far more options than ever before. Just think of the array of communication tools available today: smartphones, tablets, and laptops. On the Internet, you can meet people through Facebook, LinkedIn, and using other social media tools, including dating websites. These tools make communicating easier, but they also use up a lot of our time and energy. How much is too much?

Though the apostle Paul didn't have modern electronics, he knew what stress was. He wrote, "When we came into Macedonia, we had no rest, but we were harassed at every turn—conflicts on the outside, fears within" (2 Corinthians 7:5).

The result of too much stress for too long a period of time is burnout. And who is most at risk?

- The person who needs to succeed to feel worthwhile
- The overcommitted person
- The extremely competent individual

Are you at risk? You budget your money so you won't run out, but as my husband sometimes asks people, "Are you budgeting your energy?" Where are we going to draw the line?

I can't answer that for you. You must decide before God what He wants you to do. But I do know that if you don't set limits for yourself, you can sabotage your future and end up useless to yourself, the Lord, and those you care about.

Mayo Clinic oncologist Edward T. Creagan warns us about stress: "Is it worth dying for?"[1] Stop and ask God to help you set limits.

[1] http://www.mayoclinic.com/health/stress-blog/MY00067, accessed October 16, 2008.

Then they sat on the ground with him for seven days and seven nights.
No one said a word to him, because they saw how great his suffering was.

JOB 2:13

The Power of Presence

While visiting the ancient city of Petra in Jordan, one of our group members felt faint and needed to lie down. I stayed with her as the others continued to explore the area. Soon some local men politely sat near us to show their concern, not saying a word.

My mind went to Job. When he lost his wealth, his children, and his health, three of his friends came to comfort him. "Then they sat on the ground with him for seven days and seven nights. No one said a word to him, because they saw how great his suffering was" (Job 2:13). Presence is powerful!

Kay Warren says that as she was going through breast cancer, she found the greatest comfort "not in the verses of scripture people sent me or the fantastic meals prepared by loving church members or the books on living with cancer. What comforted me was the presence of family members and friends who were willing to sit with me, sometimes without saying a single word. They brought the supernatural comfort of the Holy Spirit to my suffering just by being with me."[1]

When people we care about suffer tragedies in their lives, we are sometimes hesitant to visit them because we don't know what to say. When we are God's children, He lives within us, so let's not hesitate to spend time with those who suffer. We are taking the presence of Christ to them—even without our saying a word.

[1]Kay Warren, *Dangerous Surrender* (Grand Rapids, MI: Zondervan, 2007), 142.

*Then I heard the voice of the Lord saying, "Whom shall I send?
And who will go for us?" And I said, "Here am I. Send me!"*

ISAIAH 6:8

Here Am I—Send Me

The prophet Isaiah had a vision of heaven with the Lord seated on a throne. He heard the Lord asking, "Whom shall I send? And who will go for us?" God had a message He wanted conveyed to His people on earth. Quickly Isaiah responded, "Here am I. Send me!" and God used him to carry His message (Isaiah 6:8).

What a contrast is Isaiah's response to ours! Christian writer and speaker Jill Briscoe wrote a book she humorously titled *Here Am I—Send Aaron.* She was referring to Moses' response when God called him to lead His people out of Egypt to the land He had promised them. Unlike Isaiah, Moses made excuses—"Who am I that I should go? . . . What shall I tell them? . . . What if they do not believe me or listen to me and say, 'The LORD did not appear to you'? . . . I have never been eloquent. . . . Please send someone else." Eventually, in anger, God told him to take his brother Aaron to be his mouthpiece (Exodus 3–4).

Let's not be too hard on Moses. Under the same circumstances, we, too, might have responded, "Here am I, Lord—send Aaron." Moses had fled Egypt forty years earlier because he was wanted on a murder charge. He had no idea what reaction he would get in Egypt. Of course, *we* know the end of the story—God used Moses in a mighty way.

What is God asking you to do? Perhaps you think it's far beyond your abilities? If He calls you, He will also enable you, as He did with Moses. I hope you will respond, "Here am I, Lord—send me."

Selected verses from Psalm 150

Refreshing Words from Psalms

This familiar psalm tells us where to praise God, what to praise Him for, and how to praise Him—with everything we have.

> *¹Praise the LORD.*
> *Praise God in his sanctuary;*
>   *praise him in his mighty heavens.*
> *²Praise him for his acts of power;*
>   *praise him for his surpassing greatness.*
> *³Praise him with the sounding of the trumpet,*
>   *praise him with the harp and lyre,*
> *⁴praise him with timbrel and dancing,*
>   *praise him with the strings and pipe,*
> *⁵praise him with the clash of cymbals,*
>   *praise him with resounding cymbals.*
> *⁶Let everything that has breath praise the LORD.*
> *Praise the LORD.*

Praise to You, my God, from whom all blessings flow!

O send out thy light and thy truth: let them lead me;
let them bring me unto thy holy hill, and to thy tabernacles.

PSALM 43:3 KJV

In the Right Place at the Right Time

In 1949, when Billy Graham held his first big tent revival in Los Angeles, some of Hollywood's most famous accepted Christ. Among them was Jim Voss, an electronics genius who was a wiretapper for gangster Mickey Cohen.

After the meetings, Billy asked Jim if he would come to Boston and give his testimony in the Boston Garden, which seated over fourteen thousand. Jim was excited, but he discovered he had already committed those days to a little church in Los Angeles. So Jim kept his word and spoke in the small church.

One evening after one of the revival meetings, FBI agents met him. "You are under arrest for your part in the Brinks robbery," they said. At that time the Brinks robbery was the largest in the history of the United States—the crime of the century. The stolen cash alone amounted to 1.2 million dollars.

"Well," Jim told them, "I wasn't in Boston."

In court, Jim had a couple hundred people who testified that he was in their church every night during the time of the robbery. Had Jim gone to Boston, he would have had great difficulty, with his record, proving he didn't play a part.

Jim learned that God truly directs our steps. Like the psalmist, may we also ask the Lord, "Send out thy light and thy truth: let them lead me" (Psalm 43:3 KJV). God's light directs us—not as a dazzling spotlight that illuminates the whole horizon of our future, but as a flashlight that gives us enough light for the next step.

"For my yoke is easy and my burden is light."
MATTHEW 11:30

Crazy Love

Pastor Francis Chan says that we're missing something important when we look at our relationship with God as a chore, a sacrifice. He writes, "What we need is to be consumed. . .to be *obsessed*—with nothing and no one else but God."[1] When we love Him that intensely, says Chan, we will find that His commands are easy to obey instead of an unpleasant duty. The following allegory illustrates this truth.

Alex was an outstanding young man—handsome, with a good job, a born athlete, and a leader. Naturally, girls were attracted to Alex, and he thought they were pretty special as well.

On Monday night Alex took Emily out. On Tuesday, he took out Chelsea. On Wednesday, it was Christine—every night a different girl. After a while, however, a special girl named Grace came along, and Alex fell in love with her.

Monday night it was Grace; Tuesday it was Grace; Wednesday, Thursday, Friday—he was with her all the time.

Alex's friend said, "Poor Alex! It's just Grace, morning, noon, and night!"

Alex said, "Look, don't feel bad for me. I love Grace, and I want to be with her every day."

When you really love Jesus, it's going to be easier to say no to being the Emilys and Chelseas of this world, when you are in love with Him, you know who truly matters. When we are "crazy" about Him, we will understand the truth of Jesus' words: "My yoke is easy and my burden is light" (Matthew 11:30).

[1]Francis Chan with Danae Yankoski, *Crazy Love*, excerpted by *Christian Book Summaries*, Vol. 4, Issue 19, summarized by Kristyn Chiapperino, July 2008, 7.

The mind governed by the flesh is death,
but the mind governed by the Spirit is life and peace.

ROMANS 8:6

The Battle in Our Minds

She had obsessive feelings that she was a bad mom. My friend, who knows her well, says she is actually a great mom. So what was she to do with her sense of failure in this all-important role? A counselor gave her advice that would help any of us disturbed with negative thoughts. She directed her to Philippians 4:8: "Finally, brothers and sisters, whatever is true, whatever is noble, whatever is right, whatever is pure, whatever is lovely, whatever is admirable—if anything is excellent or praiseworthy—think about such things."

The counselor then had her make a Truth Card for each of the six descriptive words in that verse telling us what to think about. For example, for the word *true* she was to write on the card:

- Definition of the word *true*
- Bible verse that applies: John 8:32, "Then you will know the truth, and the truth will set you free."
- Personal truth: I am a good mother, not perfect; God loves my children more than I do. I will trust God.

Holding up her feelings to the truth, she soon saw she was being attacked and discouraged by the devil. Her Truth Cards became her constant companion.

The battles of life are often waged in our minds as the devil tries to get us to think wrongly about ourselves and God. But we don't have to give in. The Bible says, "We demolish arguments and every pretension that sets itself up against the knowledge of God, and we take captive every thought to make it obedient to Christ (2 Corinthians 10:5).

The next time you are besieged by negative thoughts, hold them up to God's truth. "The mind governed by the Spirit is life and peace" (Romans 8:6).

"My Father's house has many rooms; if that were not so, would I have told you that I am going there to prepare a place for you? And if I go and prepare a place for you, I will come back and take you to be with me that you also may be where I am."

JOHN 14:2–3

I Will Come Back for You

Have you seen the look of uncertainty in the eyes of a toddler when his mom leaves him with a friend or relative for a few hours? She assures him, "Don't worry, in just a little while I will be back for you."

I'm so glad Jesus, too, assured us that He will come back for us. Just before He died, He told us, "My Father's house has many rooms; if that were not so, would I have told you that I am going there to prepare a place for you? And if I go and prepare a place for you, I will come back and take you to be with me that you also may be where I am" (John 14:2–3).

What a comfort these words are when life is tough! When your world falls apart, focus on the reality that this life is not the end. Author Max Lucado writes,

> *[Jesus] pledges to take us home. He does not delegate this task. He may send missionaries to teach you, angels to protect you, teachers to guide you, singers to inspire you, and physicians to heal you, but he sends no one to take you. He reserves this job for Himself. "I will come back and take you home."[1]*

I like that. Just the thought that one day Jesus will personally come back for me to take me to be with Him in His house forever gives me courage to wade through the muck that life brings. May you, too, say with conviction the concluding words of the familiar Psalm 23, "I will dwell in the house of the LORD forever" (v. 6). At the end of life's day, your Shepherd will be there to lead you home.

[1]Max Lucado, *Traveling Light* (Nashville, TN: W Publishing Group, 2001), 84–85.

"A new command I give you: Love one another.
As I have loved you, so you must love one another."

JOHN 13:34

Loving the Unlovable

Jesus said, "Love one another. As I have loved you, so you must love one another" (John 13:34). Gulp! That's hard!

Oh, it's not hard to love those who are nice to you, but what about those who are not? Author Eugenia Price asks the hard questions:

> *What about the rigid souls who judge us by their own inflexible*
> *standards? . . . For that matter, how successful are we at loving*
> *a tight-lipped, humorless person who not only takes himself too*
> *seriously but misses all the sparkle of our great wit? What about the*
> *touchy soul around whose personality we must tread softly? The self-*
> *righteous one who has yet to admit his first mistake?[1]*

She answers her own questions with a bold, "Yes. Or Jesus was wrong."

Now, understand that the command to love one another in no way means that we have to *like* everyone. But we can love everyone with the love God puts in our hearts when we have a relationship with Him. "God's love has been poured out into our hearts through the Holy Spirit, who has been given us," so every believer has the Holy Spirit living within them (Romans 5:5).

Eugenia says, "Learning to love with God's love requires no special feeling on our part. It requires only doing."[2]

Ask God to help you act loving even toward those you don't like. That would be quite an accomplishment, wouldn't it!

---

[1]Eugenia Price, *Make Love Your Aim* (Grand Rapids, MI: Zondervan Publishing House, 1967), 45–46.

[2]Ibid., 69.

Turn my eyes away from worthless things;
preserve my life according to your word.

PSALM 119:37

The Shopper's Prayer

Here's a verse in Psalms I call "The Shopper's Prayer": "Turn my eyes away from worthless things" (Psalm 119:37).

How easy it is to see something attractive and want to buy it. Of course, the marketers have spent a lot of money to create that desire in us.

But if I want something more than I want God, then that becomes idolatry. "Idolatry occurs when one holds any value, idea, or activity higher than God or morality," says Dr. Laura Schlessinger and Rabbi Vogel.[1] That means God is the one who should have the final say in how I spend my money, or else I'm making an idol out of "things."

Praying before you shop is a very practical test of whether or not you really need the article. You'll find it hard to pray for something you don't really need.

According to the Federal Reserve, in March 2008, US consumers had a record $957 billion of credit card and other types of outstanding debt.[2] Meanwhile, China's Central Bank announced that the number of Chinese credit cards almost doubled in the first quarter of 2008, with 105 million now in circulation.[3]

A financial planner said, "If more people would pay as they go, they might catch up paying for where they've already been." The Bible says, "Let no debt remain outstanding, except the continuing debt to love one another" (Romans 13:8). *Yes, Lord, turn my eyes away from worthless things.*

[1]Dr. Laura Schlessinger and Rabbi Stewart Vogel, *The Ten Commandments* (New York: Cliff Street Books, 1998), 59.

[2]Andrew Leonard, *The Wall Street Journal*, June 2, 2008, http://www.salon.com/tech/htww/2008/06/02/refinancing_credit_card_debt/, accessed July 11, 2008.

[3]Zhang Fengming, "Number of China's Credit Card Holders Doubles in Quarter," published on ShanghaiDaily.com, June 25, 2008, http://www.shanghaidaily.com/sp/article/2008/200806/20080625/article_364455.htm, accessed October 16, 2008.

Selected verses from Psalm 68

Refreshing Words from Psalms

I'm glad to know that the God who "rides on the clouds" also fathers the fatherless, defends widows, and daily bears our burdens. He is both mighty and compassionate.

> *⁴Sing to God, sing in praise of his name,*
> *extol him who rides on the clouds;*
> *rejoice before him—his name is the LORD.*
> *⁵A father to the fatherless, a defender of widows,*
> *is God in his holy dwelling.*
> *¹⁹Praise be to the Lord, to God our Savior,*
> *who daily bears our burdens.*
> *²⁰Our God is a God who saves.*
> *²⁸Summon your power, God;*
> *show us your strength, our God, as you have done before.*

Lord, thank You that in the busyness of life I do not have to carry my burdens alone. Every day You offer to help me if I will just cast all my anxieties on You, for You care for me.

This is how we know what love is: Jesus Christ laid down his life for us.
And we ought to lay down our lives for our brothers and sisters.

1 JOHN 3:16

What Can I Give Him?

You don't have to think very long about Christ's sacrifice for you before you feel a profound sense of debt for what He did. As the apostle John wrote, "This is how we know what love is: Jesus Christ laid down his life for us" (1 John 3:16).

Hymn writer Isaac Watts, who penned the words to "When I Survey the Wondrous Cross," so beautifully expressed the immensity of God's gift:

> *Were the whole realm of nature mine,*
> *That were an offering far too small;*
> *Love so amazing, so divine,*
> *Demands my soul, my life, my all.*

If we owned all the galaxies in the universe to give to God in appreciation, it would be, as Watts puts it, a gift "far too small." The only thing we actually possess to give God is ourselves: "Love so amazing, so divine, demands my soul, my life, my all."

When we sang this hymn when I was a child, we would repeat the last line with one slight change: "Love so amazing, so divine, *shall have* my soul, my life, my all." That always sent a shiver up and down my spine. Even at that young age, I wanted God to have just that—my all.

Don't think I haven't had trouble keeping that commitment! My selfish nature wants to renege and take back control. But the good news is we can make that dedication anew every morning. We can pray, "Lord, today, I want You to have all my day, my energy, my devotion in response to Your great love for me." It's the only way I know to say, "Thank You."

You will keep in perfect peace those whose minds
are steadfast, because they trust in you.

ISAIAH 26:3

Perhaps someone has e-mailed you this memo:

> *This is God. Today I will be handling all of your problems for you.*
> *I do not need your help. So, have a nice day. I love you. P.S. And,*
> *remember. . . If life happens to deliver a situation to you that you*
> *cannot handle, do not attempt to resolve it yourself! Kindly put it in*
> *the SFGTD (Something-for-God-to-Do) Box. All situations will be*
> *resolved in My time, not yours.*
>
> *Once the matter is placed into the box, do not hold on to it by*
> *worrying about it. Instead, focus on all the wonderful things that are*
> *present in your life now.*

Do you have a Something-for-God-to-Do Box? It's a splendid idea for those times when you just can't stop worrying about a problem close to your heart. It is much better to *do* something with your worry. First, tell the Lord about it. Then decisively put your worry in an SFGTD Box.

Of course, this box has no lid, so it's very easy to reach inside, take your worry out, and—well, worry about it some more. Adopt a hands-off policy and trust God. The prophet Isaiah wrote, "You will keep in perfect peace those whose minds are steadfast, because they trust in you" (Isaiah 26:3).

To trust God does not imply that you are neglectful. On the contrary, trusting Him means that you are choosing His solution. You are simply telling God, "I believe You are a good God who wants the very best for me, and I am choosing to leave the problem in Your hands to answer in Your time and Your way." I think you will be surprised at the peace that fills your heart.

*"Very truly I tell you, whoever hears my word and
believes him who sent me has eternal life and will not
be judged but has crossed over from death to life."*

JOHN 5:24

Eternity

Trying to think of eternity is frustrating because everything that we have ever known—except God—has existed in time. John Bate, whose writings inspired Isaac Newton's scientific investigations, told this story: " 'What is eternity?' was a question once asked at the deaf and dumb institution in Paris, and the beautiful and striking answer was given by one of the pupils, 'The lifetime of the Almighty.' "[1]

The joys of eternal life begin not when we die but from the day we begin a relationship with Jesus. He said, "Very truly I tell you, whoever hears my word and believes him who sent me has eternal life and will not be judged but has crossed over from death to life" (John 5:24). Eternity is forever. Are you ready?

[1]http://www.giga-usa.com/quotes/topics/eternity_t001.htm , accessed October 17, 2008.

May the God of hope fill you with all joy and peace as you trust in him,
so that you may overflow with hope by the power of the Holy Spirit.

ROMANS 15:13

Let Go

My friend who is fighting cancer sent me a helpful newsletter from the support group The Cancer Connection.[1] Following are excerpts:

> *One of the hardest things we have to learn to do in this life is to "let go." Especially as we see things that we want to "fix" . . . .*
>
> *This compulsion to "do something!" can become maddening when we are faced with cancer.*
>
> *The best advice we have ever received is to do what we can in terms of caring for ourselves and caring for others who need us but not to the point of exhausting ourselves. After these things, let go. Surrender whatever your cares and worries are to [God].[2]*

Are you suffering from a serious illness? "May the God of hope fill you with all joy and peace as you trust in him, so that you may overflow with hope by the power of the Holy Spirit" (Romans 15:13).

[1]Because the editor uses "whatever Higher Power you believe in" for "God" to appeal to all faiths, I have taken the liberty to insert the name of the only One who can truly help us, our heavenly Father.

[2]July 2008 newsletter of "The Cancer Connection," www.thecancercrusade. com.

"When anyone hears the message about the kingdom and does not understand it, the evil one comes and snatches away what was sown in their heart. This is the seed sown along the path."

Matthew 13:19

A-E-I-O-U

Need an easy-to-remember way of studying your Bible? It's as easy as A-E-I-O-U, says author Carole Mayhall.[1] Take Psalm 23:1 for an example—"The Lord is my shepherd, I shall lack nothing."

> A– Asking questions. Who said this and why?
>
> E– Emphasis. Try placing the emphasis on different words in the verse and see how that focuses your attention on different truths. *The Lord* is my shepherd. The Lord *is* my shepherd, and so on.
>
> I– Illustrations. A story you've heard about shepherds or even a hand-play that will help you remember the truth you are studying. For instance, Carole notes that by touching your thumb for "The," then your index finger for "Lord," your middle finger for "is," etc., you will soon have the verse memorized.
>
> O– Other verses that relate. A Bible concordance will help you find them.
>
> U– Use. What does God want you to do about this verse?

Jesus told the story of a farmer who sowed seed. As he scattered the seed, some fell on the path where he was walking. Quickly the birds came and ate it up. Later Jesus explained the story to His disciples (Matthew 13:19). The devil's job is to steal the "seed" of God's message.

Anything we can do to hold on to God's Word is a good thing. Maybe A-E-I-O-U will do just that for you.

[1]Carole Mayhall, *Can a Busy Christian Develop Her Spiritual Life?* (Minneapolis, MN: Bethany House Publishers, 1994), 56.

"I, even I, am he who blots out your transgressions,
for my own sake, and remembers your sins no more."

ISAIAH 43:25

God Forgets

Mention any date since 1980 to Jill Price, and she can tell you what happened to her on that day—"Who[m] she met, what she did, what she ate. In effect, she is a human diary."[1]

The problem is that Jill can remember every mistake she ever made as if it had just happened. "Most have called it a gift. But I call it a burden," she says. "I recall every bad decision, insult and excruciating embarrassment. Over the years it has eaten me up. It has kind of paralyzed me."[2]

Can you imagine how painful it would be to remember the intricate details of everything you had ever done wrong? It would be a nightmare.

Even though we don't have Jill Price's memory, we do generally remember for a very long time what we've done wrong. In contrast to ours, however, God's memory works differently. Yes, He is all-knowing, but the Bible tells us that when He forgives our sins, at that point, He chooses to forget them completely. God says, "I, even I, am he who blots out your transgressions. . .and remembers your sins no more" (Isaiah 43:25). Those sins can never be brought against us for all eternity.

Are you living with a load of guilt because of what you've done in the past? If you have asked God to forgive you, those sins are gone—forgotten by God. So, why don't you let them go, too, and enjoy His gift of grace today.

[1]Barry Wigmore, "The Woman Who Can't Forget Anything," May 8, 2008, http://www.dailymail.co.uk/news/article-564948/The-woman-forget-ANYTHINGWidow-ability—curse—perfectly-remember-single-day-life.html, accessed October 17, 2008.

[2]Ibid.

Selected verses from Psalm 121

Refreshing Words from Psalms

When we take care of children, we carefully watch them so they don't get hurt. God, our heavenly Father, not only watches us in daytime but also stays awake at night to keep us from harm.

> *¹I lift up my eyes to the mountains—*
>   *where does my help come from?*
> *²My help comes from the LORD,*
>   *the Maker of heaven and earth.*
> *³He will not let your foot slip—*
>   *he who watches over you will not slumber;*
> *⁴indeed, he who watches over Israel*
>   *will neither slumber nor sleep.*
> *⁵The LORD watches over you—*
>   *the LORD is your shade at your right hand.*
> *⁷The LORD will keep you from all harm—*
>   *he will watch over your life;*
> *⁸the LORD will watch over your coming and going*
>   *both now and forevermore.*

Lord, if You are not going to sleep tonight. I guess I might as well. There's no use in both of us staying awake!

Some of those present were saying indignantly to one another, "Why this waste of perfume? It could have been sold for more than a year's wages and the money given to the poor." And they rebuked her harshly.

MARK 14:4–5

Extravagant Love

The scene took place in Bethany where Simon was giving a dinner party for Jesus just days before He would give His life. Lazarus and his sisters, Mary and Martha, were present, along with some of the disciples, including Judas.

All at once the guests became aware of the wonderful fragrance of nard, a costly perfume from India. A woman was liberally anointing Jesus' head and feet with this scent that cost a year's wages—an extravagant gift.

Judas harshly criticized her. "Why this waste of perfume? It could have been sold. . .and the money given to the poor" (Mark 14:4–5). Of course, Judas was being a hypocrite when he said this, for Jesus revealed that as treasurer for the disciples, Judas would help himself to what was put into the money bag. But Jesus commended her extravagant gift: "Leave her alone. . . . Why are you bothering her? She has done a beautiful thing to me. . . . She did what she could. She poured perfume on my body beforehand to prepare for my burial. Truly I tell you, wherever the gospel is preached throughout the world, what she has done will also be told, in memory of her" (Mark 14:6–9).

The woman went beyond obedience to extravagance. She poured out a costly gift that became a memorial of her love for centuries to come—in fact, wherever the Bible is read throughout the world.

We cannot give God anything He needs. He owns everything already. But we can give Him something He wants—and that is the love of our hearts.

Have you ever given Him something extravagant simply because you love Him so much? It's something to consider.

The widow who is really in need and left all alone puts her hope in God and continues night and day to pray and to ask God for help.

1 TIMOTHY 5:5

Single Again—After a Long, Good Marriage

"Single after sixty good years of marriage"—not a stage of life women want to think about. That's why I asked two women going through this uncharted period of their lives to share their thoughts.

Michelle told me, "We really had a good marriage with a lot of fun packed into it. I miss having someone to talk to and to make decisions with." Victoria wrote, "No one can take the place of your best friend and lover. At night you especially feel the reality of death and your own fragile vulnerability to it." Friendships also change. Some don't call because they don't know what to say.

"It gets somewhat easier with time," Michelle observes. "Someone told me that grief is like powerful ocean waves that pound the shore. As time goes by the waves don't come with such regularity but when they do come, they are just as intense."

Author Eugenia Price wrote, "We limit [God] when we think of his being in charge of the death only [of a loved one]. God is also in charge of the one who is left behind."[1] God wants to be our all every day of our lives regardless of the life stage we're in—single, married, or single again. The apostle Paul said, "The widow who is. . .left all alone puts her hope in God and continues night and day to pray and to ask God for help" (1 Timothy 5:5). Widow or not, that's what all of us should do.

Day by day the Lord will give you clear direction for the future as you put your hope in Him, asking how He would have you serve Him at this stage of your life.

[1]Eugenia Price, *Make Love Your Aim* (Grand Rapids, MI: Zondervan Publishing House, 1967), 97.

For here we do not have an enduring city,
but we are looking for the city that is to come.

HEBREWS 13:14

Are We There Yet?

Have you ever been confined in the car on a trip with small children who continually ask, "Are we there yet?" The questioning usually starts after about ten minutes and recurs periodically until you finally reach your destination.

We sometimes get just as impatient. "How long is it going to take for my boss to recognize my good work and give me a raise?" "Are my teens *ever* going to accept responsibility?" "When will God send me a husband?" In the Bible I found eight instances where someone asked, "How long, O Lord?"

We're often anticipating what's next instead of enjoying what is now. My husband has a friend who used to sign his letters and e-mails with the message, "Focus forward!" But then he noticed that when he was always focused on what's ahead, he missed a lot of beautiful scenery along the way.

"When I go running," he confessed, "instead of enjoying the fresh air, the sights, and the exercise, I find myself thinking, 'I can't wait until this is over.'"[1]

So he made adjustments in his life and began to enjoy each moment. He now signs his mail, "Seize Today!"

I do look forward to the day when I can see Jesus face-to-face, and at times my heart cries out, "Are we there yet?" Hebrews 13:14 said, "For here we do not have an enduring city, but we are looking for the city that is to come."

In the meantime, I need to make the most of today's opportunities. The fact that God has put me here on earth is proof that He has something for me to do today.

[1]Harold J. Sala, *Today Counts* (Manila, Philippines: OMF Literature Inc., 2006), Preface.

Whoever fears the LORD *has a secure fortress,*
and for their children it will be a refuge.

PROVERBS 14:26

Always on the Job

Dorothy Nicholas and her husband were talking to their next-door neighbors, a young couple who had helped them on many occasions.

Out of the blue, the neighbor began to tell them of his difficult past. As a teen growing up in Greenwood, South Carolina, he had become involved with the wrong crowd and ended up spending a year in juvenile prison. When he was released, he had problems finding a job.

In desperation, he decided to rob a gas station to get enough money to leave South Carolina. He stole his father's car and gun and drove to a local station before closing time. He was about to demand all the money from the woman manager when he looked up and saw a sign over the service window that read GOD IS OUR SECURITY GUARD—ALWAYS ON THE JOB. Suddenly he realized he just couldn't rob that place. Guilt laden, he rushed home and prayed all night, asking for forgiveness and courage to go right. And with God's help, he did.

Hearing the story, Dorothy looked at her husband. Both were thinking of a night thirteen years earlier in that same town of Greenwood when they worked on ideas for a sign for their business. Finally the right words came. The slogan Dorothy's husband put on the sign at the small gas station they managed was this: GOD IS OUR SECURITY GUARD—ALWAYS ON THE JOB.[1]

Yes, God was truly "on the job" that night—and always will be. Psalm 121:3 says, "He will not let your foot slip—he who watches over you will not slumber." Your greatest security rests in God.

[1] *His Mysterious Ways,* vol. 2, compiled by the Editors (Carmel, NY: Guideposts Associates, Inc., 1991), 12–13.

"Surely I am with you always, to the very end of the age."
MATTHEW 28:20
(THE WHOLE STORY: MATTHEW 28:18–20)

The Word of a Gentleman

In 1865, David Livingstone, renowned missionary and explorer in Africa, had to pass through land controlled by a chief who had aggressively been opposing his work. Livingstone was warned that warriors were in the jungle ahead creeping toward his camp.

Going alone to his tent, Livingstone opened his Bible to Matthew 28:18–20. Then he wrote the following in his journal:

> *January 14, 1856. Felt much turmoil of spirit in view of having all my plans for the welfare of this great region and teeming population knocked on the head by savages tomorrow. But I read that Jesus came and said, "All Power is given unto Me in Heaven and in Earth. Go ye therefore, and teach all nations. . .and lo, I am with you always, even unto the end of the world." It's the word of a Gentleman of the most sacred and strictest honour, and there's an end on it! I will not cross furtively by night. . . . I feel quite calm now, thank God![1]*

The next morning, while the chief and his men watched from the jungle's edge, Livingstone instructed the expedition to cross the river. He deliberately chose to be in the last seat in the last canoe, making himself vulnerable to attack.

"Tell [the chief] to observe that I am not afraid,"[2] said Livingstone, never looking back. The entire group crossed safely. God kept His word.

In the uncertainty of your circumstances, you, too, can hold on to God's promise to be with you always. You have the word of a Gentleman.

[1]Schapera, ed., *Livingstone's African Journal 1853–1856,* vol. 2 (London: Chatto and Windus, 1963), 374.

[2]Ibid.

He tends his flock like a shepherd: He gathers the lambs in his arms and carries them close to his heart; he gently leads those that have young.

ISAIAH 40:11

God's Compassionate Heart

You've probably heard the saying "People don't care how much you know—until they know how much you care." It's true, isn't it?

Let's say that I have a problem with my computer. No matter how hard I try, I can't fix it. As I sit in front of a blank screen, increasingly frustrated, along comes a guy who has a degree in computer science. He stops at my desk and looks at what I'm doing. Almost immediately he figures out the problem. He tells me what is wrong—and then walks off, leaving me to continue my struggle. I'm more frustrated than ever! This guy knows what the problem is, but he doesn't care enough to help me. He only wants me to know how smart he is.

I'm so glad that God is not like that. He who has all knowledge also has all compassion. He deeply cares for us. The prophet Isaiah pictured Him as a tender shepherd who looks after His flock: "He gathers the lambs in his arms and carries them close to his heart; he gently leads those that have young" (Isaiah 40:11).

When Jesus was here on earth, "he saw the crowds, [and] he had compassion on them, because they were harassed and helpless, like sheep without a shepherd" (Matthew 9:36).

Friend, I hope you will think of God not only as the One who knows all about you but also the One who cares for you more than any other. God not only knows the facts of your situation, but He also sympathizes with you. He cares. Find comfort today in His love. Let Him hold you close to His heart.

Refreshing Words from Psalms

There is nothing about us that God does not know. We are never outside His concern and care.

> ¹You have searched me, Lord,
>   and you know me.
> ²You know when I sit and when I rise;
>   you perceive my thoughts from afar.
> ³You discern my going out and my lying down;
>   you are familiar with all my ways.
> ⁴Before a word is on my tongue
>   you, Lord, know it completely.
> ¹³For you created my inmost being;
>   you knit me together in my mother's womb.
> ¹⁶Your eyes saw my unformed body;
>   all the days ordained for me were written in your book
>   before one of them came to be.
> ¹⁷How precious to me are your thoughts, God!
>   How vast is the sum of them!
> ²³Search me, God, and know my heart;
>   test me and know my anxious thoughts.
> ²⁴See if there is any offensive way in me,
>   and lead me in the way everlasting.

Lord, You know my anxious thoughts. Speak peace to my heart today.

I was shown mercy so that in me, the worst of sinners,
Christ Jesus might display his immense patience as an example
for those who would believe in him and receive eternal life.

1 TIMOTHY 1:16

Pretty Enough for God to Love You

Amy was delighted to discover a beautiful doll under the Christmas tree. Clasping her lovely new doll, she hurried to hug her grandmother, who had given it to her. "Thank you, thank you," she cried.

All day long Amy played with her new doll. But toward the end of the day, her grandma noticed she was cuddling her old doll—the one that was ragged and missing one eye.

"It seems, Amy, that you like that old doll better than your new one," her grandmother commented.

"Oh, Grandma, I like my new doll so much," Amy rushed to assure her. "But I love this old doll more, because if I didn't love her, no one else would."[1]

Perhaps you are like the beautiful new doll—everyone likes you because you are so lovely. Thank God for His special gift to you and use it wisely to make good friends and brighten the lives of others.

But maybe you feel more like the other doll—worn out, used, not pretty or special. Be encouraged that God loves you every bit as much as He loves the seemingly more gifted person. Just as Amy loved both of her dolls, so God loves you just as you are. He won't fling you aside.

The apostle Paul, before becoming a believer, had persecuted Christians. He wrote: "I was shown mercy so that in me, the worst of sinners, Christ Jesus might display his immense patience as an example for those who would believe in him and receive eternal life" (1 Timothy 1:16).

Rest in the arms of the One who loves you with unconditional love.

[1]*God's Little Devotional Book for Women* (Tulsa, OK: Honor Books, Inc., 1996), 235.

They made the bronze basin and its bronze stand from the mirrors
of the women who served at the entrance to the tent of meeting.

EXODUS 38:8

A Gift for God

Before the temple was built in Jerusalem, the people of Israel met in a portable "tent of meeting." Inside was an altar for sacrifice as well as other articles, including a bronze wash basin for the priests.

At the time the tent was constructed, God's people were in the wilderness, and bronze was not available at their local hardware store. So where did they get it? The Bible says they made the basin "from the mirrors of the women who served at the entrance to the tent of meeting" (Exodus 38:8).

We really don't know what their responsibilities were, these women who gave up their mirrors for God's house. The word *serve*, however, tells us that their hearts were devoted to the Lord.

Since glass mirrors had not yet been invented, women used polished plates of brass. Just like us today, they cared about their appearance enough to carry these with them as they moved from place to place. But when their precious mirrors were needed for God's purpose, they willingly gave them up.

There's nothing wrong with caring about how you look. I believe we honor God when we have an attractive appearance. But we should be ready to give up things for the Lord. When the hearts of these women were touched with the need of God's meeting place so deeply, they were willing to give up one of their most treasured possessions for Him.

Which is more important to me—how I look or what God wants? It's a matter of the heart.

*"Glory to God in the highest heaven, and on
earth peace to those on whom his favor rests."*

LUKE 2:14

Peace

How often at Christmastime we hear the angels' message: "Glory to God in the highest heaven, and on earth peace to those on whom his favor rests" (Luke 2:14). A glorious, joyous declaration of hope.

On Christmas Day 1863, the American poet Henry Wadsworth Longfellow wrote the poem "Bells on Christmas Day."

> *I heard the bells on Christmas day*
> *Their old familiar carols play,*
> *And wild and sweet the words repeat*
> *Of peace on earth, good will to men.*

When Longfellow wrote the poem, his focus was on the American Civil War. Six months before, fifty thousand men had died within three days at the Battle of Gettysburg. With an aching heart, he wrote another verse,

> *As in despair I bowed my head:*
> *"There is no peace on earth," I said,*
> *"For hate is strong, and mocks the song*
> *Of peace on earth, good will to man!"*

Today, wars continue. Volatile situations keep nerves on edge even as Christmas Day approaches. But, one day peace will reign when Jesus returns to this earth. Until that day, you can have peace as you let Him rule your heart. "May the God of hope fill you with all joy and peace as you trust in him, so that you may overflow with hope by the power of the Holy Spirit" (Romans 15:13).

For to us a child is born, to us a son is given, and the government
will be on his shoulders. And he will be called Wonderful Counselor,
Mighty God, Everlasting Father, Prince of Peace.

ISAIAH 9:6

All You Need

Sometimes Bible verses become so familiar we gloss over them without see-ing how they apply in a practical way to our lives. Isaiah 9:6 is one of those. "For to us a child is born, to us a son is given, and the government will be on his shoulders. And he will be called Wonderful Counselor, Mighty God, Ever-lasting Father, Prince of Peace."

We generally assign that verse to the Christmas season, for it prophesies the coming of our Savior, Jesus, some seven hundred years before the event hap-pened. Yet look again and you may find there exactly what you need for today, for the verse contains four different names for our Lord.

Do you need wisdom and guidance today? He is your "Wonderful Counselor" who has all knowledge and sees the end from the beginning. Perhaps you need a big job done, something that *only* God can do. Remember that He is your "Mighty God," with all power in heaven and on earth.

Are you hurting and you need God's comfort? Isaiah says He is your "Ev-erlasting Father." God is more attentive and loving than the best earthly father.

Is your heart in turmoil? Then you need the "Prince of Peace," who can bring the calmness you so desperately yearn for. Pour out your heart to Him. Let Him carry the weight of your concern. There is no peace so complete as what you will experience when you give the Lord your burden.

Friend, don't wait until a difficult situation drives you to call on God as your Wonderful Counselor, Mighty God, Everlasting Father, and Prince of Peace; turn to Him today.

Love never fails.

1 CORINTHIANS 13:8

(THE WHOLE STORY: 1 CORINTHIANS 13)

1 Corinthians 13–Christmas Version

The unknown author of this Christmas version of 1 Corinthians 13 must be a woman who struggles with priorities during the busy Christmas season.

If I decorate my house perfectly with plaid bows, strands of twinkling lights, and shiny balls, but do not show love to my family, I'm just another decorator. If I slave away in the kitchen, baking dozens of Christmas cookies, preparing gourmet meals, and arranging a beautifully-adorned table at mealtime, but do not show love to my family, I'm just another cook. If I work at the soup kitchen, carol in the nursing home, and give all that I have to charity, but do not show love to my family, it profits me nothing. If I trim the spruce with shimmering angels and crocheted snowflakes, attend a myriad of holiday parties, and sing in the choir's cantata, but do not focus on Christ, I have missed the point.

Love stops the cooking to hug the child. Love sets aside the decorating to listen to a friend. Love is kind, though harried and tired. Love doesn't envy another's home that has coordinated Christmas china and table linens. Love doesn't yell at the kids to get out of the way, but is thankful they are there to be in the way. Love doesn't give only to those who are able to give in return, but rejoices in giving to those who can't. Love bears all things, believes all things, hopes all things, endures all things. Love never fails. Video games will break, pearl necklaces will be lost, golf clubs will rust, but giving the gift of love will endure.

Let love help you set your priorities this Christmas season. If you do, this could be your best Christmas ever.

"Be strong and courageous. Do not be afraid or terrified because of them,
for the LORD your God goes with you; he will never leave you nor forsake you."
DEUTERONOMY 31:6

A Russian Christmas Story

In 1994, two American teachers invited by the Russian government to teach biblical ethics visited an orphanage. It was Christmas, so the Americans gathered the abandoned and abused children together to tell them the story of the first Christmas.

Afterward they gave the children pieces of cardboard to make a manger, tissue to tear into straw, flannel for a blanket, and a tiny baby cut from tan felt. The orphans busily assembled their mangers as the Americans walked around to offer help.

When one of the teachers came to where six-year-old Misha sat, she was startled to see not one, but two babies in Misha's manger. Quickly, she called for the translator to ask why there were two. The boy repeated the Christmas story accurately—until he came to when Mary put baby Jesus in the manger. Then Misha related,

> *And when Mary laid the baby in the manger, Jesus looked at me and asked me if I had a place to stay. I told Him I have no mama and papa. Then Jesus told me I could stay with Him.*
>
> *But I told Him I couldn't, because I didn't have a gift to give Him like everybody else. But I wanted to stay with Jesus so much. I thought maybe if I kept Him warm, that would be a good gift.*
>
> *So I got into the manger, and then Jesus looked at me and He told me I could stay with Him—for always.*

You, too, can have Jesus with you always. If you invite Him, you have His promise, "The LORD your God. . .will never leave you nor forsake you" (Deuteronomy 31:6).

Selected verses from Psalm 147

Refreshing Words from Psalms

There is no limit to God's understanding. He knows the secrets of the universe—and of the human heart. You never have to worry that He doesn't understand your situation.

> *¹Praise the LORD.*
> *How good it is to sing praises to our God,*
> *how pleasant and fitting to praise him!*
> *³He heals the brokenhearted*
> *and binds up their wounds.*
> *⁴He determines the number of the stars*
> *and calls them each by name.*
> *⁵Great is our Lord and mighty in power;*
> *his understanding has no limit.*
> *⁷Sing to the LORD with grateful praise;*
> *make music to our God on the harp.*
> *¹⁰His pleasure is not in the strength of the horse,*
> *nor his delight in the legs of the warrior;*
> *¹¹the LORD delights in those who fear him,*
> *who put their hope in his unfailing love.*

Lord, even when life doesn't go the way I want it to go, I know that You love me. You demonstrated Your love on that first Christmas Day!

Thanks be to God for his indescribable gift!
2 Corinthians 9:15

The Christmas Jacket

I've told you before how much I admire my pastor friend Eric Denton, who every Sunday night takes a group to feed the street people of Los Angeles and give jackets to those who need to stay warm. He has done this for many years. But one December evening was special.

A man was standing alone on the street, finishing his dinner, when Pastor Eric approached him and asked if he would like to have the jacket he was wearing. The man looked like he had won the lottery as Eric helped him put on the warm jacket.

But then a beautiful thing happened. The man surprised him by saying, "I've got a son who's twenty-five. Every day I've wondered what I could get him for Christmas. He's got a good life: married, living right. I think this jacket would be something he'd like. Would that be okay with you?" With a hug, Eric told him he thought it would be a perfect Christmas present.

As he walked on, Eric couldn't help thinking that the man's son would never know the price his father would pay that winter to go without this jacket—that there could hardly be a gift that would rival it in its value of love.

How like Jesus' Christmas gift to us! He gave us a gift that cost Him dearly so that we could have forgiveness and eternal life. Jesus was willing to come as a helpless baby, experience life as we experience it, and then be stripped of His seamless robe and die an agonizing death on the cross to pay for our sins.

"Thanks be to God for his indescribable gift!" (2 Corinthians 9:15).

Therefore, when Christ came into the world, he said: "Sacrifice and offering
you did not desire, but a body you prepared for me."

HEBREWS 10:5

Jesus—One Cell

Stop for a moment and come with me. We'd better tiptoe.

See that manger? Look inside. Nestled in the hay is a newborn baby, wrapped tightly. No ordinary baby—the very Son of God in human form. Who but God would come up with a plan to have a relationship with us that would begin with a baby?

Jesus was willing, at that special moment of divine conception, to be reduced to *one cell*—the size of a pinpoint. The One of whom the apostle John wrote, "Through him all things were made" (John 1:3). The designer of DNA! The architect of galaxies! Yet all that indescribable creative power and genius became *one* cell in the body of Mary! The ultimate miniaturization—God in one cell! Yet it was His plan, for Jesus said to His Father, "A body you prepared for me" (Hebrews 10:5).

Because Jesus became one of us, He understands our limitations and frailties, our grief and loneliness. Psalm 103:14 says, "For he knows how we are formed, he remembers that we are dust."

Because His crib was a manger, none can say, "I am too poor to approach Him." All of us can come with our worship and requests. No wonder the angel said, "I bring you good news that will cause great joy" (Luke 2:10).

But there's more. The angel's message goes on: "A Savior has been born to you" (v. 11). Because Jesus came, we can surrender to Him our sins and find forgiveness. For this little baby in a manger was later crucified to pay for all the wrongs we have done.

He's waiting for you to worship Him today.

*May these words of my mouth and this meditation of my heart
be pleasing in your sight, LORD, my Rock and my Redeemer.*

PSALM 19:14

The Day After Christmas

The Christmas season is often stress filled—shopping, decorating, cooking. Parties and church activities, as wonderful as they are, require energy. The day after Christmas, most of us are "spent"—and it's not just our money that is gone. So is our ability to bounce with life. Tempers are short. Harsh words are spoken.

Michael Bright's poem "Silver Boxes" speaks to my heart during such times:

> *Lord, help my words be silver boxes,*
> *Neatly wrapped up with a bow;*
> *That I give to all so freely,*
> *As through each day I gladly go.*
> *Silver boxes full of treasure,*
> *Precious gifts from God above;*
> *That all the people I encounter*
> *Might have a box of God's own love.[1]*

Today, perhaps people would delight in receiving from you "Silver Boxes" filled with kind words along with a special portion of patience.

Today might just be the day to pray with the psalmist David, "May these words of my mouth and this meditation of my heart be pleasing in your sight, LORD, my Rock and my Redeemer" (Psalm 19:14).

[1]Michael Bright, "Silver Boxes," quoted by Florence Littauer in *Silver Boxes* (Dallas, TX: Word Publishing, 1989), page unknown.

And we all, who with unveiled faces contemplate the Lord's glory,
are being transformed into his image with ever-increasing glory,
which comes from the Lord, who is the Spirit.

2 CORINTHIANS 3:18

Your Face

Do you like your picture on your ID card? Probably not. But you're stuck with it, right?

Most of us are not satisfied with how we look, so we go to a lot of trouble to make our faces look as good as possible. Stores carry products claiming to help us look younger, prettier, and healthier. In the US alone, $18.8 billion is spent annually on cosmetics.[1]

Let's face it, people sometimes judge us by how we look. But not even the best cosmetic can mask the emotions our faces reveal—joy, anger, peace. Because we women easily pick up the signals, we read people's faces to see what is going on in their minds.

For followers of Christ, the apostle Paul declares, "We all, who with unveiled faces contemplate the Lord's glory, are being transformed into his image with ever-increasing glory, which comes from the Lord, who is the Spirit" (2 Corinthians 3:18).

The picture Paul paints is that when we focus on the Lord, we become more like Him. The better we know Him, the more we reflect Him to others, just as light reflected by a mirror makes a face glow. The wonder is that in the process of learning to know the Lord, we are changed into His likeness by the Holy Spirit. Now that is true beauty!

Mrs. Wang stands out in my memory for the glow of God's presence on her face. Her husband, Wang Ming-Dao, was the "father" of the house church movement in China. Because she was a Christian, she spent twenty hard years in prison. Yet when I met her, I saw no bitterness—only the love of the Lord in her face.

The more closely we follow Christ, the more we will be like Him.

[1]http://www.crescatsententia.net/archives/2003/12/10/, accessed July 1, 2008.

I would like to learn just one thing from you: Did you receive the
Spirit by the works of the law, or by believing what you heard?

GALATIANS 3:2

After You Become a Christian

Most of us understand we can't earn eternal life. Sinners by nature and by choice, we have no way to become right in God's sight except through faith in Jesus' death for our sins.

After we become believers, we begin to work very hard at being good Christians. But do you realize it's impossible to do that by your own efforts?

Paul asked believers: "I would like to learn just one thing from you: Did you receive the Spirit by observing the works of the law, or by believing what you heard?" (Galatians 3:2).

The answer is pretty obvious. By believing the good news of God's grace, we became His children, and His Spirit came to live in us.

Then Paul continued: "Are you so foolish? After beginning by means of the Spirit, are you now trying to finish by means of the flesh?" (v. 3). Just as we become God's children by the work of His Spirit, so too do we mature in exactly the same way. We can no more become like the Lord by our own efforts than we can make ourselves grow physically.

When you plant a vegetable garden, you water the soil, pull the weeds, and fertilize the plants to get a harvest. But you can't "make" the vegetables grow. The results come only by cooperating with God.

So, too, we must feed our spiritual lives and pull the weeds that sap our spiritual strength. But God brings the growth.

Stop trying to be a Super Christian by your own efforts and ask God to take over.

*Then Peter came to Jesus and asked, "Lord, how many times shall I
forgive my brother or sister who sins against me? Up to seven times?"
Jesus answered, "I tell you, not seven times, but seventy-seven times."*

MATTHEW 18:21–22

Turning Over a New Leaf

"Turning over a new leaf" means changing for the better. This also entails
being forgiving. Yet, author Ray Pritchard points out,

> *Every year in January we talk about turning over a new leaf. [But]
> we don't turn anything over; we just carry our burdens and hurts
> from one year to the next—haunting memories, injured feelings, and
> thoughts about the past that we can't get out of our minds.[1]*

It takes courage to forgive—to give up resentment, anger, and hurt.
Pritchard says, "Only the brave will forgive. Only the strong will have the courage to let go of the past."[2]

Forgiving does not mean saying, "What you did was okay." No, the offense
was wrong. But if you don't forgive, you will be the loser, continuing to carry a
heavy backpack of garbage from the past. And garbage stinks!

Oh, I know—those memories keep coming back, and you go through the
emotions all over again. Then you must forgive again and again. The apostle
Peter asked Jesus, "How many times shall I forgive my brother or sister who
sins against me? Up to seven times?" (Matthew 18:21). Jesus' reply? Not just
"seven times, but seventy-seven times" (v. 22). In other words, every time that
memory haunts you, forgive again—and again.

Paul instructs us, "Bear with each other and forgive one another if any
of you has a grievance against someone. Forgive as the Lord forgave you"
(Colossians 3:13). The Lord's unlimited forgiveness is our pattern to follow.
With God's help, you *will* turn over a new leaf this new year.

[1] Ray Pritchard, *The Healing Power of Forgiveness* (Eugene, OR: Harvest House Publishers, 2005), 47.

[2] Ibid., 26.

Selected verses from Psalm 145

Refreshing Words from Psalms

As we soon start a new year, how good it is to know we have a great God who walks beside us every day.

> ³*Great is the LORD and most worthy of praise;*
>   *his greatness no one can fathom.*
> ⁸*The LORD is gracious and compassionate,*
>   *slow to anger and rich in love.*
> ⁹*The LORD is good to all;*
>   *he has compassion on all he has made.*
> ¹³*Your kingdom is an everlasting kingdom,*
>   *and your dominion endures through all generations.*
> *The LORD is trustworthy in all he promises*
>   *and faithful in all he does.*
> ¹⁴*The LORD upholds all who fall*
>   *and lifts up all who are bowed down.*
> ¹⁵*The eyes of all look to you,*
>   *and you give them their food at the proper time.*
> ¹⁶*You open your hand*
>   *and satisfy the desires of every living thing.*
> ¹⁸*The LORD is near to all who call on him,*
>   *to all who call on him in truth.*

Thank You, Father, for Your faithfulness to me this past year. You truly are faithful to fulfill Your promises. I look to You for all I need.

Wash away all my iniquity and cleanse me from my sin. . . .
Create in me a pure heart, O God, and renew a steadfast spirit within me.
PSALM 51:2, 10

Inventory Time

When I went to the store, I stopped short at the door. The sign hanging there said CLOSED FOR INVENTORY. Through the windows I could see people sorting and counting, but they made no move to unlock the door for me. It was time for them to take stock of last year's goods, remove soiled merchandise, and display the current fashions.

I need to take spiritual inventory from time to time as well—stop "business as usual" to take stock of what is going on in my life. Is there some "soiled merchandise" that needs to be dealt with? David cried to the Lord, "Wash away all my iniquity and cleanse me from my sin. . . . Create in me a pure heart, O God, and renew a steadfast spirit within me" (Psalm 51:2, 10).

In preparation for Passover, every orthodox Jew matriarch cleans her house from top to bottom to be sure there is not one particle of leaven or yeast, for leaven is a symbol of sin. Anything she finds that contains leaven is burned with this prayer, "All leaven or anything leavened which is in my possession, whether I have seen it or not. . .whether I have removed it or not, shall be completely considered naught and ownerless as the dust of the earth."

We don't have to declare our sins to be "ownerless," because Jesus died to take them away. Whatever we did last year, or any time in our lives, can be washed away—gone forever. Let's take inventory: ask the Lord to purge us of any sin so we can worship Him with clean and holy hearts.

We would love to hear from you!

Please share with us how this book has helped or blessed you.
Or for additional needs, contact Darlene Sala at Guidelines
International Ministries, 26161 Marguerite Parkway, Suite F,
Mission Viejo, CA 92692. Or by e-mail at darlene@guidelines.org.

COMING SOON!
From Darlene Sala

Encouraging Words for Women
Can you truly trust God with the details of your life? According to bestselling author Darlene Sala, the answer is a resounding, "yes!" Since its 2002 release, more than 400,000 women have been inspired and encouraged by Darlene's *Encouraging Words for Women*. Now this popular title is available again in a great new format! In fifty-two devotional chapters, you'll be reminded of your worth in God's eyes, and of His affirmation, protection, and guidance. You'll be assured that, whatever their circumstances, our God is a Father you can always trust.
Paperback / 978-1-68322-127-2 / $4.99 / May 2017

Journey into Grace
Life is a journey of joyful moments and painful moments, including twists and turns that threaten to undo us. But if we allow God to work through the joy and the pain, that journey can lead to the life-sustaining richness of His Grace and an intimate relationship with Him. That truth is the core of international speaker and teacher Darlene Sala's new women's devotional, *Journey into Grace*. With Darlene's heartfelt voice alongside two coauthors, including her daughter, Bonnie, the 150 readings explore themes such as fear, forgiveness, learning, loving, prayer, and relationships.
Paperback / 978-1-68322-285-9 / $12.99 / September 2017

Pressed for Time?
Get These 3-Minute Pick-Me-Ups!

Too Blessed to be Stressed: 3-Minute Devotions for Women
by Deb Coty

Women will find the spiritual pick-me-up they desire in *Too Blessed to Be Stressed: 3-Minute Devotions for Women*. 180 uplifting readings from bestselling author Debora M. Coty pack a powerful dose of comfort, encouragement, humor, and inspiration into just-right-sized readings for women on the go.
Paperback / 978-1-63409-569-3 / $4.99

Daily Wisdom: 3-Minute Devotions for Women
Daily Wisdom for Women has touched the lives of more than three quarters of a million readers since its release nearly two decades ago. Now in a great "3-Minute Devotions" edition, this devotional will continue to encourage new generations of women as they seek the true wisdom only found in God's Word.
Paperback / 978-1-63409-689-8 / $4.99

Special Editions of *The Bible Promise Book®* for Everyday Encouragement

The Bible Promise Book® for Morning & Evening

This *Morning & Evening* edition features Bible promises arranged into morning and evening readings—including God's Word, Wisdom, Faith, Prayer, and more—each scripture will draw readers ever closer to their heavenly Father. Scripture selections for each morning and evening are complemented by a brief devotional and prayer, for a refreshing blend of Bible promises and encouragement!
DiCarta / 978-1-61626-410-9 / $14.99

The Bible Promise Book® for Women

A beautiful gift edition for women features more than 60 relevant topics—including Adversity, Duty, Friendship, Modesty, Protection, Sincerity, Strength, and Zeal—you'll find nearly 1,000 total verses included. Each topic includes a brief introductory comment to put the verses into a 21st-century context. Handsomely designed and packaged, *The Bible Promise Book® for Women* makes an ideal gift for any occasion.
DiCarta / 978-1-61626-358-4 / $9.99

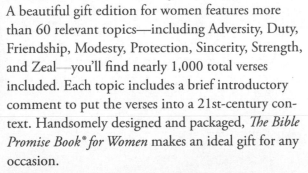